THE WORLD OF

Big-Game Hunting

SINCE 1895
FIELD & STREAM
THE SOUL OF THE AMERICAN OUTDOORS

CREATIVE PUBLISHING international
MINNETONKA, MINNESOTA

Field & Stream
The World of Big-Game Hunting

Introduction by David E. Petzal

CREATIVE PUBLISHING international

Chairman: Iain Macfarlane
President/CEO: David D. Murphy
Vice President/Retail Sales & Marketing: James Knapp
Director, Creative Development: Lisa Rosenthal

Executive Editor, Outdoor Group: Don Oster
Project Leader and Article Editor: David L. Tieszen
Managing Editor: Jill Anderson
Associate Creative Director: Brad Springer
Art Director: Joe Fahey
Photo Researcher: Angie Hartwell
Manager, Production Services: Kim Gerber
Publishing Production Manager: Helga Thielen

Special thanks to: Jason E. Klein, President, FIELD & STREAM; Slaton White and the staff of FIELD & STREAM magazine

Contributing Photographers: Charles J. Alsheimer, Chuck & Grace Bartlett, Alan & Sandy Carey, Alissa Crandall, Michael H. Francis, Donald M. Jones, Jess R. Lee, Tom & Pat Leeson, Keith McCafferty, Bill McRae, Wyman Meinzer, David E. Petzal, Jerome B. Robinson, Conrad Rowe, Rodney Schlecht, Dusan Smetana/The Green Agency, Ron Spomer, Jeff Vanuga

Contributing Illustrators: Norman Adams, Luke Frazier, Craig P. Griffin, R. Scott, Shannon Stirnweis, John Thompson

Cover Photographer: Mark Raycroft

Printed on American paper by: World Color

10 9 8 7 6 5 4 3 2 1

Library of Congress Cataloging–in–Publication Data

The world of big-game hunting.
p. cm. -- (Field & stream)
ISBN 0–86573–098–9. -- ISBN 0–86573–099–7 (softcover)
1. Big game hunting--North America--Anecdotes. I. Creative Publishing International. II. Title: Big-game hunting. III. Series: Field & stream (Minnetonka, Minn.)
SK40.W67 1999
799. 2'6--dc21 99–38861

FIELD & STREAM is a Registered Trademark of Times Mirror Magazines, Inc., used under license by Creative Publishing international, Inc.

Table of Contents

Introduction

LAST NOVEMBER, I STOMPED into a New Brunswick deer-camp cabin tastefully covered with a coat of ice from sitting motionless for three hours in a freezing drizzle. One of my hunting pals said, in the cracked voice of an old man:

"Tell me, pilgrim, were it worth the trouble?"

My reply was as rigidly codified as any religious text: "Eh? What trouble?"

This was not a conversation; it was the recitation of dialog from the 1974 Robert Redford movie, *Jeremiah Johnson,* the highly sanitized story of a real-life mountain man named Liver-Eating Johnston who would have sent Charles Manson screaming off in terror. *Jeremiah Johnson* is more than the all-time favorite movie among big-game hunters; it's an object of worship, and the true believers, such as myself, have seen it so often that we know the dialog by heart.

Why the attraction? I think it's because the film did a superlative job of showing a man who was at large in some of the most magnificent wilderness on earth. He was self-sufficient, and free beyond our concept of the word. It is a movie about a man who Got Out There and lived his life on his own terms.

Mountain men were misfits and loners. They found the constraints of even early 19th century America intolerable, and so they were willing to risk unparalleled danger and hardship in return for a life of absolute liberty. They didn't care if they made money trapping beaver. It was an excuse to Get Out There.

Big-game hunters today are no different. It is still possible for us to Get Out There—to experience real hardship and peril. It is still possible for us to set foot where no man has ever planted a boot and none may ever do so again. It is still possible to succeed wildly or fail dismally with the wilderness for a backdrop.

Many years ago a friend and I hunted elk for two weeks in the Montana Rockies. We were in our early thirties and tougher than railroad spikes. We hunted every day until we could not put one foot in front of the other. The last night of the hunt, I went down in the cabin cellar to get potatoes for dinner, and it took me ten minutes to climb the ten stairs back up.

For all that, we never saw an elk. And today I would eat municipal sludge at $35 a pound if I could make that hunt again. I don't think about the elk we never saw; I think about what it was like to stand on the top of a divide in the Rockies in October with the aspen leaves turning to gold.

A few years ago a friend of mine went on a marathon walk after bighorn sheep; it was the last day of the only hunt he would ever make for them, and it was do or die. He walked until his blood soaked through his boots, and he got his sheep, and the next day he could not walk at all. And today, when he tells the story, he has a dreamy look in his eyes—the blood-soaked boots are far, far away—because he Got Out There, and because he now knows the topgraphy of his own soul as very few people do.

Out There does not have to be the Rocky Mountains. It can be a South Carolina swamp, an Illinois woodlot, a Wyoming sage flat...or this book. Out There is just beyond this next page.

David E. Petzal,
Executive Editor, FIELD & STREAM

Antlered Game

North American big-game hunters are uniquely blessed. We have the biggest, the most spectacular, and the smartest animals on earth right here. Nothing is bigger than a moose, or smarter than a whitetail deer, or more spectacular than an elk or a caribou. The antlered animals are mythic. Even experienced hunters, when confronted with a record-book example of these species, are struck dumb. I've seen more than one hunter of international experience come completely unglued in the presence of a big whitetail. Such a deer may live literally in your back yard, but it is the equal of any big-game trophy anywhere.

SINCE 1895
FIELD & STREAM
THE SOUL OF THE AMERICAN OUTDOORS

By Norman Strung

Whitetail WAYS

EAST, WEST, NORTH, AND SOUTH, BUCKS ARE A CHALLENGE UNTIL KNOWLEDGE OF THEIR HABITS HELPS THE HUNTER MAKE FEWER MISTAKES.

TANGO WAS HIS NAME, and he had a tar paper hunting camp near Windham, New York. I don't remember much about him except that he wore long-handled underwear beneath red suspenders, and had a belly of sufficient proportions to all but obscure a sizable belt buckle. It was there at Tango's place that I underwent several rites of passage: my first choking taste of raw whiskey; my first experience among men who did not treat me as a boy; and my first whitetail kill.

That came on the fourth day, on doe day, after a heavy flurry had passed through the mountains. I was standing at the edge of a willow swamp and she emerged from a tunnel of snowclad hemlock. I can still recall my wonder at the sight of her; not just that I encountered my first deer in the woods, but the texture of her coat against the grays and greens and whites of the forest. The contrast was surreal, as if she were phosphorescent; her sleek, brown coat fairly glowed in that dim light. She glanced behind her and stood motionless for a second. I raised my lever-action carbine and delivered the shot.

I was still shaking when I dragged my proud trophy into Tango's yard.

"Nice shot, son," the old man said.

Someone patted my back. "Your first deer, I'll bet."

I nodded, and my forehead was annointed with blood. It took the combined pleadings of both my parents, plus the threat of lifted hunting privileges for a year, to get me to wash off that spot before going to school the next morning.

That happened more than twenty years ago, but my fascination with the species hasn't diminished. I have hunted whitetail in a dozen states, East and West, with bow, gun, and camera, and I must confess that each time a liquid doe or regal buck materializes from the ether of the forest, I am struck with the same adolescent awe. Still, if all those years of chasing white flags through the woods have a lesson, it is that these deer are incredibly cunning, but once you understand them, you can bag one every season.

First and foremost, whitetail deer are skulkers, creatures whose survival instincts center around hiding. Even when hunting season is months away you will rarely see one of these deer standing out in the open. When whitetails move from one place to another they will choose brush-choked trails rather than open paths. They lie in shade, never sunlight, and their most active periods occur during subdued light, or at night.

True to this nature, when whitetails perceive a direct threat, their first line of defense is to hide from their pursuer. They'll crawl into a willow thicket or flatten out in waist-high brush, watching and waiting until the danger passes. Reluctant to move unless they sense they have been seen, they rely upon the element of surprise and their considerable speed to find safety in another hiding spot.

Herein lies the difficulty of whitetail hunting. You must seek out a perfectly camouflaged creature who usually knows where you are and what you are up to. However, within those conditioned reflexes lies an Achilles' heel. In order for them to hide, they've got to know what they are hiding from. As a result, a whitetail will often "hunt" you just as surely as you are hunting him.

I recall a day that found me in a tree stand with a bow in my hands. I'd climbed up just as dawn was breaking and hadn't been there 15 minutes when a fine buck emerged from the brush 100 yards down the trail. He looked right and left, then stepped out into full view and lowered his head to sniff the ground. Suddenly he froze stock-still, tail rising to half mast. He peered down and up the trail once again, then did a little head-bobbing, hoof-tapping dance that brought him full circle. He stretched his neck straight out and sniffed the air, knowing I had passed the spot, but not in which direction.

THEN SLOWLY, LIKE a cat walking on quail eggs, he came down the trail, testing every breeze, examining every bush. He would pause and listen, checking his back-trail often, then resume his careful steps.

He wasn't trying to avoid me, he was trying to find me so he could avoid me, and his need to know brought him within my range after 5 anxious minutes.

This behavior suggests the key to successful whitetail hunting: that it is a game of hide and seek, but a game in which the wise hunter alternates from an active to a passive role.

The hunter as pursuer must find habitat with good populations of deer before he ever gets down to serious hunting. A perfectly good way to meter activity levels is to string 2-pound-test monofilament at midthigh levels across major game trails. Do this in the evening so you don't end up counting hunters, and pocket the mono when you examine it the next morning. (Birds have a nasty habit of getting tangled up in the stuff when they use it to build nests in the spring, so don't leave any of it behind.)

There are a few other ways to learn if a section of field and forest does indeed have a good population of whitetails. A deer's habitat is divided into three areas of activity: feeding, moving, and bedding. When I'm sizing up an area's potential, I look for evidence in all three categories. For example, when I'm in a feeding area, I search the ground around me for tracks, grazed browse, and droppings. If I don't find these signs, I take a dozen steps and look again. If I still find no sign, I move ahead and look once more.

I do the same thing along trails and in bedding areas, and if I come across fresh evidence of deer activity one out of three times, I consider the place worth hunting. I should also add that I make these "tests" as much a part of my daily hunting habits as quiet walking and slow, deliberate body movements, for I have found whitetail populations can shift location overnight.

Perhaps the most misinterpreted aspect of whitetail nature is that of their home territory. Myth has it that these deer are permanently rooted to a definable range where they cunningly evade hunters. Like most myths, this has some basis in fact; given low to moderate disturbance by hunters, whitetails do prefer to remain within a familiar environment, but when hunting pressure is heavy or constant, they are not at all reluctant to move into quieter quarters.

THE BEST EXAMPLE of this that I have been witness to occurred on a river island in Montana. The island rated as top whitetail habitat, an even mix of tall but open timberland and low, brushy browse such as primrose, willow, and honeysuckle, roughly a mile wide by a mile-and-a-half long. Before and during the first week of hunting season the place was saturated with deer; I sighted up to thirty-five in one day! But I also sighted a substantial number of other hunters. A place with concentrations of deer like that is a hard secret to keep.

Then, during the second week of the season, the deer sightings dropped dramatically. In fact, I had a hunch that I was seeing the same doe and two fawns every day. My conclusion was that the resident deer had smartened up, that they were using their much-touted ability to crawl into gopher holes and pull them closed behind them to avoid me. I hunkered in and resolved to learn where they were hiding. I waded through primrose patches so dense that it was like walking on bedsprings, and bellied my way through willow tunnels where it seemed only a pheasant could run. I climbed trees. I overturned rocks. I looked into hollow logs—and every so often I would jump a doe with two fawns.

That Thursday, it snowed. Not a heavy storm, just 2 inches of wet and white, but ideal stuff for determining the age of tracks and beds, and thus get a rough estimate of the numbers of deer that were giggling behind trees. I made my accustomed rounds, and by the soaking-wet end of that cold and thankless day I had encountered three beds and three sets of tracks, obviously those of a doe with two fawns! The evidence was overwhelming; most of the deer had left the island for a quieter sanctuary.

When the signs point to a healthy population of deer, however, it's time to switch to a hiding game.

At its simplest, hiding amounts to taking a stand. Find a place of concealment close to a heavily used trail and wait for your quarry to come to you. You'll gain substantial advantage stand-hunting if you'll gain some altitude by placing yourself atop a stump, on a fallen log, or best of all, up in a tree. Getting up off the ground, even if it's only a few feet, helps disperse your scent, improves your vision, and extends your field of fire. I also suspect that the most frequently perceived part of a hunter's anatomy are his legs.

Since the object of stand-hunting is to intercept deer on the move, it's best practiced early in the morning and late in the evening when the animals are traveling between bedding and feeding areas. However, unnatural influences—usually other hunters—can make them move during the middle of the day.

When I encounter a stalking hunter I always find some sort of stand until he has passed well out of my range. Ditto whenever I hear a shot from my side of a mile away. Another time to stop and wait is when you see any deer on the move that hasn't seen you. Regardless of its size or sex, it's likely that something has disturbed the animal, and there may well be others along directly.

Stand-hunting amounts to an educated guess; it takes a lot of luck to bring a skulking deer and a concealed hunter together. However, one trick that turns the tables on a whitetail—that makes it the seeker while you play the hider—is to use a diversion to attract its attention, so it concentrates on that instead of you.

The idea isn't exactly original. It occurred to me after watching a buck sneak up on a surveyor's marker tied to a tree branch. A more effective lure, however, has proven to be the aluminum paper from a pack of cigarettes. Just hang it on some string from a branch off to the side of the trail, well away from your stand, and let it whirl and twinkle in the breeze. As soon as a deer spots the paper it will freeze until it figures out just what the paper is. Sometimes a deer will even snort, sniff, and stomp its way toward the sparkling attractor, trying to frighten the strange object, and thereby alerting you to its presence.

Stand-hunting relies on deer that are moving around, so it's not a very successful technique during midday hours when whitetail are usually bedded down. You can still turn them into seekers at this time, though, by a combination of silent walking and patient waiting.

A whitetail's alert system depends on a series of confirmations. Their senses of smell and hearing are far more acute than a human's, but they seem to have the need to confirm fully what those senses indicate by way of eyesight that is inferior to ours. I have heard that whitetails are extremely sharp-eyed, but my field experience hasn't proven this to be so. Their color-blindness is common knowledge, and that has to be a handicap. While deer are quick to spot movement, so long as I stayed motionless I have had whitetails stare at me, some from as close as 10 feet, without ever figuring out just what I was. I can't imagine a similar scenario involving a human looking at a deer.

YOU CAN CAPITALIZE upon this curiosity and limited vision if you walk very slowly and quietly through likely bedding areas. Keep your arms glued to your sides, take tiny steps, and every 5 minutes take a stand. Again, getting some elevation, even if it is only a few feet, increases the productivity of this technique tenfold. What happens is that resting deer are forewarned of your presence by smell or sound, but they still want to see you, just to be sure. They'll usually rise from their beds, ears alert, nose quivering, while they wait for you to step into view. Then, when you take a stand, all noise stops. That same gnawing curiosity that draws a whitetail to a strip of aluminum foil forces them to find out what and where you are, and they will actually move toward you. It takes a while to so pique a whitetail's curiosity; you should post for at least 5 minutes. But once those wheels are set in motion, you're in a great position to fill your tag.

An example of such a situation occurred three years ago in Florida. I was hunting on a ranch near Ocala, ghosting through a swampy hammock, and I took my 5-minute pause on a shell mound 30 yards away from a small clump of palmettos. Aside from blinking and a slow-motion glance at my watch to check the timing of my wait, I moved not a muscle nor made a sound. Then, scant seconds before I was due to take my first slow stride, a buck stepped halfway out of the palmettos and looked me square in the eyeball. I expected him to explode, but he never saw me! Instead, he swung his head 180 degrees and looked in the opposite direction, at which point I shot him through the shoulder with a shotgun slug.

I should also mention that a variation of this technique works so well with two hunters that I've all but given up on conventional drives. Partners walk through a bedding area far enough apart so they can just make each other out through the screen of cover, and they take 5-minute turns at standing and stalking. But they alternate both their positions and their timing. Assuming each 5-minute stalk period covers 100 yards, the standing hunter posts himself 50 yards in front of the stalker, who moves ahead 100 yards. When it is the stalker's time to post, he is 50 yards ahead of the stander, who then begins his stalking period, and so forth.

Although I have spent the greater part of my time hunting whitetails with a gun, I must confess that the majority of my learning experiences have occurred when I had a bow or a camera in my hand. The intimate ranges required for a shot with either instrument give you the opportunity to watch these creatures for long periods of time, and some of the things I've seen have destroyed a few myths and made me a much better hunter.

I have never seen a spooked whitetail circle around in back of a hunter, as some believe. Once they realized what was up, they all angled off to the left or right and ran in a relatively straight line for up to a mile before settling down.

However, I have watched whitetails who weren't sure of a hunter's identity circle downwind to catch his scent—an act that puts them at a hunter's back, since you hunt with the wind on your face.

An even more interesting reaction to the threat of a hunter finds a deer rising from its bed to face the hunter four-square, usually peering at him through a light screen of brush. As the hunter changes position the deer follows him, maintaining that same squared-off relationship. I have seen hunters pass within yards of a deer in this situation, and aside from the gradual shift in position, the animal has not moved a muscle unless it was seen by the hunter. That matter of being seen is fascinating, too. Deer seem to sense the split-second of recognition, and they are off and running before a gun is ever shouldered. With this in mind, whenever I suspect that I might be seeing a deer I keep doing whatever I'm doing—stalking, standing, sitting—and study my suspicions from the corner of my eye.

Whitetails have a warning system that alerts others of their kind, too. When these deer suspect danger they elevate their tail and flare their white rump hairs, making their rear end more apparent than ever. They also flare the glands on the inside of their hind legs and sometimes exhale air in a snort, or stomp their front feet. However, this warning system is far more prevalent among does and fawns than bucks; the bigger the buck, the less apt he is to be concerned with much more than his own hide. In fact, the big bucks I've seen didn't even flag their tail as they ran, but tucked it between their legs like a scared puppy and scrambled off low to the ground.

I have had the opportunity to carefully observe big bucks at close quarters only twice, since most of the time when I encounter them, the season is open as well as my tag, and I have a gun or bow in my hand. But both behaved the same way, and that behavior suggests another important lesson. First, they skulked with such stealth and easy grace that I did not see them until they were practically on top of me; their movements were that fluid, their camouflage that perfect. Second, they had their heads nearly flat on the ground as they moved. They would advance 10 yards at a time, slowly swinging their heads from side to side 2 inches off the forest floor, then pause and raise their heads for a different view.

The second time this happened I felt it was more than coincidence, so I dropped to the buck's eye level and discovered a whole new world. For about a vertical foot I could see further at ground zero than I could at normal height!

As those deer moved forward they weren't just sniffing the ground, they were looking under the brush, and were sure to see a hunter long before he would see them. No, that little discovery hasn't led to a trophy buck every time I enter the woods, but it did confirm the overall wisdom of getting up off the ground when you're on stand, even if it's only a foot.

Whitetail hunting brings together many skills—shooting, patience, stealth, sharp eyes—but you'll find the most dependable ally to be sound knowledge about your quarry and the mechanisms of their daily lives. Put another way, when you know what they're going to do, you can cut 'em off at the pass. But there's another dimension to becoming a student of the whitetail—you develop an appreciation of a wild and beautiful creature. It's an extra flavor that adds spice to your days afield and to the venison that will surely grace your table each season.

By Wayne van Zwoll

SADDLEBAGS

HE TAUGHT THE YOUNGER HUNTER LESSONS HE HAD YET TO LEARN—THE DIFFERENCE BETWEEN A BIG BUCK AND A FINE BUCK; AND THAT BIG BUCKS CAN BE FOUND IN LITTLE PLACES . . . IF BIG BUCKS ARE ALL YOU WANT.

HE WOULD COME into camp of an evening, but never before the opener. Mostly, he'd say, he just wanted to see our deer. We'd usually have one, or a couple. I was a pretty serious hunter.

"A fine buck, that," he'd murmur, after hearing the story of a hard hunt. It didn't matter how big the buck was; it was a fine buck if the going had been tough.

He had a peculiar way of talking, a proper English with a lilt that pinned the words together gently. After assessing our deer, he'd shuffle to the fire and hunch over it like a buzzard stooped over old meat, peering into the flames as if deciding which to pluck next.

We called him Saddlebags because the flaccid coffee-colored skin under his eyes hung in prominent loops. His sharp nose shadowed bright gray eyes, deep-sunk below hairy brows, now white. His face was always shaven. A rumpled pea-jacket hung loose on what had probably once been a muscular frame. He could have been fifty or seventy, a logger or a rabbi. To us, he was simply a local. It seems strange now that my preoccupation with deer precluded any substantive interest in the origins of our guest. Deer hunting can be a selfish thing.

Before, when the hunting had been good, Saddlebags had routinely shared our last evening on the mountain. As deer became scarce, he visited more often. Eventually I asked why.

"Visiting's good when the hunting isn't," he said. "It's an option that improves with age." It was the only time I can remember him smiling.

The next year we left early because a big snow sent the deer downcountry. We didn't shoot a buck. More importantly, I didn't shoot a buck. We chewed through drifts up to the door handles on the way out, dropping our tire chains only a couple of miles above the highway. We were shaking them clean when I heard the rattle of a laboring pickup.

Saddlebags pulled alongside, a gray wool cap clinging to his brow like the somber clouds clutching the mountains. He could have spoken to anyone, but he aimed those bright eyes at me and said evenly: "A tough year."

I slung the last set of chains into Uncle's truck and slammed the canopy shut. "It wasn't worth my time." I was cross.

His retort cut though the exhaust boiling from the belly of his Dodge. "What *is* worth your time in October?"

I didn't go back next season. Uncle said I missed comfortable weather and a near-record paucity of deer. "We got a fork; you might have done better. The deer were hanging in the steep places. Old roosters like me run out of fuel on those slopes."

I felt smug because the hunting had been poor.

"Saddlebags came the last day and said winter had taken lots of deer but that the hunting would be better next year. He told me to tell you to come back."

"How can he predict a good season?" My record on that hill was the best in camp; I'd worked hard to make it so. What could the old man show me about deer hunting?

My uncle replied dryly that maybe there was more to Saddlebags than I thought and that with my skills I might just prove him right. "Besides," he added, "you can't quit without three consecutive days at dishes. Camp rules."

Next autumn I found myself between college and a job. Uncle phoned on Labor Day. "Camp menu time. Wednesday supper's your choice. What do you want?" I could have cut him short. I said that chicken and noodles would be fine.

MUSTARD ASPENS FLUTTERED a greeting as we lurched along the dusty jeep trail, climbing toward a fresh blue sky. We set up at the old spot, below a stony basin slit by a thin white creek and capped by red bluffs.

He came that evening, the first time ever before our hunt. We'd finished supper and tended to the trail food for morning. The rifles were picketed in the notched lodgepole that had held many rifles. Saddlebags walked to it and bent over, peering at our guns like a bird might at a procession of insects, but not touching. "A dandy lot. Yes, dandies. Is that one yours?" He looked at me.

"Yes." I told him what it was, wondering how he'd picked it.

"You could use a bit more barrel for a .280 Ackley. But I see you've replaced the trigger, so you must know a smidge about such things. Do you shoot it well?"

What kind of question was that? I mumbled something humble and turned the knife on my whetstone.

"Maybe you could show me tomorrow after you get your deer." He stared without moving, the inquisitor. Shadows thrown by the fire accentuated his stoop and his corniced brow. Only a spark of light flickered from the dark recesses of his cheeks.

"I can't know if I'll kill tomorrow. I

don't shoot yearling bucks." I was prepared to explain my selectivity, but he spared me the condescension.

"Nor did I, for many years. It's good that a deer will last three winters in my freezer."

I may have smiled. I said: "Come back in a couple of days. You can shoot that rifle if you like, if I'm off the mountain."

"You could come with me tomorrow. I can show you a buck."

Before I could say no, Uncle called from the tent to say he was hunting the top loop come morning. The top loop was an ambitious trek. He'd always left it for me, and through the tent wall I told him so. "Yeah," he agreed. "But I puffed my way up there last year and kinda liked the view. Do something different tomorrow." It was as if he'd not overheard, but his timing was too good. I capitulated.

SADDLEBAGS CAME RUMBLING up in the dark before I'd washed the last of my oatmeal down with hot chocolate. I grabbed my Remington, slung my fanny pack onto the dusty seat, and climbed in. I said good morning and he said it was indeed. I almost said this is opening morning and you'd best realize I don't want to waste it.

We bumped down the main mountain road while I finished an apple, then took a spur that led north. It was a small track that soon became a tunnel through toast-colored alders that raked both mirrors flat and clawed noisily at the fenders. The mountain hid dawn, but I could feel it sneaking up on us. I fidgeted.

The pickup stopped in brush so thick I could see only an occasional star. We pried our doors open against the saplings. I buckled the pack, thumbed in four cartridges, and eased my door closed. From the other side came the muted, oily snap of a bolt locking home. Saddlebags had a rifle. "This way."

I followed him down the tunnel of alders, now just a trail. He used no light, but I was the only one to stumble. Presently a rockslide relieved us of our canopy. The sky was purple with red flanks. We were hard against the hill, shielded from sunrise.

Slowly Saddlebags picked his way over boulders the size of washing machines. Behind him, I was the noisier. The old man stopped at a tiny island of battered firs and motioned me to sit. I felt like a dog, keen to hunt but constrained by the unfathomable whims of the one who held the leash.

Saddlebags leaned against a fir, aiming a pair of binoculars across the slice and down to a small, dark meadow on its border. "Snow's there most of the year; melt brings on the forbs; deer bed below, come up for snacks." He whispered it from the side of his mouth, in a matter-of-fact way that left no room for comment. He slid down to a sit, his head dropped over his chest, and he appeared to sleep. I'd known other men like this, I recalled bitterly. To them hunting was time, not effort.

The sky smoldered a long time before dawn fired the frost on the meadow. I shivered as I watched it. There was no other place to look, no alternatives. I didn't like limiting my options.

"What do you make of him?"

I started, not yet comfortable on the flat of a rock, but so occupied with getting comfortable that I'd not seen Saddlebags sit up straight to glass. I aligned my binoculars with his, and after a bit of looking found the buck. It was only the curve of an antler at first. Then an ear popped out, and the glint of an eye. He stepped from shadow as I watched; an exceptional buck for sure, perhaps 28 inches with four long, heavy tines.

My companion's trimmed Springfield stayed on his lap. Did Saddlebags think the deer too far? My guess was 200 yards, not a long shot with my rifle; but the Springfield wore a receiver sight. The buck fed out, tawny side to us, tempting. I eased the sling over my bicep. Saddlebags remained still, watching.

The sun was up now, still blocked from view by the mountain but spilling directly into the sea of conifers below. "Not bad." I said it nonchalantly as if I'd seen better, but firmly enough to hint I was interested. The old man didn't acknowledge this attempt to make things happen. I prodded again. "He'll be back in the bushes as soon as the sun hits." Still no response. I thought then of the buzzard-like form of Saddlebags over our fire. Here was some *real* meat—but the same stony, reflective image of a deliberate man.

"Do you want him?" I had to ask. The sun was crawling into the meadow now. The buck might leave, and he was very handsome.

"Do you?" Saddlebags didn't turn around, just whispered it as if he were suddenly curious in an offhanded way.

I swallowed. Is rain wet? Of course! That's what we're here for, man! I almost shouted it, but only thought it. The buck ambled into a pocket of ceanothus that hid his chest. "You saw him first."

Saddlebags lowered his glasses and sank back against the tree. "Be my guest."

The buck was in the open again, but poking his head in the air more frequently and paying less attention to the vegetation. Twice he'd moved to the edge of the timber and come back. Next time he might slip into that blue-green deep, submerging like a fish that's decided it will sulk on the bottom.

My crosswire nodded gently on the buck's third rib.

WE GOT BACK late, with the buck lashed to packframes in the pickup bed. The others were in the tent, eating. Uncle came out to meet us: "Well?"

"He shot a fine buck," said Saddlebags. "How did you fare on the top loop?"

"A tough trip it was," my uncle lied. "But no deer to show for it. Come eat."

Saddlebags hunched over the fire, warming himself. The stars were bright and the air had snap. "Thank you, no. I'll help the young man take care of his deer, then I must be off." He turned toward the pickup and waved me to his side. "We'll spread the meat a bit in the sacks, so it will cool."

After the Dodge had rumbled away down-canyon, my campmates came out and gathered around. Only one other buck had been shot: a yearling. They admired the antlers on my pack-board. "A secret spot, no doubt," probed some-one. "High or low?" asked another. "Was it alone?" "Long shot?" "What time?" I answered them all, even the last one: "Did you offer Saddlebags a chance?"

No, I hadn't. Well, not really. The old man had followed me up the mountain and this buck had jumped to my front. There was time for only a quick shot. I'd hit, the bullet nipping the rear of the far lung. I'd scrambled for another look as the deer raced through a strip of whitebark pine. An explosion behind me had sent the buck cart-wheeling down a shale slide, 200 yards away.

"We were on the far end of the top loop." I smiled innocently at Uncle, who gaped.

"I thought *he* was taking *you* hunting!"

"But he did. He showed me a big buck. It had long, thick points and lots of sky between them."

Someday I'd tell them that I didn't kill it because in death it would not have been as fine a buck as the mediocre deer on my packframe. I had been offered a sure shot by a man who'd earned exclusive rights to it. A bullet from my rifle would have been but a period to a sentence skillfully crafted by someone else.

"It isn't big," I said simply. "But it's a fine buck." The circle broke up slowly, my compan-ions moving off toward the fire. Most of them had not hunted hard enough to discover the difference between big bucks and fine bucks, or to care.

I cleaned the meat that night. Ebbing flames danced on dark tent walls as I eased out of my clothes and slid into my sleeping bag. Uncle was next to me; I shook him awake.

"It's not dawn yet." His voice was wary.

"I gotta know. Did you hunt the top loop last year? "

He chuckled, then shook with silent mirth. "Who showed you the top loop eight years ago?"

"You did." I was getting annoyed.

"A long time ago, someone else showed me. After I took to it, he didn't hunt it anymore. He said the steep places were for young legs, and fine bucks for men who chafed when they couldn't earn a big one. He wasn't native, just local. He had an extraordinary mind and a Spartan Springfield. He taught me a lot about hunting—mostly the parts worth passing on."

I said nothing.

"He also taught me you can find big bucks in little places, if big bucks are all you want. Good night, Deadeye."

I didn't bother him again.

By Sam Curtis

Floodplain WHITETAILS

When farmers evened out the ups and downs of nature, the deer began to flourish.

B.K. KRUPS LIVES ON the lower Yellowstone River near the border of North Dakota and Montana. He has a passion for hunting and history, and he was willing to share both the day he showed me around his ranch.

"When I was a young man in the 1940s, whitetails were so scarce that the Fish and Game wouldn't let you hunt them. My father told me things weren't much better at the turn of the century. And pictures of my granddad's homestead show the Yellowstone with hardly a cottonwood or snowberry on its banks. No self-respecting whitetail would think twice about setting up housekeeping in a place like that. Today it's different. It's a whitetail paradise around here."

What Krups and his family have seen evolve over 100 years of changing whitetail habitat on the Yellowstone is true along many rivers in the northern plains, including rivers as far south as the South Platte in Colorado, and as far west as the Columbia in Washington.

In the last half of the 19th century, bison grazing, droughts, and prairie fires kept these floodplain habitats low on trees and shrubs and tall on grass. The few whitetails that did eke out a living were almost wiped out during the turn of the century by settlers who hunted them to put dinner on the table.

Ironically, the same floodplain habitats we have come to associate with prime whitetail territory have, until recent decades, been marginal at best. Yet a turnaround for whitetails and their floodplain habitats came when people finally settled in along the rivers of the Great Plains and started growing crops.

"With the bison gone, and the wildfires controlled, and the land under irrigation," Krups said, "we sort of evened out the ups and downs of nature. Cottonwoods and willows began to think the river wasn't a bad place to hang out in after all."

In fact, in a recently completed seven-year study, deer researcher Gary Dusek concluded that this riverside cover is the most important factor supporting whitetail populations like never before along the Yellowstone and other rivers of the northern plains.

But Dusek also found that 20th-century floodplain agriculture has done a lot more than provide cover. As a crazy-quilt pattern of different crops was planted within riverside stands of cottonwoods and willows, a habitat evolved that contained a great deal of vegetable diversity and a lot of "edges." The result is whitetail heaven where deer find cover, water, and a wide variety of food within a very confined area all year long. It makes for fat, healthy whitetails that don't starve during the winter and live on a very small home range.

"You'd think that getting a trophy buck would be as easy as rolling off a rock," Krups told me as we drove along the Yellowstone, "especially since these river whitetails develop a pretty standard routine. By the time hunting season opens, they're heavy into the grainfields and the sugar beets. They hide under the cottonwoods all day and nip out for eats at night."

Pointing out fields where he'd seen some dandy bucks, Krups explained that after harvesting their crops, most of the ranchers don't immediately plow their fields, so grain and sugar beet leftovers are favorite whitetail foods during hunting season.

It certainly sounded easy enough to get a deer—until B.K. explained the problem. It seems that floodplain whitetails have found such ideal habitat along the Yellowstone and other rivers of the Great Plains that they don't have to move around much. During the day, stands of young and mature cottonwoods provide good cover overhead, and an understory of wild rose, willow, and snowberry gives them ground level cover and browse.

Krups took me into a peninsula of river-bottom forest surrounded on three sides by fields. Beneath the trail cottonwoods, brush grew head high.

"Not a bad hideout, is it? Those old whitetails can hunker down in here, and you could walk past them within 20 feet and never see a thing on the ground from here. I've had hunters come in here for days in a row. They sit at the base of a tree and all they see are bits and pieces of deer flitting through the brush."

With the grainfields so handy, Krups explained, deer only move a few hundred yards from daytime bedding spots to nighttime feeding sites. And unless you're sitting in exactly the right spot, their limited movement may very well not bring them close to you.

Another problem for the floodplain whitetail hunter is cattle. "Lots of guys don't think anything of livestock. They see deer and cows out in a field together, and they figure they kind of ignore one another. That's just not so, at least not around here," Krups said.

It seems the problem arises not in the fields, but in the woodlands where cattle move to seek shade and where they stomp around and chomp on the shrubs that whitetails depend on both for cover and for food. Where livestock use wooded areas heavily, whitetails tend to be few.

"Some hunters get hot under the collar because ranchers don't want them hunting near their livestock. I suppose we may appear overprotective of our prize bulls. But the fact is that you aren't going to get your best whitetail hunting where you find cattle anyway. Since I'm mainly into growing grain and sugar beets, I end up with a pretty good crop of whitetails, too," Krups said, grinning.

"Well, the deer may be all around, but it doesn't sound like they're very easy to get," I said as we pulled up to his ranch house.

"Particularly the bucks," Krups said, grinning widely as if there were another problem.

There was. He elaborated.

Research on tagged whitetails in the area showed that bucks move freely over their entire home range all year long with the exception of the months of October and November. At a time when you'd expect males to be on the move in their search for mates, they actually move less than females, making them more difficult to find.

"So what you're telling me," I said, "is there are whitetails all over your ranch, but they're impossible to get."

"No, they're not impossible," he said, "but there are some things you ought to know about before you go out in the morning."

He began by explaining that floodplain whitetails seem to have favorite fields that they move into at night for feeding. By the time they appear in the fields it's often too late to hunt but it's still possible to identify a good-sized buck in the twilight. And its presence in a specific field is a good indication that the deer will bed down nearby in an effort to minimize movement. So the buck you see in a specific field today may very likely return again and again to the same spot.

"In the morning and evening, the trick is to choose a spot on the edge of the field and its bordering woodland where you can see into the cover and into the field. You've got to be up in a tree. This sitting around on the ground isn't going to get you anything," Krups said.

"Those bucks often hang around under cover at the border of the forest after coming out of the fields in the morning and before going into them at night. This edge area is sort of a transition zone that they spend some time in between feeding and bedding."

Krups suggested that I spend the morning in a tree stand he had built at the edge of a field where one of his "dandy" bucks had been feeding. He would take me there well before daylight, he said.

Floodplain Tree Stands

Mature cottonwood trees are not made for portable tree stands. They're too wide, and their bark is too corrugated and too unpredictably attached to the tree. An old cottonwood and a tree stand are an unsafe combination.

Many floodplain cottonwood groves have at least one permanent tree stand, a lumber-and-nails concoction someone erected who knows when. Even if permission to use one of these homemade stands comes with assurances of its age and sturdiness, use it with a safety harness and a great deal of caution.

A young, live cottonwood that's 1 to 1½ feet in diameter can safely handle a portable stand. And among these younger trees growing closer to the streambed you are likely to find whitetail bucks during the day. This is the ideal spot to put a portable stand.— *S. C.*

Now, I've always considered "well before daylight" to be around 6 A.M. A half hour until legal hunting hours is an interminably long time to wait. But Krups had me out of bed at 4:45 and at the deer stand by 5:30.

"This way everything has a chance to get back to normal before it's light," he said as he disappeared in the dark, telling me to stay put until he returned. I wasn't sure about "everything," but I doubted that *I'd* get back to normal before the next day.

Normality, it turned out, was alive with deer. Between 6:30 and 10, when Krups picked me up, I'd seen thirteen whitetails, including one buck that I'd passed on.

"After lunch I'm going to have you try something else," Krups said after I'd filled him in on the morning.

Male and female whitetails, it seems, have different cover preferences during the day. While does move into mature cottonwood stands along the river, bucks often spend more time in the

Whitetails and Water Management

The presence of cover is the single most important factor contributing to large whitetail populations in floodplain habitats. And good cover is largely dependant on light-handed water management that allows for seasonal flooding of lowlands in order to encourage the growth of riparian shrubs and trees.

Where intense water management occurs, including such practices as river channelization or mainstream impoundment, grassland becomes the major habitat type, and whitetail populations decline.— S. C.

younger cottonwoods closer to the streambed. Because these areas have a sparser understory than the more mature riparian forests, it's possible to still-hunt for whitetail bucks during the middle of the day with some success.

The lunch I ate made it possible to move very slowly along the river that afternoon. I spooked one young buck munching on snowberry and rose hips. But the buck I really had my sights on did a fast fade into some willows.

BY 4 P.M. I was back at the ranch ready for a nap, but Krups wouldn't hear of it. "You've got to leave in the morning. Give it one more shot. I'll let you go to bed early, I promise. Here's the plan."

Krups explained how hunting season always pushed a few deer out of the floodplain and up along tributary streams during the daytime. Unlike deer that held tight, moving little, the few deer that escaped out of the river sometimes moved a mile or so in the course of coming down to feeding fields in the morning and returning to upland draws at night. This movement made them vulnerable, especially if you took a stand along the cover of a tributary stream that the deer used as a travel route between bedding and feeding areas.

"Let me take you up Corral Creek," Krups said. "There's a rock outcropping just off the ranch road. You can sit there until dark and look right down into the brush. You'll see any critter that comes through."

How could I refuse a man who filled his deer tag opening morning of every season and who knew all the floodplain whitetail tricks about as well as the deer themselves?

I must have nodded off. I sat up with a start and peered down into the growing darkness. In 15 minutes it would be too late to hunt. I thought of packing it in.

Something flicked behind branches in the spreading gloom. It came again, closer. Then the buck was right below me, moving at a steady pace toward dinner. It was clear from his rack that he had survived many a fall season by moving upland during the day and sneaking back to the floodplain croplands at night.

Over a late dinner, Krups gave me a hard time anyway. "It's pretty tasty liver for such an old buck. I'm sure glad it took you so long to get it. It gave me a chance to show you the different tactics we use on floodplain whitetails. Next year maybe you'll be able to hunt on your own."

By Sam Curtis

BACKYARD MULEYS

While other hunters head for the heavy timber, the author has scored consistently in agricultural lowlands near home.

EVERY YEAR DEER hunters trudge past my house, cross the hayfield out back, and disappear into the lodgepole forest that begins at the base of the hill. Most of them head for the ridge that marks the divide between the canyon where I live in southwestern Montana and the next canyon to the east. From there they can hunt hundreds of square miles of national forest land that is prime mule deer habitat by anyone's standards. Yet every year a considerable number of those hunters return with their deer tags unfilled.

It's not that mule deer are scarce. Plenty of those hunters see bucks that they could bag. Yet the typical lament from these deep-woods hunters is consistently the same, except for the specific name of the distant location.

"Oh, I saw a big buck back on Blue Mountain, but I wasn't about to drag it all the way out from there. Too bad. It was a nice deer."

There are other hunters, of course, who don't see muleys. And some offer excuses like, "The woods were too noisy," or "They must still be in the high country." I suspect, however, that some of these hunters have a problem with the size of the territory. There is so much of it, and the expectation of seeing a deer in the next draw—and the next one after that—is so great that they hunt too fast. They miss seeing deer in their attempt to hunt as much territory as possible.

I'm well aware of these problems of hunting in big country, and I used to cope with them myself until three seasons ago. It was then—quite by accident—that I started bagging backyard muleys. And I've taken a buck mule deer within a mile of my front door every year since then.

My education in the ways of backyard mule deer all started on opening day of the 1978 season. It was a cool, clear morning at the end of a week of dry weather. I had been scouting the woods several days earlier, and hard as I tried to walk quietly, each footfall sounded as if it were landing on a carpet of crunchy cereal. My only quiet option seemed to be in sticking to the wood road of a neighboring rancher. It wouldn't take me very far from the main canyon road and nearby houses, but it seemed my only choice.

At the top of the knoll in back of my house I paused to wait for legal daylight. Lights still shone from the houses below, and I wondered if I might not be better off having breakfast in one of those comfortable kitchens. There seemed small chance of seeing a muley so close to civilization. Nevertheless, I shouldered my rifle and strolled slowly along the wood road into the trees.

The buck seemed as surprised at my presence as I at his. He lowered his head, and his steps became tentative.

Within an hour of leaving home, I was back by the fire having coffee. And the buck was hanging in the shed.

The incident was a fluke, of course. At least that's the way I saw it at the time. The buck had been a maverick, no doubt, not yet spooked by hunting pressure. My hunting friends agreed.

However, the next year's experience suggested otherwise. In 1979 I did very little muley hunting until the end of the season. As a matter of fact, the chances of finishing the year without getting a deer looked very good as I stepped out of the house on the last day of hunting. The hour was past 9, and I knew three friends had already gone up the gulch behind the house. A shot had been fired earlier, and I was sure all the commotion had unsettled any deer in the vicinity.

But I kept remembering the backyard muley of the year before. There was no time to get deep into the woods. I'd have to concentrate on hunting nearby and hope for a repeat of the previous year.

Going directly up the steep nose of a side ridge that starts behind my vegetable garden, I gained several hundred feet in elevation before angling across to the head of a small draw. The draw is thick with timber—one of those places you have to hunt very slowly if you hope to see anything, much less get a shot at it. The deep snow helped slow me down and effectively muffled any twigs I might have snapped below its surface.

At first I wasn't sure I'd seen a movement at all. But it was worth stopping to double check. Nothing more happened for several minutes. Then, between one slit in the vertical world of trees, a horizontal patch appeared. An antlered head moved into another slit. I sat in the snow with my .30/06 readied until I saw the buck's shoulders.

Now I was beginning to wonder. Two backyard muleys in a row! One on the first day of the season, the other on the last. One when there was no snow on the ground, the other when the snow was up to my knees. Maybe there really were such things as backyard muleys.

I certainly couldn't attribute their presence to the fact that they hadn't been spooked. There had been enough people hunting in the area that year to stir up a whole herd of deer. But neither could I claim that it was just the snow that had forced them so close to human habitation. The year before the weather had been dry as a bone.

I was contemplating these matters in my living room when the three hunters who'd set out before me came wearily back through my front yard. They'd taken a shot at a mule deer heading up the gulch that morning. I said I'd heard the shot. It was the only deer they'd seen all day, and they'd gone miles back along the divide.

"You know, sometimes those muleys come down from the high country after dark," one of my friends started reasoning out loud. "They feed in the hay and wheat fields at night and then just before dawn they head back to the cover of the deep woods. That one we missed was probably running a bit late."

"Well, Dave," I said, "he or one of his friends must have continued to run late because he's hanging in the shed right now."

There was a great deal of head shaking and soft muttering following my remark. I even began to feel a bit guilty. One of the guys had been out after a deer several times a week since the start of the season.

MY FRIENDS ATTRIBUTED those first two backyard muleys to an uncommon turn of good fortune, but I was definitely beginning to believe otherwise. Last year's season made me a *firm* believer.

In 1980 I purposely decided to spend my time hunting a limited area within about half a mile of the canyon road and its adjacent dwellings. My efforts were concentrated on the gulch out back. The first week of the season I went out three times. One time I saw no deer at all; twice I saw does. The fourth time I went out was the start of the second week of the season. At the top of the gulch, resting quietly in the sun, a three-point buck convinced me of the common existence of backyard mule deer.

There is nothing unique about the area I hunt. It could be any muley country where forest and agricultural land meet. Here, it is not at all unusual for muleys to stick to the periphery of pine forests, along the edges of fields and irrigation ditches within sight of roads and houses.

I'm convinced these backyard muleys are not seen by most hunters because they don't *expect* to see them. First of all, many hunters aren't yet looking for deer because they've just gotten off the road. And, second, most hunters are moving too fast and too noisily to see deer, they're in such a rush to get into "better hunting grounds."

Even when track concentrations indicate there are deer down low, along creeks, in fields, and at forest edges, many hunters believe they are the tracks of whitetails instead of mule deer. And, even granting that this is sometimes the case, the whitetail assumption has led many a mule deer hunter past a prime buck.

Some skeptics will still balk, of course. Recently an acquaintance, who heard me mention backyard muleys, laughed at the idea of finding a good-sized buck so close to home.

"You may run into some young, inexperienced bucks that hang around close in," he said, "but it's no place to hunt if you're looking for a trophy."

I then related an incident that occurred before I believed in finding mule deer in the backyard.

Wally Hansen and I had been hunting up the canyon and back along the divide. We'd run into some tracks, and we'd seen some does, but not an antler had been visible. As a last hunch before returning home I told Wally I wanted to walk out on the nose of land that overlooks my neighbor's ranch house.

On the south side of the nose a thicket of hawthorn fills a narrow draw. It was late in the day, and I figured I might run into a buck emerging from the brush to feed. My attention was fixed on that southern thicket while I walked down the nose. But as I neared its end, a movement to the north caught the corner of my eye. Wheeling around, I watched a six-point buck sneak out of sight. It was the biggest deer I'd ever missed.

THE ONLY PLACE the buck could have been bedded was in a small brush patch of no more than a quarter-acre. It lay just above an irrigation ditch, beyond which stretched a plowed field, my neighbor's house, and the county road. Above the brush, open grassland rose a quarter of a mile before running into forest.

So much for the lack of backyard trophies.

But believing in backyard muleys and hunting them are two different things. Bagging a mule deer that is within sight of a road depends on knowing the areas where the deer hide and on hunting these areas thoroughly.

As the missed-buck incident points out, thick brush along irrigation ditches and creek bottoms is a prime location for muleys. These places are more often thought of as whitetail habitat, but muleys will also use them when they border the forested lands usually associated with mule deer territory.

These thicket areas are particularly difficult to hunt alone, though. When you are outside the brush, you can't see into it, and when you're inside you can't see more than a few yards in any direction. Lone hunters will do best to post themselves in the late afternoon at a point where a sizable portion of the thicket's periphery can be observed. From such a vantage point, you are likely to see deer that are moving out of their cover to feed.

Two or more hunters have an advantage when hunting brushy locations. One person can work through the brush while others take up positions around the outside and wait for the deer.

Thick timber bordering fields and other open land affords prime cover for backyard muleys. To hunt this type of habitat when there is no snow to cover the dry twigs and the grasses that tend to be such loud noisemakers, you'll be wise to stay on paths, wood roads, or game trails. But a covering of 8 to 10 inches of snow will offer ideal conditions for hunting heavy timber. You can move with relative quiet through the heart of the timber, and you have better chances of seeing deer against the light background of snow.

I prefer to hunt this kind of area alone. The theory that two or three hunters will push deer into one another may work in practice when hunting more open terrain, but it doesn't work in thick timber. Any deer that is being driven by another hunter is likely to be on the run, and a deer running through thick timber is a blur—not much of a target.

I'd say the key to success here is to hunt by yourself and to hunt very slowly. A silhouette is often your only clue to a deer's presence. It may be merely a hint of those mulelike ears or a subtle interruption in the color and pattern of trees. Many times I've had to use binoculars or my rifle scope to determine whether an object was a deer or an apparition.

Finally, any draws or gulches located near open fields or close to roads and houses provide good backyard refuges for mule deer. Ideally, you'll work these potential hiding places by coming down them from above. When you can't view the entire area and you are hunting alone, it's often smart to work the same gulch three different ways. Come down one shoulder of the gulch or draw, then go up the other shoulder, and finally come down the bottom of the gulch itself. To some people that may seem like beating a dead horse, but a quiet hunter can pass within a few dozen yards of an unseen deer without disturbing it, providing the wind is right. There have been times when I have not seen deer in a relatively confined area until I've been making my third pass through it.

Backyard muleys do exist. Finding them requires that you hunt their likely hiding places thoroughly, quietly, and slowly. And hunting them safely requires that you be completely familiar with the location of nearby buildings and livestock. But going after backyard bucks, in my estimation, is often more productive than hunting a large and seemingly limitless expanse of their habitat.

By John Barsness

Antlered OBSESSION

TROPHY MULEYS AREN'T FOUND BY THOSE WHO SHUN HARD WORK—OR FEAR HEIGHTS.

THERE IS A KIND OF trophy hunting far removed from head collecting or record books. My own antlered obsession involves a mystic vision much like the Pleistocene paintings in France's Lascaux Cave. At any time of day or year, I can close my eyes and see a mule deer buck, antlers high and stylized, etched in lines of ocher on clay walls. This vision flickers across my tribal memories as if I were seeing it by the light of a mammoth-grease torch. The antlers of the bucks I've killed and eaten are scattered around my house and barn, and I can visualize each deer as if it were still standing on an open ridge. But the buck that holds me is the one in the cave.

Perhaps there is a simple explanation for this obsession: the largest mule deer live on barren ridges where people and even other wild mammals rarely go; where you—and they—can turn in any direction and look down on the rest of the earth.

I found my first such buck while still in my early twenties. I saw him standing on top of a Montana mountain near the Idaho panhandle. You could get there by following a switchback trail for 7 miles, or you could climb almost straight up across talus slides and deadfall for half that distance. Being descended from Norwegians who believed that anything worth doing should be done the hard way, I went straight up.

For the first 1,000 feet in elevation, I saw plenty of deer sign and a few does. For the next 1,000 feet, I could have been hunting in pretty but empty forest. As I looked across the canyon, the opposite ridge seemed vertical. The absolute darkness of Douglas fir was broken up by yellow stands of Western larch, the needles having just turned in late October. The weather was almost muggy, and I wondered if it was foolish to hunt up here rather than in the semi-rainforest of the canyon bottom, where the damp earth between ferns showed plenty of deer tracks. And then I started climbing again.

In late morning I half-circled the mountain, 500 feet below the apex, and jumped an elk in cool timber, not getting a shot. An hour later a small bunch of deer, including one buck halfway old and large, rose from the far side of a clearing and stood there for a moment. I rested the crosshairs of the .270 gently on the buck's chest for a heart-whump, then I lowered the rifle and watched the deer go. This was the first time I'd left a legal deer in peace, and I felt as virtuous as a sergeant in the Salvation Army.

Just before noon, I neared the top of the mountain. The ground was moist under a wall of basalt on the north side of the ridge, and I sneaked along, stopping and looking, the quickness of opening day having finally left my feet. I soon saw a buck standing at the base of the rocks 75 yards uphill, his outline silhouetted against bright clouds. He gazed away down the mountain, appearing as gray-black as the basalt. He was by several sizes the largest deer I'd ever seen, and when the crosshairs went by his chest for the fourth time, there was no chance that the bullet would find anything but sky.

At the shot, he turned and ran almost straight toward me; I shot again, and he fell. He moved his head slightly and I shot him once more at the base of the neck. Enough adrenaline pumped through my arms to make rolling him over easy, but when I tried to heave his gutted body over a dead fir 10 minutes later, the task had become impossible. I left my jacket on the buck's heavy mahogany antlers to keep bears away, and returned the next day with a friend

and a horse and packed him down the switchbacks. After hanging almost a week, the buck weighed 232 pounds. His antlers are still on my guest-room wall, but it was soon after the last of his steaks were grilled that I started seeing the deer in the cave.

RICHARD JACKSON IS a good friend, a former Tennessean who claims direct ancestry of the Jackson called Stonewall. After seeing most of America and Canada, he picked Montana's Blackfoot Indian Reservation as his home, married a Cree woman, and built a life around horses. He's been a rodeo rider, knows the nearly lost art of breaking a wagon team, and has one of the best strings of mountain horses I've ever seen. He uses them in an area called the Badger-Two Medicine, a piece of the wild Rocky Mountain front surrounded by Glacier Park, the Bob Marshall and Great Bear Wilderness Areas, and the reservation. He herds cows for a local cattleman's association, guides summer campers and anglers, and outfits for black bears, elk, and (particularly) large mule deer. I had chased bears and trout with him before, and when he asked if I'd like to chase deer, there was nothing to say but yes. When you open the front door to Jackson's house, you're confronted by a mule deer head with antlers almost as thick as the fore-end of a rifle stock, and the thickness rises through the tines like the branches of an old alpine fir.

It had been fifteen years since I'd killed that deer near Idaho. In the following decade, I'd killed more big bucks, and guided people to others, from the Missouri Breaks to the Yellowstone Divide. Some had worn larger antlers, though none so dark and heavy, and while several weighed around 200 pounds, none had possessed an equally massive body, almost as large as a spike elk. It had been five years since I'd killed my last one, on top of the rimrocks of the Musselshell Breaks. Throughout those autumns, I'd watched literally hundreds of other bucks, both in deep breaks and on high mountains—but that old mystic vision kept my rifle silent. Mystic visions have a way of restricting your life, as any saint, Sun Dance warrior, or prospector will tell you.

Opening morning was dark and the canyon wind was blowing when we saddled up and rode several miles down Badger Creek. It grew lighter as we headed up a side canyon, following a trail above a cliff, and by the time we entered the timber, it was shooting light. Jackson whispered for me to dismount and walk ahead on the trail, my rifle ready, while he waited behind. Fresh elk droppings covered the earth a half-mile up, but we saw no elk. When the trail turned uphill I stopped, and soon Jackson showed, leading my horse. He had seen the elk sign too, and shrugged. We both hunt elk, but we chase mule deer, something not admitted to in many Western circles.

I remounted, and we rode up a switchback trail, resting the horses at every bend. As the switchbacks ended, the trail went straight up; the big Douglas firs thinned, and small alpine firs appeared. We got off and led our steeds, stopping every 100 yards to rest.

The trail finally began to level off on a ridge made of limestone gravel and scattered alpine fir. As we neared the top, I looked around and got that mule deer feeling, the sensation of looking down on the rest of the world. Even bighorn sheep and mountain goats don't live right on top of ridges; sheep prefer the shouldering grassy meadows, and goats, the lichened cliffs.

Chief Mountain, a rock pinnacle as steep and identifiable as the Matterhorn, was visible at least 50 miles to the north where it ran along the eastern edge of Glacier Park. To the east I could see one lower ridge, and then the high plains stretched to the twin buttes of the Sweetgrass Hills, 100 miles away. To the west and south were unending limestone reefs and

Mule Deer in Trouble

Despite having the largest antlers of any deer of the genus *Odocoileus* (which includes whitetails and blacktails), mule deer don't get much respect. Looked upon as the dumb cousins of the whitetail, even their ancestry was misunderstood until recently. DNA analysis has shown that rather than whitetails and mule deer being the two main species of American deer, with the various blacktails as subspecies of mule deer, mule deer are actually crosses between whitetails and blacktails. This information, along with other fascinating facts about mule deer, can be found in *Mule Deer Country* (NorthWord Press, 1999), a book written by the noted big-game biologist Valerius Geist, featuring great photography by Michael Francis.

After enjoying very high population growth in the 1950s and 1960s, mule deer went into a deep decline throughout much of the West during the late 1970s. Though muleys have made something of a comeback recently, they're still not in great shape. More glamorous big-game species such as elk and bighorn sheep have long had large foundations to promote their welfare, but mule deer are just now getting some respect and help, which they need far more than elk or even wild sheep. — J. B.

peaks, some topped with early snow. We tied our horses to a couple of firs, then took our rifles and binoculars and eased up through a stand of smaller firs to the far edge of the ridge where we could look into a big basin of open parks. We were at least 25 miles from the nearest trailhead, which was farther than I would have walked even fifteen years before. And then we heard the wolf.

Jackson wasn't sure what the sound was, but I'd been in the Northwest Territories six weeks before and had heard several wolves howl, and this was it: long and low, with a cadence as patient as a mountain. Wolves have returned to that part of Montana in the past decade; there is nowhere else south of Canada where you can find whitetail and mule deer, elk, moose, bighorn sheep, mountain goats, black and grizzly bears, mountain lions—and wolves. We listened to the wolf, heard it pause, and a coyote yipped somewhere else, sounding as impatient as a running stream.

We watched the basin for a while, but nothing showed. Back on our horses, Jackson told me to be alert; this was a ridge known to hold big deer. If we saw any deer I was to dismount, grab my rifle, and get ready to shoot. I nodded and we started off along the shoulder of the ridge, traveling along the first line of scattered alpine fir, with Jackson in the lead. We rode perhaps 200 yards before he hissed, "Deer!"

I reined hard and swung out of the saddle, right into the dry branch of a dead fir. Jackson rolled his eyes heavenward as I slid my rifle from the scabbard and dropped the reins. Resting the .270 over a level chest-high branch, I looked slightly downhill into a shallow ridgetop saddle and saw the dingy, white rump-patch of a mule deer. The scope revealed that the deer was a buck, and not a small one. He was walking directly away from us, his antlers spreading beyond his ears.

By this time Jackson was standing a few feet to my left, his binoculars up. "Take him," he whispered, just as the deer walked behind a fir.

I shook my head. "He's not big enough." I knew he was a big buck, but he didn't seem as big as the one in my vision. He walked directly away from us, then stopped and fed, his head hidden, in some low brush behind a fir. The breeze quartered past him, and if he wandered much farther to the left, its line would intersect his nose.

The deer started to move again, up the far side of the saddle. "Look again, buddy," Jackson said, quite seriously. The buck moved into a patch of fir, and I looked through the scope at an opening in the middle. When the deer moved through the opening, sideways now, there were long tines lifting everywhere in the shadows, and he looked remarkably like a deer in a cave.

The crosshairs moved to his shoulder, but before I could shoot, he was behind three more trees. The rifle moved with him. When he came out of the trees only the top half of his body showed, and the crosshairs drifted across to his shoulder and the rifle went off. His hindquarters eased down, his high antlers tilted back, and then he disappeared behind the gray ridge.

Without speaking, Jackson turned to the horses, and I turned downwind and circled, putting another round in the chamber. I marked the three trees in my mind and walked quickly, not running so I wouldn't be breathing hard. A long minute or so later I eased up next to the three trees and saw why his antlers hadn't looked big enough: he was fully as large as a spike elk.

Jackson walked up behind me as I stood there looking down at the buck, at the heavy six-pointed antlers that lay on limestone gravel, and at the massive curve of his body. Jackson shook his head and said he'd told me so. Then he asked if it would be all right if he said a Blackfoot prayer. I nodded, and he sat down a few feet to my right, cross-legged, his palms turned up on his knees, and said his prayer. I sat by the buck, my left hand on his warm side, and looked down at the ridges below. When we were done praying we gutted him, then took the head and cape and a backstrap to eat that night. After draping a rain slicker across his body to keep bears and eagles off until we could come back with a packhorse, we rode down the mountain, the buck's head in my lap, one antler braced across my left thigh and the other held in my left hand, above my shoulder.

From the time I saw him, and all through

that ride and the rest of the week—even while we tracked an elk for half a day without ever catching it—the buck grew and grew. At the end we rode out of Badger Creek in a blizzard, the buck's antlers and meat riding far ahead of me in the packstring, and in my mind he kept growing. I felt an odd detachment—not from the deer, because he would always be part of me, but from the hardness of the earth, the rocks and twisted alpine fir, and even the hard cold snow from the sky. It was as if something had come out of the mountains and touched me, as if skill and patience and perseverance had nothing to do with the meeting between me and the deer. As if I'd accidentally wandered into a lost cave and had no choice but to follow its erratic tunnel to the last room, where someone had mixed ocher with melted fat and painted a deer and a man, the man always following the deer.

Where to Find Large Mule Deer

What's a large mule deer? Many people claim any buck with antlers spreading less than 30 inches isn't a real trophy. No other antlered game animal—including elk, whitetails, caribou, blacktail deer, or even moose—has such an arbitrary number hung on it separating big from small.

Realistically, a 30-inch spread says almost nothing about a mule deer's antlers, and is to some extent a regional prejudice. A great many 30-inch heads have spindly antlers that just happen to flop out to the sides, and such antlers tend to occur more often in southern mule deer range. Some zoologists believe this might be a function of vegetation. In the Southwest and Mexico, for example, brush tends to grow sparser and lower, and even the forests have open understories and wider-spaced trees. Deer with widespread, low-slung antlers can hide better in widespread, low-slung brush. At the opposite end of mule deer range, in British Columbia, Alberta, northern Idaho, and Montana, forests are much thicker and taller, and mule deer antlers tend to grow more up than out. They may be just as large, but they don't spread as widely.

In some ways, the Boone and Crockett record book tries to remedy this difference by judging antlers on overall mass and size rather than spread. Their *Records of Big Game* also provides a good look at where large-antlered (if not large-bodied) mule deer live. For years, Colorado was the place to hunt trophy bucks, and it still claims far more heads in the record book than any other state. But in the past decade, Idaho and Utah have produced significantly more record heads, and states like Wyoming, Montana, and Oregon are not far behind.

Colorado's trophy decline is probably due to overhunting; for years it was the only Western state that sold unlimited numbers of nonresident deer licenses.

Significantly more big mule deer come from the mountains, rather than the plains. In part, this is also because of hunting pressure: plains bucks are more accessible. There are more of them, however, and you'll see ten times as many bucks on a hunt in the Wyoming sage or the Montana breaks than you will in any mountainous region. For a first-time hunter after a representative buck, I'd recommend a plains hunt.

But the great deer live back in the mountains, where they can grow old. I also suspect a superior diet has something to do with the growth of impressive mountain antlers–not just in terms of mineral content, but also seasonal growth. The greatest amount of rainfall on the plains occurs in May and June, but July and August—when antler tines are growing—are usually hot and dry. This may be why plains deer often have heavy-based antlers, but rather spindly tines. In the high mountains, where deer food stays green all summer long, bucks grow heavier, longer tines.

In any high-mountain wilderness, from Mexico to Alaska, you won't see many deer, but the odds are good that the ones you see will be really big. In the eight days I hunted with Richard Jackson, we saw exactly four deer, two of which were bucks. The second buck was not as big as the one I took, but it was a good buck just the same. One of Jackson's hunters on the next trip got it (or one just like it), and it green-scored 180 Boone and Crockett points. The rut begins in earnest during that later hunt, and more bucks are usually seen.— *J. B.*

OUT WEST THERE ARE MULE DEER APLENTY, BUT ACCESS IS LIMITED. TO FIND A REALLY FINE BUCK, YOU MUST SET YOUR SIGHTS HIGHER.

By Keith McCafferty

UP-COUNTRY *Mule Deer*

A FEW MONTHS AGO I drove into a valley south of my home to bring back venison for the freezer. I got a late start, and as I drove through the first washes of light, indistinct outlines of deer receded into the fields on either side. They were a part of the landscape at this hour, as numerous and fleeting as my thoughts. Dozens more, sharply defined in the headlights, fed on the steep shoulders of the road cuts. The deer did not so much as pick up their heads as I passed. Twenty miles up the valley I turned off onto gravel, then dropped into dirt ruts that bent toward the ridges of the mountains. I parked in thin snow at the hem of the forest, with neither a deer nor a hoofprint in sight.

This is the paradox of today's hunting in much of the West, and as I uncased my rifle and started to climb into the pines, I felt the slight tug of irony that must have accompanied many who trod this path before me. It is an inescapable fact that mule deer populations here have reached the highest levels in recorded history, and that the sight of these animals has become as unremarkable as a flight of starlings in a city. At the same time, the opportunities for hunters to control deer populations in the open lands and at lower elevations are even fewer. There are two reasons for this: One is that ranchers have closed their gates and leased hunting rights to a fortunate few. The other is that more and more Western ranchers are just auctioning off the cattle and selling their property to speculators, and as the subdividers come in the hunters go out.

A man who comes West today with expectations of big skies and bent-grass prairies may be seriously disillusioned. The public-access road will bypass the vista of his dreams to end in a cul-de-sac among trees. Beyond those trees his eyes will lift to find ridge upon ridge of trees, but unless he learns how to hunt in timber and at an oxygen deficit, he won't see many deer.

It is country where that spotting scope all the experts told you to buy just adds pounds to the pack. However, a few of hunting's axioms do apply in these steep quarters, and one of the most important is that the hunter have a rifle in his hands on opening morning. Mule deer are widely regarded as being inferior in intelligence to whitetails and elk, but all three species have an uncanny knack of disappearing off the earth's face once a few shots have been fired, and I believe that of all our deer, the big bucks with the double-forked horns are the quickest to react to pressure.

Nowhere have I found better examples of this behavior than in the mountains where I live. This isolated range is oriented along a north-south axis, with dozens of side ridges dropping off the high shoulders and angling east or west into the bordering valleys. The northern faces of these side ridges are densely clothed in lodgepole and fir, but the south-facing slopes are more or less open, gouged at irregular intervals by ravines choked with juniper and pine and studded here and there with brilliant patches of aspen. This is excellent habitat, and if left undisturbed, the mule deer will feed on the open slopes and bed down on vantage points above the ravines. Twice I've hunted these south-facing slopes opening day, and on both occasions counted upwards of fifty deer, including a dozen or more bucks, in the first hour of daylight.

Three years ago, two of the biggest bucks I've ever seen bounded out of a ravine and stopped within 15 feet of me. It was early dawn of the opening morning and very cold. The deer whirled round and blew smoke out their nostrils, looking back down the slope where a hunter was working his way up the creek bottom. I had an old pork-pie hat on my head and flipped it toward the bucks. The hat caught on the tine of an antler, tilted for a second, then fell to earth. Both deer recoiled in horror, leaving me in an avalanche of stones and with a memory I will cherish far more than the rack of antlers I might have obtained with the press of my finger.

I never saw those deer again, nor, in the four days I hunted that country for elk, did I see any other bucks. Excepting a handful of does, the south slopes were barren. It would have been difficult to convince anyone that the range supported 10,000 head.

Where did all of the animals go? They went into timber, of course, but there are a lot of trees in the forest and a man can't look behind every one. In this kind of hunting, there is no substitute for local knowledge. An outsider has to start somewhere, however, and it's my belief that a man who's looking for a big buck should begin by searching out pockets of cover that are either at very high elevations or very low. That's where the hunting pressure is slightest.

IN MOST RANGES, the lower skirts of the forest border upon the private property in the valleys. Deer that feed in the hayfields or on the pale green furrows of winter wheat will back up onto the lower slopes in the morning, then bed down on flat shoulders where the ridges staircase down toward the valley. Public access points to the mountains are usually in major drainages that are several miles apart. A man who wants to hunt the toe slopes that fan out between the points will have to hike up and down these little ridges, with no hope of dragging a deer out in one piece if he's lucky enough to bag one.

This is a prospect that stops most hunters, especially resident hunters, before they ever leave the truck. It brings up an interesting point about Westerners and the differing attitudes they hold about hunting elk and deer. To most locals a deer is nothing more than a piece of meat, and the closer it stands to a road, the better it looks in the crosshairs. But a man who wouldn't climb an anthill for a buck will rise at 2 in the morning, chain up all four tires, lurch 20 miles, and then hike across three mountaintops and rappel down a cliff to shoot a spike bull elk. Afterward, he'll round up six of his friends, gas up a chainsaw to cut alleys in the downfall, and work right on through a 20-below night to haul the beast out.

This attitude allows deer on the rugged toe slopes between accesses to sleep free from fear. It also explains why big mule deer bucks are also found at very high elevations, for few men out for deer will make the climb and the elk hunters who drink thin air wouldn't dream of packing out a mere deer that's standing 4,000 feet above the valley floor. While this perspective is beginning to change, it is still prevalent enough to disperse mule deer into fairly predictable neighborhoods during the middle weeks of the season.

Especially in the upper elevations, the deer share living quarters with elk, and it is not unusual to discover them feeding side by side in the openings on any given evening. But whereas elk take great pains to secrete themselves in the deepest pockets of cover during the day, mule deer stay closer to their feeding grounds. They see the light coming, top over the ridge onto the north face, tiptoe a few hundred yards into the timber, and lie down. The hunter who makes the effort to get into these places, who slowly still-hunts upwind among the openings at first light when deer are less alert to movement, and who carefully pokes his nose into the trees where the bucks rest their hooves in the afternoon has a decent chance of filling his freezer.

One helpful tool when hunting such country is an altimeter (good ones can be had for under $100, and are available from outdoor catalogs and many sporting and mountaineering shops). This compass-size instrument records altitude via atmospheric pressure, and used in conjunction with a topographic map, is of great aid in navigating steep pine slopes where visibility is limited. Deer go to ground in timber for security. Man, on the other hand, is reluctant to leave the sunlight behind. The altimeter builds confidence, and the hunter who is confident in the woods is apt to hunt more slowly and focus on the job at hand.

He will have to in order to earn his meat. Don't let anyone tell you that hunting deer in the trees is easier than hunting elk. In fact, a bedded buck is more difficult to surprise in cover than a bull elk. For one thing, his color and size make him harder to see. Also, deer do not carry the heavy odor of elk, which takes the edge from hunters who have learned how to use their noses. And bedded deer are every bit as alert and quicker to react. Elk, in my experience, are more likely to rise to their feet deliberately, to look over their shoulders, to open their nostrils.

In all the years I've hunted in the Rockies, I've twice taken elk that never rose from their beds, and I've shot several others just after they stood up. But I have yet to take a decent buck under these circumstances. The Achilles' heel of a mule deer—the tendency to stop after being jumped and look back—is an adaptation to life in open country, where four-legged predators could not strike from long range. But in timber a spooked mule deer behaves no differently than a whitetail, and once he's out of the blocks, that pogo-stick gait makes him harder to hit.

Hunting muleys on steep, tree-covered slopes is hard work—but that's where the big bucks are most likely to be.

It is only after the heavy snow falls and the necks of the bucks start to swell that they become vulnerable to hunting pressure. As November progresses, the tracks of the does begin to exert a magnetic force and the bucks are led down the mountain noses to the ground, often into those midrange elevations that receive the most hunting pressure. For this reason, a hunter who is looking for a trophy buck during the rut should avoid areas where hunters congregate along routes of elk migration. Mule deer in those places will seldom live long enough to fork out their antlers.

In fact, some of the biggest racks come out of ranges that are not known for either elk or deer populations. Such a range casts shadows over a river 100 miles east of my home. The soils here are poor and the talus slopes extend right down to the water's edge. It's too rocky for elk and the vast majority of deer in the area graze behind barbed wire on tall-grass ranches owned by celebrities 20 miles downstream where the canyon opens into a valley. You have to drive past 500 deer to wind up and around into doghair-pine country, where you'll be lucky to see just one. But what deer there are grow gray hair on their muzzles. Twice now, on the day following Thanksgiving, I've seen bucks that are carrying too much weight on their heads for the good of their health, and someday I hope to be rewarded with one.

But even if that card never falls, hunting in this country is a fine way to end a season. By the time I drive out of the canyon, the grasses will be molten in the evening sun, while the sky will have turned the deep cobalt blue that heralds winter. Every burnished peak trails a feather of snow. But there are shadows in the fields and not all of them are rocks. One took out the left front panel of my car last year. I try to keep my eyes on the road where they belong.

By Byron W. Dalrymple

Exquisite ANGUISH

WHEN YOU'VE HUNTED MULEYS FOR DECADES, YOU KNOW WHICH KIND OF HUNTING YOU PREFER. IF IT'S DESERT DEER, YOU OFTEN WONDER WHY.

IT WAS THE AFTERnoon before the opening of deer season in the vast, barely populated Big Bend country of far west Texas. Ever since we'd splashed the horses across the trickle of San Francisco Creek, we'd been climbing. I recalled that an old cowpoke from the Big Bend region, when asked where it was, thoughtfully replied, "I reckon it ain't close to nowhere." Pressed for what could possibly be good about it, he said, "It's lonesomer than any place else."

On some Texas maps the area where we were, southeast from the village of Marathon on the huge Gage Holland ranch, is deservingly labeled "Hell's Half Acre." Holland, riding ahead, wanted me to see it and its totally unmolested deer. At that time there were no ranch roads here, no windmills, and thus no cattle. It was a virgin land of ancient desert mountains. Riding into it was like turning the clock back 100 years.

The horses labored up the steep slope, the insecure footing of deep, small rock shards making them slip and plunge. I was musing that when you've hunted deer for several decades, as I had, quite literally coast to coast, border to border and beyond, and in every conceivable habitat they'd managed to colonize, you know emphatically the kind of hunting you most enjoy. If it happens to be, as in my case, desert mule deer, sometimes you wonder why.

We topped out and paused to let the horses blow. The view was awesome. Jagged haze-blue mountains hulked southward toward the Rio Grande. The enormous fault called the "Devil's Backbone," with its colossal lizard-scale contours, undulated across the panorama. As we slumped in our saddles, resting, a magnificent buck with massive mahogany antlers appeared skylighted atop the ridge above us. Broadside, it stared down at these strange interlopers in its remote domain.

Musing ceased. Suddenly I knew why I prefer desert hunts to all others. Those blocky, pale-gray deer that make you suffer in settings where deer seem not to belong—they and their surroundings were the reason. Without question this is the most dramatic, intriguing deer hunting extant, a unique challenge. Desert mule deer country, compared to any other deer habitat, is conscienceless, contemptuous of the anguish it may deal the unwary. It's the classic example of "buyer beware." And yet, it's mesmerizing.

My first tenderfoot hunt years earlier had

offered a prime example of both. In the mountains south of Tucson, Arizona, I watched a buck ghost through a dense cholla cactus thicket whose countless crooked arms festooned with millions of straw-colored spines appeared impenetrable. The buck came out upon an open rocky slope, framed between two giant saguaros. Desert mule deer were this easy, eh?

I raised my rifle and rested it against the trunk of the shrub screening me. A thorn slit my palm. I jerked back. My right foot struck a piece of what natives call "jumping cholla." It flipped up, the stiff spines pinning it to my calf. In pain, I started to pry it off with the only available tool, my gun barrel. Then, something I saw froze my movement. A rattler lay coiled within strike range. Unaware now of the cholla pain, I eased back. Meanwhile, the buck disappeared over the ridge.

All this doesn't mean desert mule deer country is prohibitively perilous. Those living in it would scoff. After all, many deer ranges have snakes; you could fatally fall from a New England tree stand; break a leg on a Pacific slope; or tangle with a Montana grizzly. Desert settings simply make you pay closer attention—or chance suffering more than elsewhere. To compensate, there are the unique surroundings and the excitement of seeing these splendid animals, evolved from their highly specialized environment, spang out in the open almost every day.

The desert mule deer, *Odocoileus hemionus crooki,* is perhaps the most interesting North American deer. Its range, confined to the continent's harshest deserts, is restricted to southern Arizona and New Mexico, western Texas, and south far into Mexico.

These are animals of the desert floor and mountain foothills. Water is always scarce, except on ranches where windmills or tanks furnish it for cattle. Some naturalists insist that the deer can go for long periods of time with water only from plants. Clumps of low-growing sotol, for example, have a cabbage-like center that desert deer eat for both food and liquid. I've watched them munching juice-filled prickly pear pads, somehow braving the spines. In Arizona I once observed a buck rip apart a stiff-barbed barrel cactus with it's antlers, then eat the watery pulp.

When I began this desert hunting, I assumed that the animals would be thin and the meat leather tough. To date I've tagged thirty-odd desert deer, and all were fat and tender. I've eaten venison from throughout the nation and desert mule deer are always the best. They're marvels of adaptation, withstanding weather conditions ranging from 120-degree heat to the occasional bitter cold and snow.

Watching desert muleys utilize spare cover is

a lesson for hunters everywhere. One day on the Holland ranch, Gage and I drove during midday, glassing the open slopes. Only scattered shrubs and cactus broke the vast expenses of sparse ground vegetation. We located eight bucks in 2 hours, each bedded in the spot of shade from a single bush. Daytime thermals rising from valleys warn them of danger below. Stealthy approach from the open slope above is impossible.

Once on such a slope I saw a ten-point buck bound from its bed beside a sotol clump not 2 feet high. It ran up into an area where a half dozen scattered yuccas were the only consequential vegetation. It whirled behind one, dropped flat, and stretched its head and neck out on the ground. On several occasions I've stood glassing bucks as they fed along open ridges. Each stared, moved slowly ahead to the first bayonet, yucca, or cholla, then in slow motion lay down behind the meager cover.

Desert mule deer are somewhat smaller than Rocky Mountain deer. Some biologists believe the scientific rule applies that animals in hot regions have lesser body mass in relation to surface area in order to more efficiently dispel heat. Most big bucks I've taken weighed 140 to 170 pounds field dressed. The largest, shot on Holland's place during one of the dozen seasons I've hunted there, field dressed 195.

Desert mule deer are paler than their mountain relatives. The dark brow area is also lighter and smaller. The antlers often lack brow tines, or have comparatively small ones. The tail may have a faint black stripe down its base.

It's true that the measurements of maximum-sized antlers are less for desert deer. One reason, little known among hunters, is that all skull measurements of this subspecies are also smaller than those of the mountain type. Nonetheless, antlers of adult desert bucks reach gratifying proportions. I've shot several with 22 to 24 inch spreads, and seen one of 28 and another of 30. However, a look at any eight- or ten-point buck in this wide-open country is guaranteed to make a hunter quiver.

That gets us to one really important focus of this hunting. It *isn't* often record oriented. That's one reason it's so enjoyable. Coping with desert surroundings, and the delights of watching and hunting deer in this incongruous habitat are the others. I vividly remember a day when Gage Holland and I drove in a 4x4 all day on his enormous spread. We didn't hunt; we watched, glassed, and photographed deer, counting over 100. I still see in my mind's eye a photo that I couldn't get—seven eight- and ten-point bucks posed together on a bald rocky hummock a few hundred yards away.

That image suggests easy hunting, and in truth, many Texans do have it so. Success also is highest here. That's because hunting is done almost entirely on private lands—ranches of a few thousand to a hundred thousand or more acres. Deer, and hunter numbers, are carefully managed. Most hunting is done by vehicle—glassing the foothills—and thus covering much territory. Walking is in brief stalks or scouts of canyons and deep washes. A few ranches offer horseback hunts.

On Texas' public lands, and on a few ranches where season leases can be acquired, hunters do it the hard way—they walk. This approach is standard in New Mexico and Arizona on the vast public lands where vehicle trails are scarce. An indication of how difficult this hunting is can be seen in Arizona's harvest figures. In that state the desert mule deer kill and that of the extremely wary little Coues whitetail often run about equal, or even higher for the whitetail.

These figures are also indicative of the comparatively small number of sportsmen who hunt desert mule deer. The Texas hunter total is also low. Ranchers who charge fees keep the numbers in check. The modest number of hunters throughout the range points to a further delight: hunting is never crowded.

Occasionally you wish that you had others with whom to share your misery. A southeastern Arizona hunt I made years ago in the Chiricahua foothills presented a wryly amusing vignette of desert deer and desert coping. The guide was a white-bearded former cowpoke, the alleged cook was his buddy. In those years this was primitive country. We headquartered in a dirt-floored adobe shack and would make bets on who'd win the nightly scorpion kill pot. The cook worked one-handed over an outdoor fire while his free hand gripped the neck of a tequila bottle. I marveled that he never fell in the fire and avoided asking what it was he served, figuring I was better off not knowing.

We walked the slopes, ridges, and draws, and climbed the rimrocks. Those are prime bedding places, with spots of shade available in giant crevices. It was hot—just right for snakes. We climbed warily.

Desert vegetation and rocks are the chief annoyances hunters in this country fight. If you think southwestern desert mountain country has sand underfoot, think again. Sharp-edged rock rubble litters slopes, covers ridges, and often the desert floor as well. Boots must be tough. I was then only mildly desert experienced. By the end of the second day my feet and legs were killing me.

Vegetation is perhaps your worst enemy. If you horseback, you'll need leather chaps. If you walk, tough brush pants are mandatory. None were then available. Short catclaw thorns shredded my clothes. My hands had several thorns buried in them, along with the hair-fine cactus spines you can't see but feel at every move. Virtually every desert plant waits either to stick you or stab you.

Lechugilla is a particularly vicious species. It grows in patches among rocky ground cover on slopes. The plants, which grow densely close together, reach about a foot high. A whorl of upright thick, stiff leaves with knife-like points invites disaster. Deer dig them out and eat the juicy leaf bases. I walked across a patch and badly sliced one leg. Nail-like thorns of low ground mesquite pierced one boot sole.

The comic relief came at third-day dawn. Cookie sat on a rock by his fire, awesomely hung over, and loudly complaining about the pain in his feet. He wore old pointy-toed cowboy boots—and had each on the wrong foot! Even with this corrected, he still wailed about violent pain in his left big toe. He'd forgotten to shake out his boots, a morning ritual in such places, and a squashed scorpion that had stung him before its death was stuck to his sock. That morning I shot a forkhorn near camp, an excuse for getting out of there.

Over the years I learned the ways of the desert, which any desert mule deer hunter would be wise to do. The preponderance of my hunts in Texas have been less painful. The more I chased desert mule deer, the more they mesmerized me and the more the desert mountains enchanted me. If I were to select a hunt that rates as the most memorable, it would be one on Gage Holland's place.

Some 20 ranch-road miles from headquarters there was a huge butte-like rock pile that heaved up from a broad flat. At daylight you would often find deer on the flats or on lower slopes. By midmorning most have moved up to bed beside a bush, under a rim, or among the enormous rock chunks atop the upthrust. Holland knew I was familiar with the place.

He told me, "There's a ten-point that lives around that hump with the biggest body I've seen this year."

About midday I started the steep climb. Even in December the day was a scorcher, and the 4,000-plus altitude had me winded. I rested briefly, then stealthily padded across, jumping narrow breaks. Rattling shale brought me up short with my rifle unslung. I couldn't see the buck until it hit the flat running all out. I'd botched it, and I wouldn't try a tail-on running shot.

Disgruntled, I muttered epithets at the deer. Apparently that helped. The deer stopped and turned broadside. It was too far away, though; I guessed its distance from me to be perhaps 375 yards. I hunkered down and laid my left hand palm up on a rock, with my .264 barrel across it. Temptation nudged. I held midway on the ribs, compensating for the steep downward angle. The bullet struck the buck just below the backbone.

It was the heavy deer Gage had seen, and the largest desert deer in antlers and weight I've ever tagged. I had the head mounted and presented it to Holland. It still graces a ranch headquarters wall.

By Wayne van Zwoll

Hunting the Other MULE DEER

BLACKTAILS WILL SHOW YOU WHETHER YOU'RE A WOODSMAN OR NOT—AND IT HELPS IF YOU'RE NOT CLAUSTROPHOBIC AND DON'T MIND RAIN.

THE LAST SHOT JERKED the bead off the buck's rib as a blur of wild blackberries swept in behind it. The boy stood alone, the carbine's four quick blasts ringing in his ears. He listened to them once again in his mind and once more heard the hit—the rap of a knuckle on a pumpkin. The track led him through an alder tangles and over a pile of soggy logs that the river had dashed against the thicket. The pumpkin sound had come here as the buck had cleared the logs. He found a drop of blood on one of them. Twenty steps beyond lay his deer.

The irascible woodsman who had sent him here would be pleased. The buck had a black face and a rich chestnut coat and thick dark antlers that forked twice. Its tail was black on top, not ropy like a muley's, nor quite as broad or long as that of a whitetail. *It's gosh-awful pretty,* he thought, fingering the antlers. Rain had put a slick, dark finish on the coat. Blacktail deer, the woodsman had said, were pretty even when wet.

YOU DON'T HAVE to like rain to hunt blacktails in the Pacific Northwest, but it sure doesn't hurt. Wet weather probably accounts for the fact that you can buy over-the-counter blacktail licenses in Oregon and Washington. Everybody likes to sit on a sunny rock and glass for mule deer, but few hunters will wade through salal and blackberry thickets in a downpour to find a blacktail.

My best blacktail hunts have been in the rain. Once, poking along the hem of Oregon's Willamette River, I jumped a fine buck from a small patch of grass. Swinging hard as he sped toward the timber, I fired my .257 Roberts twice. He fell only a few yards from the river and a short swim to safety. Droplets dimpled his sorrel coat as tendrils of mist snaked up through the alders. After the shooting, when you hear only rain, blacktail cover becomes a religious place.

Rain can work in your favor, especially during November's rut. These hunts offer the best chance at bucks because the deer are most active then, and early winter storms have raked off the alder and vine maple leaves so you can see perhaps 30 yards instead of 30 feet. Rain also helps you by quieting the forest floor, confining your scent, and veiling your movements.

Even without curtains of rain to isolate you, dense coastal timber is a fitting haunt for the secretive blacktail. Behaving more like whitetails than their mule deer cousins, blacktail bucks will lie tight and let you walk by, or they'll vanish like a swirl of mist in the alders. In typical security cover, they can be out of sight in two blinks.

Blacktails live where they can eat well. Bedding in jungles of tall second growth, they dine at the edges, where the sun warms the earth and speeds plant succession. Novice blacktail hunters often spend too much time in old growth—dark, wet chasms under skyscraping spruce and Douglas firs big enough to cut for schooner masts. The truth is that second growth loses out where a towering overstory excludes sunlight, so until those giants fall in a storm or succumb to fire, there's nothing for deer to eat.

Blacktails do use such sanctums to evade hunters and—particularly in coastal Alaska—to get out of deep snow. Dense, mature timber intercepts the snow and, in hilly ranges below the Canadian border, can make north slopes more appealing to deer than more open souths in the winter, no matter what you read about sun and wind clearing the souths. Mule-deer surveys I've run have shown concentrations of deer on the norths, where shade also keeps snow from periodically melting and refreezing, so it remains soft. But in Oregon and Washington, snow rarely affects wintering blacktails—or lasts long enough for tracking.

Blacktails (and wet blacktail cover) were made to order for still-hunters. Poking along a deer trail or skid road, rifle at the ready, is hunting at its purest. But stands in the right places also produce, especially at dawn and dusk and on dark, misty days.

Blacktails are less predictable than whitetails but easier to pattern than mule deer. Mainly that's because the dense cover in which they live has well-established trails. Trail-watching for blacktails inside cover may show you more deer than a stand at the edge, where you can see farther. To combat claustrophobia, just tell yourself that you don't have to see far because all those limbs blocking your view also funnel deer onto the trail 40 feet in front of your muzzle. Of course, you're smart to find a place that puts you some distance off-trail to keep your scent pool from flooding it. Listen carefully and scan the cover methodically. Move your eyes, not your head.

Like whitetails, blacktail deer thrive near cropland. In western Oregon they pilfer wheat and alfalfa and orchard crops. I once sneaked up for a close shot at a buck stuffing himself with filberts. Waiting at the edge of a field or orchard late in the day is a good idea—provided you've not just hunted through the cover you're watching.

Morning stands at the edge of cropfields can also be productive if on the approach you stay downwind and inside timber's edge. Trouble is, the blacktail cover that fringes farmland in the Pacific Northwest is commonly hemmed by jungles of vine maple, alder, and wild blackberries.

Head high, with thorns that can mince flesh and stems as thick as gun barrels, blackberries are impenetrable in places. Even deer avoid the densest thorn. Where blacktails do slip in, their trails resemble tunnels, and you must crawl. Forget about shooting or moving quietly.

Once I fired across the Willamette River at a buck easing through willows. He humped at the shot and scrambled out of sight. After wading the narrows, I found tracks in the mud and a wine-colored stain. I followed the sparse blood sign until it stopped at a wall of blackberries. It seemed impossible that the buck could have breached this barrier, as solid as a porcupine's back.

I dropped to hands and knees and crawled along the edge. Not far from the last of the blood, I found a thin spot in the blackberries. I'd already bloodied my hands, so I wriggled in on my belly. About a dozen feet down this barbed tunnel, I came nose-to-hoof with the dead buck.

Blacktails prefer easier places. On a morning thick with fog, I sloshed across a river in the dark and eased into a finger of alders denting a patch of alfalfa. At field's edge I stopped to peer through my 7x35 binocular. Almost immediately a deer slipped from the cement-colored mist. At 50 yards I saw antlers and traded binocular for rifle. The young buck angled closer, not at a walk, but cavorting, kicking up his heels like a frisky colt. I just had to thumb the safety back on.

WHILE VALLEY FARMLAND may be posted, national and state forests in the Cascade and Coast Ranges offer open access and good hunting. Private timber companies like Boise-Cascade also allow hunting on much of their land, but with some travel restrictions. Road closures benefit both the deer and hunters who value sport. Labyrinths of logging roads open to traffic draw windshield warriors, who cruise the cuts and park on landings. Blacktails, which would normally browse in the cuts and travel the roads as they might deer trails, are forced into heavy cover.

Thoroughfares kept free of vehicles are a first bet for still-hunters. My favorite blacktail tactic is to poke along skid trails and logging roads early and late, glassing across stumpfields—especially those that are two or three years old. A cut will provide several years of forage and security cover for deer as second growth comes on. Hunting is best just before new brush is tall enough to hide the bucks.

Minding the wind is crucial in close cover because your scent pool will sometimes reach to the edge of your vision. While in mule deer country you can move fast enough to keep at the leading edge of a scent pool drifting slowly with you, most blacktail covers demand that you put the wind to your face. Be aware that treetops can rake wind from the sky and splash it onto the forest floor like liquid. Rain confines and dilutes human odor, but you'll do well to keep ground-level air to your front to tuck scent back into you when the rain stops.

A binocular makes sense even if you're headed for heavy cover. I once spied a buck as it slipped into a riverbottom thicket. Circling to get crosswind, I entered the alders slowly, one step per minute, glassing carefully. With visibility at less than 30 yards, I worked hard to sift out the close-range detail. My perseverance paid off when I spotted a doe's ear. She was watching me. I held the binocular stiff and systematically "read" the field again, from left to right, top to bottom, then again. And suddenly it popped out—the eye of the buck. Easing the rifle to my shoulder, I sent a bullet just left of that eye, under the beaded antler.

In small woodlots and strips of timber, deer drives can bring results. To my mind, noisy drives with lots of people are no more effective than two or three riflemen who can still-hunt cooperatively. These still-hunts also preserve the silence of the woods. Deer routed by a stealthy hunter will commonly move out slowly because they want to monitor the hunter's step.

You're smart to limit cooperative hunts to small chunks of cover. Many drives are too long and take in too much territory, so bucks slip between people. The biggest blacktail that I've killed appeared in front of my rifle after my partner missed it with a shotgun slug only 40 yards to my left.

Marshy places hold blacktail deer, especially in areas pressured by hunters. These deer swim readily and often bed at the brushy edge of a slough. But to stay sharp hunting blacktails,

which build rapidly into dense forest. These high meadows and the dark timber below create the perfect elk habitat.

Early in the season, before the snows force them down, there are herds of elk on Mutiny Mountain.They bed in the dark timber below, where it's almost impossible to hunt them. In the evening, they filter upward, where they feed and rut in the high basins throughout the night. In the morning, they reverse course and drift back down into their timbered sanctuary.

THERE ARE VANTAGE points that, from a distance, allow you to glass the basins and meadows that drop off Mutiny Mountain. Of an early autumn morning or evening, you can almost always glass the tawny forms of elk here. Getting to them is another story.

A few years back my outfitter buddy, Tom Tietz, glassed a big bull, a magnificent elk with seven good points on each side. Tom got his hunter up the mountain, across the rounded top, and onto the ridge on the back side. They needed to cover another quarter mile, and then they could look down into the first basin and shoot the elk of a lifetime. At that point the hunter said, "No more." He wasn't the only hunter to quit on Mutiny Mountain—but it was he who gave it its name.

If that last quarter mile was really beyond him, then he did the right thing. Someday we all reach a point where we can do no more. The trick is knowing if it's real or if it's time to take a deep breath and push forward anyway. The problem with Mutiny Mountain is that when you take that deep breath, it comes above 12,000 feet.

THE EVENING BEFORE the season, we made our way to a lookout. This part was easy; a road brought us close, and we had only to sidehill up a few hundred yards. In that short distance I felt the pull in my flatland legs, and my sea-level lungs complained.

We set up the spotting scope on a knife ridge. Mutiny Mountain loomed above and to our left, but from here we could look past the mountain and into the series of undulating basins that fell off its northwest slope. It was late afternoon, and the elk were already there.

A vast herd was spread out and feeding. There were tan cows and larger, paler bodies. The distance was too great and the light too far gone to count points, but we could catch the occasional hint of antlers. A few made their sex obvious by sparring in the graying brush or stretching out their dark necks to bugle. Before light left us, we counted more than 20 bulls.

The moon was bright when we left the truck at three the next morning. Picking our way slowly through low brush and jumbled rock, we could walk without flashlights. Tom knew the general route, but we couldn't really see ahead. Sometimes that's better.

Stopping often to blow, we made the top of Mutiny Mountain. Slowly we made our way along the bread loaf, skirting the boulders of dimly seen side canyons. The sky was pink behind us when we reached the junction of the mountain and the sharper ridge to the west. The basins lay to our right front, still cloaked in deep shadow.

We waited while the light grew, shivering from chilled sweat. In the earliest gray we could see the first basin far below. It was empty. This was expected; the elk should have fed uphill through the night, and we should find them somewhere along the high, open ridge. Except the ridge was also empty. Beyond the first basin, just above some of the uppermost fingers of trees, a herd of tawny forms trooped out of a little cut, headed down.

Perhaps there was too much moon, and they'd finished feeding. Although it was not quite dawn on opening day, we were almost too late. Two fine bulls trailed the cow herd, their lilting bugles echoing up through the still air.

"We still have a chance," Tom said, stuffing his binoculars under his vest. "Can you run?"

Probably not, I thought, gulping oxygen. I kept that to myself and just nodded.

Tom took off. Cinching my packframe belt tight, I gripped the rifle in one hand and launched after him. The first few hundred yards were easy—straight down the mountain to the cover of the first basin. Then we would have to sidehill west, cross the intervening ridge, and just maybe intercept the elk in the first strands of timber in the next valley. We dropped more than 1,000 feet at a slipping, sliding jog. Despite the downhill, my chest ached and my breath was a harsh rattle long before we reached the first dwarfed firs. Tom looked back to make sure I was with him, then angled to the left, following a game trail that wandered along a little shelf above the first trees.

With the footing less treacherous now, he speeded up, and the time had come for me to quit and let the elk win this round … or to suck it up and go. It was possible. I'm a runner; I just don't run at 11,000 feet. But I was no longer on an elk mountain. I was back in Officer's Candidate School, in the green Virginia hills, and I was on a platoon run. All that mattered in the world was keeping pace with the man in front of me. I plunged ahead, and we skirted the trees, crossing through a narrow fringe of timber to look into the basin beyond.

"The time had come for me to quit and let the elk win this round … or to suck it up and go."

We pulled up short behind a screen of gnarled conifers, Tom looking and me doubled over, gasping, hands braced on knees. We were too late; the second basin was also empty. Then, just below us, hidden behind one of the narrow fingers of altitude-stunted trees, a three-note bugle sounded. Tom looked at me carefully. He was no longer the Great Satan, my platoon sergeant, just Tom—a little younger, a lot thinner, and a whole lot more used to altitude than I. "Are you okay? We can still catch them if we hurry."

I straightened up, nodding. Maybe 400 yards. I could do it.

Trotting again, we followed the trees down, then circled back up. A bugle sounded just ahead, across a clearing and beyond the next finger of timber. Slowly now, we crossed the opening. I loaded the chamber, tried to get some air, and side by side we stepped into the trees.

THE ELK WERE just on the far side, tan cows dimly seen, and then a big bull, viewed through a fringe of aspen as if behind a picket fence. He bugled again, not 30 yards from us. I got the rifle up but couldn't hold it steady. The crosshairs did lazy eights, wobbling from buff shoulder to white aspen and back again. I took a breath, but it did no good. Trying to time the wobble, I finished the squeeze. The rifle went off, and bark flew. I'd hit a tree.

The herd shifted, uncertain, while I frantically worked the bolt. The bull danced to the left, then stopped. More bark flew—another tree. Spots danced before my eyes. I threw the bolt again while the herd shifted left, panicked now. Antlers floated above the brush, and then a head and neck and shoulder came into a narrow lane. No longer under my control, the rifle went off again. This time the bull collapsed.

We ran to him, pure adrenaline at work, and I took in the six long points and thick beams. Then I collapsed as well, sinking into the low heather and trying to suck oxygen into my starved lungs. A long time later, still shaky, I could run my hands over those walnut antlers and enjoy the warm sunlight just hitting this sheltered basin.

LATER THAT DAY, with a packframe full of elk, I struggled my way slowly and painfully back to the top of Mutiny Mountain. On the crest of the bread loaf, I turned around and eased the heavy load back against the slope, letting myself down into a thick carpet of lichen. I sat for a long time, looking west across those lovely basins to the shining mountains beyond. A warm sun cut through the cool breeze, and the two together quickly dried the sweat from my face and neck. The breeze rippled the sparse Alpine grass, and the same sunlight that I bathed in glinted off distant snowcaps along the crest of the Rockies. The tension drained from my tired legs and back, and, more slowly, my breathing returned to some semblance of normal. I lay back against the pack and watched a couple of high, fluffy clouds drift across the deep-blue sky. Sometimes "No more" is the right answer—but I was thankful I didn't say it on that perfect day on that perfect mountain.

By Ed Park

Any Elk is a GOOD ELK

"DON'T EVER USE THE WORD 'JUST' WHEN TALKING ABOUT AN ELK..."

EXHAUSTED AND DISappointed at the end of a hunt, you sometimes need to be reminded of what really matters.

I WAS DOWN, wallowing in the frustration that comes when your hopes run out of time and you must settle for second best. I even wondered why I'd tied those little elk antlers onto the front bumper for all to see, except that it's customary in our part of the country. I sure wasn't bragging about them.

I was hungry, tired, and cold—a good part of the problem—so I stopped at the first town for dinner. As I got out of my rig I glanced at those antlers on the bumper. They certainly weren't what I'd planned on, but . . .

"Congratulations," a voice interrupted my thoughts. "Looks like you've got a good one there."

The old-timer meant well and wasn't prepared for my reply. I said I couldn't see anything great about a yearling bull, and went into the diner. I slid into a booth and stared blankly at the menu, my mind wandering back over the past few months and all my great expectations.

I had wanted a trophy bull pretty badly, so I had chosen my area and my guide with care. The Snake River Unit is one of the better places in Oregon, and Calvin Henry is one of the best guides. He knows his game and his country, works hard for his hunters, has a good camp and equipment, and has a high hunter success rate each year.

I'd driven to Cal's base camp on Lightning Creek and met Cal and his assistant, Linn Hatton. The other six hunters were already there, so we had a complete round of handshaking. The actual hunting began at four-thirty the following morning. It was bitter cold, but everyone was eager, so we rolled out at first call, dressed, and staggered to the kitchen for breakfast.

We climbed into our freezing saddles and left right after we ate. We rode several miles up Sleepy Creek, meeting dawn along the way, and ascended a steep trail up Jakey Ridge. The plan was to ride the ridge tops, then hunt on foot down through the timbered draws and pockets while Cal and Linn took the horses back around to meet us below. Ride up, hunt down—a good way for elk.

My route was down a sharp ridge. I was to watch for elk that might be pushed from one timbered draw to another. Others would still-hunt the brush or guard similar ridges. I'd chosen the open ridges because I like to take lots of time to sit and glass, soak up the solitude of that vast country, and enjoy the meager warmth of the November sun.

The others jumped elk from the dense cover, and a couple would have been easy shots, except that nobody saw horns—all cows and calves. One large, lone set of prints I cut farther down indicated that at least one bull had slipped out, unseen by any of us.

Each day we saw elk, and each day we saw tracks of elk we didn't see. The ones we saw were cows; the tracks of the unseen indicated bulls. The hunted bull elk has to be one of the cagiest game animals we have. The statewide success rate in Oregon the past few years has run only 13 to 14 percent. If you get an elk—any kind of elk—as often as every seventh year, you're doing better than average. No elk comes easy.

On the last day, we were to hunt Lightning Creek Trail, which was too rough for the horses to climb. That meant we'd be hunting uphill, but it was the only logical way to work that particular area. Each of us would hunt a draw from bottom to top and back, and the one I was assigned was particularly rough but with a promising strip of timber.

In this country the south slopes are barren of timber; the summer sun bakes them so hot that trees cannot survive. But the cool norths and sheltered pockets hold timber, and there the elk are. My general technique was to climb the off-side, the open, grassy slope, then ease to the ridge crest now and then to search the timber. I was alone, so there was no one to help me or foul me up. That draw was all mine.

The wind was vicious all day, with showers of snow to emphasize that nature still had control of things. The open ridge was a brutal place to be, and I knew all too well why the elk were holed up in the heavy stuff.

All morning long I worked my way up the grassy side, with frequent pauses to glass and search the timber and brush. Finally I was within a couple hundred yards of the top of the draw. The crest of Haas Ridge was just beyond that. I decided to stop and eat lunch before working out this last pocket.

After a good rest I eased to the ridge crest one final time and peered into the shadows. Nothing. The strip of timber was quite narrow near the top, and I noted that I could very easily take anything that might break out the far side. I thought about rolling down a few rocks to see what spooked.

I spotted a good, basketball-sized rock to my left and climbed down to it. I glanced down the slope to see just where it would roll and saw—

Elk!

There, directly below me, a good 100 yards down, stood a cow rubbing her head against a small fir. I sat down in the snow, and, as I did, I noticed a second cow lying in the snow maybe 10 yards from the first. It was just past noon.

I searched every shadow with my binoculars, found nothing more, but decided to just sit and wait. In time the one cow quit scratching her itch and wandered off to feed, simply melting into the heavy brush. Eventually, the resting cow got up and disappeared. With nothing to watch, the minutes oozed by slowly, and I became painfully aware that my butt was soaked from snow. But I was determined to sit and wait it out until I was sure there was no chance of a bull.

At 12:43 I glanced at my watch and wondered if I'd be smart to give it up and roll that rock, but as I looked back down into the timber, I spotted one of the cows coming into view again. I put the binoculars on her.

Bull!

A spike, browsing on brush, had materialized. He wasn't the royal I'd wanted, but it was the last day. I centered the crosshairs on his shoulder and squeezed. The shot boomed through the canyon and echoed from the ridges.

Below me, nothing moved. I sat for several more minutes, then I eased down the hill to where the bull had stood. There was no blood, and his tracks led downhill in great bounds. I followed them for maybe 25 yards, spotted a small splotch of blood, and then found him, piled up against a fir.

Once I was sure he was dead, I fired the prearranged three signal shots and got down to the work of dressing, skinning, and quartering. By the time I'd scrambled down the mountain, daylight was gone. Linn had taken the other hunters back to camp while Cal had waited to ride back in the darkness with me.

The following day Cal, Linn, and I took the horses up Haas Ridge, along its crest, and down the canyon to my bull. We loaded him on two horses and packed him back down. It was a grueling seven hours in the saddle.

AND NOW, AS I sat in the restaurant, thinking over that hunt and others, I was sorry for my shortness with the old-timer. I started to get up, embarrassed and annoyed with myself. But as I did he was just coming through the door. I waved him over.

"Buy you coffee? I feel better now."

His smile indicated that he understood, and he accepted.

"Didn't get the big one, huh?"

I shook my head.

"Well, I know how you feel. I used to hunt those elk every year, but the country is tougher than I am now, so all I can do is dream about it—like a lot of things.

"I've taken my share, but there were lots of years when I found nothing, when those elk outsmarted me and I came home empty. I learned to respect elk like I respect nothing else. They're the greatest game animal in the country.

"So when you said that yours was 'just a spike,' I shrugged and went on. But then I got to thinking, and I came back because I wanted to pass on one word of wisdom. Don't ever use the word *just* when talking about an elk, be it a big bull, a cow, or a spike like yours, because any elk is a good elk."

By Norman Strung

FULL BUGLE

THOSE LUCKY ENOUGH TO EXPERIENCE ELK AT FULL BUGLE WILL BE ENCHANTED BY THEIR EERIE MUSIC.

FULL BUGLE. ALTHOUGH I have hunted elk for three decades I doubt I've seen it happen more than a dozen times. There is no formula to pick a predictable date nor even a guarantee that it will occur every autumn, and perhaps that's what it should be; an unexpected gift, or maybe just a reward for perseverance.

I can say this however: if it is going to happen, it will follow the first cold snap of fall that plunges the thermometer deep into the teens. Spot conditions have proven to play a part, too. Clear, frosty mornings when the air is still and you can hear a normal conversation from half a mile away seem to urge them on and so does the phase of the moon. Every time elk go crazy, the moon has either been full or newly on the wane. It's an element that borders on the poetic for in their reckless behavior a kind of lunacy is loosed upon the land.

Full bugle describes elk when they are not only at the peak of their rutting period, but whipped into a wild frenzy by some rare concurrence of hormones and atmosphere. The woods crackle and snap as males spar with brush, branches, and each other; and the hills and valleys of the high country are alive with their reedy, trilling music. If you are lucky enough to be there when it happens, it is an experience you'll never forget.

The first time I encountered full bugle was in Montana's Bull Mountains. A rancher friend had called to let me know the elk were "tootling pretty good" on his place and I arrived that very evening. The next morning he dropped me off on a bench above a timbered coulee where he'd heard them the day before.

I was largely untutored in the art of calling elk, my education consisting of some how-to tapes and one brief meeting with a raghorn who proved indifferent to my deceits. I nearly fell over when my first notes got an immediate response. Then I dove for cover when a second bull answered, followed by a third!

These elk challenged me, then one another. As near as my ears could tell, they were roughly equidistant—triangulated around the forested draw, each refusing to budge from his harem and fortress, but daring the next guy to do so. It was still dark in the tail timber so I picked a careful, quiet path to the center of the action.

I set up on a little hill surrounded by sparse juniper and began to call again. The instrument I used was pretty primitive by today's standards, capable of producing only two notes, but finesse was not the order of that day. In their agitated state, the elk would probably have been provoked by a pennywhistle.

The bull at the top of the triangle seemed to zero in on me. While the others bleated and bellowed randomly, his responses were immediate to my calls and more urgent. Not knowing much elk talk, I simply followed his lead. When he coughed, I coughed; when he broke branches, I broke branches; when a resonant grunt began deep in his lungs then went up the musical scale to high C, I tried to do the same.

We dueled vocally for half an hour, the other bulls often squealing in chorus. Our timbre and tempo grew. The air crackled with sound and fury.

AT LAST THE bull could take my taunting no more. With an anguished bellow that ended in a gravelly scream, he strode from his vantage straight for me, his hooves thudding in the soft duff. I found I was shaking, not from fear but from the fevered pitch of the moment.

He strode into a clearing below me not 35 yards away, shoulders rolling, neck extended, lips curled in a sneer, wearing a crown of sagebrush he'd wrenched from the earth. When he looked away I drew my bow. My arrow clattered in its rest. When I released the string, he exploded into action.

I can only guess what happened. I am sure I hit him because of his reaction, but I must have struck a hard bone—a knucklebone, his scapula, or the burl of an antler. The arrow lay on the ground where the bull had stood, unbloodied with a bent tip. Disappointed? Not on your life! Never before had I known such an electric confrontation. I shook for another 15 minutes among the junipers, listening as the three antagonists drifted off to some distant mountain beyond my hearing.

While the term "full bugle" is a fair description of this time, I have always wondered who had what in mind when they coined the phrase "bugle" to describe the call of rutting elk. The overtures of agitated males are not the sounds of brassy horns but those of woodwinds: piccolos, clarinets, and especially flutes. The mature bulls are the accomplished musicians, blowing sweet, clear melodies with astounding tonal variation. The young bulls, on the other hand, sound like they're practicing: sharps go flat, high notes are missed, and voices crack like adolescents trying to sing.

One morning dawned upon that kind of wild disharmony in the form of a squabble above me. A mature bull was raging and some squeaky spikes were answering him. As I worked my way toward the confusion, I found the source of the big bull's anger; two young spikes were trying to get into his harem while he parried and thrust to drive them away. His actions and their reactions resembled some primitive machine whereby his charges provided the power to propel his young challengers round and round the harem like horses on a merry-go-round. He was surely distracted enough for me to get a shot, but every time I tried to get within range, another spike would come around, one almost bowling me over. My predicament was finally resolved by the wind. At about nine it began to blow upcanyon as the valley below warmed. The herd caught my scent and the whole dog-and-pony show changed their tune and bolted for the high country.

The spectacle of a bunch of bulls bugling in concert can also confuse the uninitiated. One day when they opened up I was hunting with my I friend Willie, who'd never heard an elk bugle, much less four at the same time. Since he was new to the area, I drew him a map, pointed him in the right direction when we split up, and assured him he'd know the place where I suggested he wait because some woodcutters had been working there.

My hunch proved correct. As dawn eased over the horizon, a quartet of bulls began working up the ridge where he waited. I called and called from across the valley but the elk were so preoccupied with each other that I couldn't draw one to me. No matter, for I felt sure that Willie would get a shot. They were walking right into his lap.

We met as planned at 10, at the juncture of two logging roads. His hands were clean and as he approached, he lowered his eyes and slowly shook his head. "Those guys sure got here early," he muttered.

"What guys?"

"The guys in the truck."

"What truck?"

"The one up on the hill. And boy were those guys good callers! Not to be a wiseguy, but they were ten times better than you. I could hear the difference from every place I moved. Those guys were tops and I didn't want to mess up their plans by getting in their way."

I was puzzled. We were the only ones with permission to hunt there that day. Then I remembered an old pickup the woodcutters had left on the ridge.

"Willie, those were elk, not hunters."

As I laid out the facts, reality registered in tiny increments—our exclusive permission, the old pickup, the expert calling.

At last his face went blank and his eyes rolled back into his head. "Oh no!"

"Oh yes," I assured him, and we still laugh about "those guys" today.

For all the mistakes made by man and beast during this momentary madness, I still find it curious that I've never killed an elk on a day when they were in full bugle. Some unexpected glitch always arises to botch an otherwise sure shot or to blow my cover.

While the others bleated and bellowed randomly, his responses were immediate to my calls and more urgent.

THE LAST TIME I witnessed their symphony there were three of us. We walked up a moonlit trail paved with fallen, frosted aspen leaves that glowed like silver dollars. Half a dozen bull elk were calling, some so close that the clarity of their notes raised hairs on the back of my neck.

We knew that as dawn broke they would work uphill, so we each took a stand on one of the three ridges that led from the green alfalfa fields below to the mountains above.

It was a five-star performance. The draws below us were like amphitheaters that echoed fluting refrains. They bugled for 3 hours, and so help me, during one spectacular crescendo, they were joined by a bull moose and a pack of coyotes, the croaking moose sounding like a frog among nightingales, while the coyotes *ya-hooed* and *yip-eed* as if for a curtain call. At that instant I fought the impulse to give them a standing ovation.

We rejoined, smiling, and recounted the wonder of it all. Dick said, "I never moved or tried to make a play. It sounded like they went by me 100 yards away, but I just wanted to listen."

Bill nodded. "Me too. It was so beautiful... "

At that moment I realized that I had done the same. Two bulls and a dozen cows had passed within gunshot on a gametrail I knew well, yet I made no effort to intercept them. Stranger yet, the thought never occurred to me. It was as if in their manic state, like Pan with his pipes, the elk enchanted all who heard them. I had been bound to the spot and charmed by their eerie music, unwilling and unable to break the spell cast by full bugle.

By Keith McCafferty

OFF THE EDGE *of the Map*

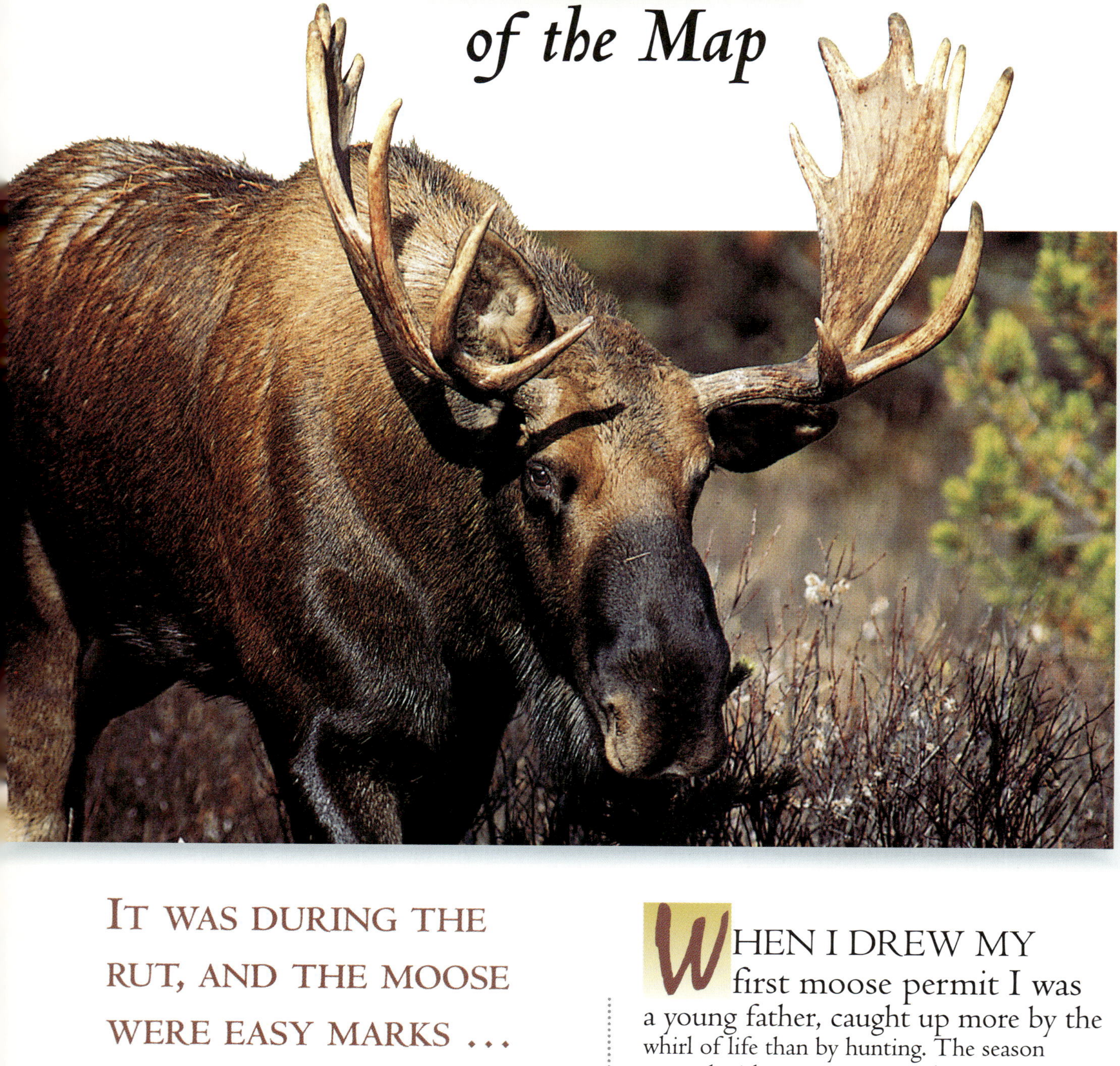

IT WAS DURING THE RUT, AND THE MOOSE WERE EASY MARKS ... TOO EASY FOR A TRUE HUNTER.

WHEN I DREW MY first moose permit I was a young father, caught up more by the whirl of life than by hunting. The season opened without my notice. The moose came into rut, lost interest in one another, and left the willow bottoms for the high country. By the time I found a bull, people were buying turkeys for Thanksgiving and the moose had climbed high up on the ridges of the Spanish Peaks, where they fed in the tag alder understory of the lodgepole pines. The kill I made that year was 3 miles up Burnt Creek in 2 feet of snow; we had to bone the beast out and pack him down through the shintangle to the river, then pull on frozen waders to cross. Working this way, it took three of us three days to get the meat out. I went back in alone to pull my camp, again to pack the hide, once more for the head. Ten days after shooting the moose, I peeled my socks off and stuck my feet in a bucket of hot water to thaw.

I told myself I'd never do that again, a promise that ought to have been easy to keep, because the odds of my ever drawing another permit were next to none. But God punishes people in strange ways. And so it was that early this fall, on the morning of our first hard frost, I found myself bumping up along an old gold mine trail in the Pioneer Mountains, with my brother at the wheel and my old John Wilkes double rifle in the backseat. We had made our trip early to catch the moose in the season of their rut, having been told by a game biologist that if we did so it would only be a matter of picking out the piece of meat we wanted and winching it up to the truck. I figured that would turn out to be one of those "you should have been here yesterday" stories. But here we were and there were the moose. By sunset of that first day we had seen fifteen feeding among the willows in the serpentine bends of the tributaries.

This came as good news to my brother, who was along solely for the strength of his back and who had made it clear that the difference between a good moose and a bad moose depended upon the distance it stood from the road. Considering my previous experience with the species, I ought to have been relieved. But the emotions that stirred in me were complex. I'd always had to work hard to find game. And I'd always hunted close to the bone of necessity, because my family depends upon the meat. This trip, too, was primarily for meat, and I asked myself whether it really made a difference if for once my quarters might be packed across a creek to the road, rather than over several intervening ridges, where most of the game I've found has chosen to wander. Twice, with this question turning uneasily in my mind, I had uncased the rifle and stalked across the willow bottoms to get a closer look at the bulls. The first moose had been small. But the second was an immense animal, gone gray with age and with his bell reduced to a dewlap. Like many old bulls, his rack had begun to lose its palmation. His right antler was branched like that of an elk, while his left consisted of a single, short spike.

Kevin had watched my stalk from the rig. Upon my return he muttered unintelligibly and then said in a loud voice, "Well, he looked big to me." My explanation, that my wife had a place cleared over the mantel for the skull and that a one-horned rack would throw off the symmetry of the room, seemed to have little impression on him.

"You know what the Indians did after killing a moose, don't you?" he said as he started the engine.

"Yes," I said wearily, "made camp."

He nodded his head wisely.

I knew what he was trying to say. But the fact is that I could not find the place in my heart that would allow me to shoot a moose we had seen from the road, and I believe he would have felt the same way were our situations reversed. It is one thing to justify taking a life for the meat, but it is another to pull a trigger. Some of us need first to have hunted. "Maybe tomorrow I'll just strike out on foot," I told him.

And that was what I did, fording a pool of Lacy Creek on a log that cracked paper panes of ice when I stepped on it at 6 the next morning. As the dawn drew a band of pale light on the horizon, I dunked a pair of brass hulls into the double, anticipating its use at any moment. But by 9 o'clock, I was no longer sure. These moose were spread out over big country. I found I had to climb way up into the sliderock to see down into the willows. It was slow going and I didn't need anyone to tell me that I'd have seen more moose by riding a steering wheel.

And so the day passed and I remained mooseless. The next day was no better. Kevin took his bow into the mountains for elk while I scoured the willows in several creek bottoms.

We both saw a lot of squirrels. Kevin summed up the situation that night when we were sitting around the fire. "Too hot. Too dry. Too many Rockies and not enough Bullwinkles," he said.

ON THE FOURTH morning of our hunt, I abandoned the willows to hike up onto a timbered bench above Lacy Creek, where I suspected moose were bedding down during the heat of the day. I had the thrill of coming onto the one-antlered bull, who rose stiff-leggedly and then made off through the gloom in his silent gait. A moment later his bass grunts resonated through the thicket. I could feel the hair rise up on my forearms.

Anyone who's hunted has been carried away by the beating of his heart. Before I jumped that bull, my moose hunting had been tempered—at least in some degree—by my brother's caution to stay within reasonable distance of a road. But the grunt of a bull moose, like the bugle of an elk, is the sound and the lure of wilderness. I could no more ignore it than I could watch a trout kiss the surface of a stream without feeling my chest tighten. The fact that I did not want that particular moose was of no consequence. I wanted what he represented, country unfettered by the encroachment of man, and I wanted the feelings of insignificance and mortality that hunting alone in such places provide.

I found what I was looking for several mornings later, near a creek that ran just off the edge of my map. I had been sidehilling a ridge of pines that swept in long fingers toward the meadow below when I heard a clacking sound, like a sound that fencers might make were they fighting with sticks. Drawn down one of the fingers by this sound, I found that it emanated from the meadow, which at this hour lay submerged under a pool of mist that was as solid as a cumulus cloud. Cold beads of water formed on my face when I approached the meadow. The tall grass was silvered with frost, and I recall turning to look back at the dark trail I had made through it and thinking about going back. I am not ashamed to say that I was afraid, in the same way that I am afraid of sounds in the dark. I also knew that once I found the source of the noise—and I was pretty certain what it was—that I would put that fear behind me and once again be a hunter.

Ten minutes later the black bulks of two moose loomed up in front of me. It was an eerie sight. Tendrils of mist shrouded their bodies, and without any bushes or trees in the foreground to lend perspective, I could not determine how far away they were. It might have been 50 yards or 150. The dry sound their antlers made seemed to cross a great distance before reaching me, providing the sound track for an otherwise silent film of two grainy figures moving back and forth across an empty screen. Occasionally, as the moose shoved at each other, one or both would edge off the screen, to be encapsulated in the cloud, and I'd slip forward a few more yards.

I raised the rifle once. But the moose were seldom still and their antlers blended with the mist to become almost invisible, so that there was nothing I could do but stand there and feel my heart pound. Finally, one of the bulls broke the engagement and trotted off. A moment later a series of grunts came from the direction in which he had disappeared. They sounded bottomless and mournful and cold, as though echoing from the depths of a well. The remaining bull lowered his head and raked through the tall grass with his antlers. Then he started to back up on stiff legs. He swung his head up and turned sideways to me, his dark, suddenly immense outline powerfully etched in the thinning mist.

The rifle would not hold still. I lowered and raised it back up, slowly, making myself draw down through the shivering vortex of my excitement to find the calm at the center. The front blade settled into the V on the standing leaf of the quarter rib. *Boom!* The bull started forward into the mist. *Boom!* The brass hulls pinged back into the wet grass when I opened the rifle. I slipped in two more and waited in the silence, my head ringing with the concussions. The air was heavy with scent. Suddenly, two moose came into sight on my left, tall-shouldered, stroking through the mist in their swimming, long-legged strides. Bulls. A third bull wheeled by on my right. He let out a thunderous grunt, then stopped as he reached the limit of my vision and grunted again, turning back, seeming to seek out the source of the confusion.

Very slowly, I backed toward the edge of

the meadow. Then I turned and climbed out of the pool of mist, scarcely noticing the hill rise under my legs. I was well up into the sage before I sat down. Below me I could hear the bull grunting as he hunted back and forth through the meadow. Although I felt like a coward, I knew that retreat had been the right thing to do. It would have been foolhardy to have stayed there, to risk a chance that I'd have to stop a charge, not knowing whether he was the moose I had shot at or a rival bull.

I stayed high until the sun rose over the pines and burned through the mist. All the moose were gone by then, and down in the meadow I could find no blood, no torn earth, not even a lingering scent to indicate that they had been there. I dropped my hat where I thought the bull had been standing when I fired. Then I started walking in widening circles. Forty-five minutes later I found the moose dead in the shade of some willows. I leaned the rifle against his antlers—he was a fine bull with about a 40-inch spread—and sat down on my pack to reflect. A few days before, I had made a choice about hunting, and as a result of that choice a moose lay dead in country where the sound of an engine would never penetrate. Now I was going to pay the price of that decision.

I had told Kevin I would meet him on the road at 3. That was 7 hours away, and those hours would prove to be among the most back-breaking and frustrating of my life. I had a small block and tackle in my backpack and 100 feet of rope. The moose was lying on its side. By anchoring the block and tackle to the willows, I thought I would be able to lift his uppermost hind leg a foot or so, then tie it off with cord, attach the block and tackle to the front leg, and lift it. By alternating back and forth, it did not seem unreasonable to assume that I could work the moose over onto his back for skinning. But all I managed to do was tear out the willows by the roots, and I ended up dressing the animal by lying on my side in a pool of blood and working my knife inside the body cavity by feel alone. Had anyone seen me sitting by the side of the road that afternoon as I waited for Kevin, they might have thought I'd crawled to the fringes of civilization after being attacked by a grizzly bear.

Kevin was not so sympathetic. "You really know how to ruin a man's day," he said when he stepped out of the truck.

"Better bring your flashlight," I told him.

THAT NIGHT, WHEN the moon rose over the ridge, my brother and I, smeared with gore to the elbows and with sweat cold on our chests, helped each other struggle to our feet after slipping our arms through the shoulder straps of the packs. One last load now and we would be out. But before I had taken more than a step, I craned my neck to look in the direction a coyote had barked and fell heavily. I wound up on my back like a turtle rolled onto its shell. Kevin slumped down beside me and for a minute or more nobody spoke. I thought wryly then of the Shoshone, who had hunted moose in this valley a century before and who had the sense to move their people to the moose rather than move the moose to their people.

"What do we do now, big brother?" Kevin said.

I told him we better make camp.

By John Barsness

The FELLOWSHIP of Moose Hunters

SOMETHING SPECIAL HAPPENS WHEN BIG GAME FALLS: A SPIRIT OF TOGETHERNESS EMERGES, AND HELP CAN APPEAR FROM ANYWHERE.

IT WAS NOT A PARTICULARLY large bull moose—which is like saying the Empire State Building is not particularly large among today's skyscrapers—but that was the size we were looking for, an eating bull. The animal walked off along the creek-bottom willows, then stopped and looked back over his black shoulder. Moose can see, I think, as well as most other deer—as well as we do, if not better—but like dogs, they trust their nose and ears. A moose's nose is five times the size of a bloodhound's and its ears spread wider than a big deer's antlers, but on this morning the breeze drifted toward us across the mountain canyon and the bull stood still, waiting for something to happen.

It did not take long. I could see, on occasion, the orange vest worn by my wife, Eileen, as she quietly stalked through the scattered lodgepole timber below. She moved up behind a stand of three trees and sat, elbows on her knees, .270 in her hands. The bull began to doubt she was a cow moose and took two steps, then stopped again, angling slightly away, the length of its body looking too black in the mountain's shadow, like the rectangular mouth of a cave. At the shot the moose's long head turned away and he started to trot, grayish legs sliding through the willows, but in less than three steps the legs folded like the legs of a

cheap card table, and the moose's body disappeared into the green willows as if falling into a black hole. "Good shot," I said, something I seem to say around her several times each fall, and the man next to me guessed that the moose wasn't going anywhere.

I didn't even know the man's name, or that of the fellow standing next to him, but they followed me down into the willow bottom to where Eileen stood, still breathing slightly fast after the shot. "Where'd you hold?" I said. She touched the bottom of her ribs with a thumb. "Right there." I nodded. All four of us eased down into the creek bottom, Eileen in front with the rifle, pushing the waist-high willows aside, and found the bull lying on its right side, its head toward us. Eileen cautiously prodded it with the rifle muzzle, but as the man said, he wasn't going anywhere. Then she circled the moose, looking along its long, gray legs as if staring upward at an unscalable cliff. "My God," she said.

That was when I discovered I'd left my saw in the pickup, which I'd left parked on the logging road up the mountain. I searched my pack twice, to no avail. You do not go moose hunting without a saw, unless you have a front-end loader.

"Here," one of the men said. "Use mine."

He handed me his compact sheath-saw, and we introduced ourselves. We'd all found the moose at about the same time, seeing him from the logging road above, but since I'd seen him first (by perhaps 2 seconds) and they were looking for something a little bigger, they'd deferred to Eileen.

"Actually, we'll probably wait for the sun to come up and take some pictures first. It isn't every year you get a bull moose," I said. Eileen stood nodding, looking at the bull, still a little moose-shocked.

The bigger guy shrugged. "We'll go hunt for a little bit. I saw a big bull last week just down the creek. We'll look for him, then come back and help."

I shook my head. "You don't have to do that."

He nodded emphatically. "This isn't—," he said, naming another state where he said every hunter was out for himself.

So Eileen and I waited awhile for the sun and took a few photos. At that point our fellow moose hunters returned and helped hold the moose's legs and roll the carcass while Eileen and I gutted the bull. When she'd shot the animal, the temperature had been around 40 degrees, but the forecast was for the mid-80s, and we knew we had to get the bull's hide off and at least quarter him before the day grew warm. I persuaded our new friends that we could handle it ourselves, that they should go hunt. They said they'd be back to help us get the moose up to the road.

One thesis of human evolution suggests that we are what we are—social, cooperative tool-makers—because of our hunting heritage. That when a few pitiful little fruit-eaters came down out of the trees to prey on other mammals in an increasingly dry Africa, they had to evolve into rock-throwing team members to survive. In the process, numbers, brains, and opposable thumbs were substituted for size, fangs, and claws, and we became who we are today because we hunted together in small bands, eventually growing efficient enough to kill mammoths and herds of *Bison antiquus* with rocks and spears.

The more cynical among us might suggest that that evolutionary direction has continued: Now we live in much larger bands, such as Greater Los Angeles, and kill much larger pieces of the earth, like rain forests. But to me, the strongest evidence of our evolutionary course comes not from the "progress of civilization," but from what happens when large game falls to modern hunters.

When big game falls, something emerges from our Paleolithic core. Antelope are the smallest North American game—even a large buck dresses out at well under 100 pounds—but on one hunt another hunter helped me dress my buck, then escorted me to his camp, gave me a soft drink, and drove me to my pickup, which I'd left parked 3 miles of dusty dirt roads away.

This factor increases proportionately with game weight. Help appears from anywhere, from truckstops to the halls of academia, when an elk goes down. I've hauled out as many as three wapiti in a week, as part of a gang of four, each man dragging an elk quarter down a mountain in the snow for a mile or more. The odd thing is that everybody does this rather cheerfully, as if they were on a sleigh ride rather than performing aerobic exercise of the most gruesome sort. Marathoners do not run Boston dressed in heavy boots and two or three layers of wool, dragging 100 pounds of protein through foot-deep snow and over Douglas fir deadfall. If they did they would not smile so frequently.

Such communal hunting is going out of style. We've drifted away from extended families and the cooperative hunt. Much hunting has become competitive, the status going not to the hunter who provides the most meat for the clan, but to whomever kills the biggest antlers for himself. This isn't necessarily bad—it's been a long time since the old "party hunt," where one hunter filled everyone's tag if he got up on a herd of deer or elk, served any essential purpose. But the modern hunter who's never been part of a late-season cooperative steak-drag with family and good friends has missed something far more satisfying than Boone and Crockett antlers.

Or even with strangers. Eileen and I talked about our two new acquaintances as we skinned her moose. We'd planned to remove the hide and break the bull down into pieces small enough to cool in the creek bottom shade, then cover it with brush and go get some friends who'd agreed to help haul it out. But we realized we might have help right here.

First we tied the two left legs to willow clumps and skinned the topside of the bull down to the humped ridge of the backbone, laying the hide flat in the open space we'd cleared among the willows. Then we rolled the moose over and skinned the other side. By then the lower legs had lost their usefulness as braces, so we cut them off, slicing through the knee ligaments until we could break the joints. Then we sliced the shoulders away, sawed the neck and head off, and cut the hindquarters away from the rib cage. This left us with six pieces of moose—head, hide, shoulder, rib cage, and hindquarters. In the pickup we had a plastic toboggan (one of the more useful hunting tools—this one had already hauled pronghorn, whitetail deer, mule deer, and elk, but never before a moose) and aluminum packframes. I hiked up and got the frames and lashed a shoulder—weighing perhaps 50 pounds—to one and the head, festooned with orange ribbons, to another. I took the shoulder, Eileen the head, and we worked our way carefully first through the willows and then up the more open pine slope to the road.

By the time we got there our saw-loaners had not returned, so we decided to go get our friends and come back for the really heavy quarters. We drove down the logging road for 2 miles to where it entered the main canyon road. There were two four-wheel-drive vehicles parked at the turnoff, one a pickup with a bull moose in the back.

We stopped and said hello. Two young men had killed the bull farther up the canyon, but this moose had been on the uphill side of their truck and they'd managed to drag him down in two pieces. The other vehicle held a man and his wife and two kids, a boy and girl of about ten, all of whom were dressed in orange vests and looking for a moose.

While we talked, they discovered we had a moose, and that I knew where a live one might be found. Eventually all three vehicles headed back up the logging road, and eight people swarmed down the hillside. The two young moose hunters and I slid the rib cage and hindquarters up the mountain in two trips on the plastic toboggan, one man on each side and the third pulling on the lead rope. Eileen packed out the hide on a packframe, which almost toppled her into the little creek, and the other moose hunter carried the other shoulder. Between trips Eileen explained the different internal organs to the young girl—for some reason females are generally more interested in gutpile anatomy than males—and the young boy carried out the heart. When the moose was in our truck, the two young men gave everyone a cold, canned drink from the enormous cooler they'd packed for a week-long moose hunt, and I explained to the family-style moose hunter how to find a spring on the other side of the ridge where moose often hung out.

As we stood there, the moose hunters who'd loaned us the saw drove back down the logging road, surprised to find our moose already sixthed and loaded. We had the bull back in a cool garage, out of the flies and heat, before 11 in the morning.

But that's the way it works in the fellowship of moose hunters, a Pleistocene organization that's existed far longer than the family farm. Like Old Man River, it just keeps rolling, and sliding and tugging and sweating, along.

By Jim Rearden

Hunting the World's LARGEST DEER

SMOKE FROM OUR dying fire curled from the tent stovepipe as Terry, my eleven-year-old son, and I eased into the frosty dark-before-dawn. Spire-top spruces stood black against the faint light of the eastern sky. It was September 18, and the moose in the Deep Creek Valley of the Kenai Peninsula were rutting. We hoped to find a bull there before he sneaked into the timber to his daytime bed.

Our shoepacs crisped against the morning rime, and I shivered from the 28-degree air—or was it from the excitement of the hunt?

We had pitched our wall tent the previous evening on a ridge above Deep Creek, 60 miles from our home at Homer, on the tip of the Kenai Peninsula, where I am Outdoors Editor for *Alaska* magazine. The tent-pitching, sawing and splitting wood, and the night in the tent had helped us to adjust to the wilds. Our senses seemed sharper this morning, and the cold spruce-scented air was like wine. During the night we had heard the fierce deep calls of a horned owl; a cow moose had wailed several times within a mile of our tent; and just before I had fallen asleep I had heard the answering grunts of a rutting bull moose.

"Ready?" I asked Terry, who knows the value of silence. He nodded and we shrugged into packboards and started sneaking along a trail that headed east, toward the bottom of Deep Creek Valley.

Moose meat is a favorite with my family, and during my thirty years in Alaska we've eaten more moose than any other kind of meat. Richer in flavor than beef, it isn't as fat, and we much prefer moose to beef. I've taught each of my three boys in turn how to hunt moose and how to care for the meat. Our annual moose hunts are high points in our lives.

This was Terry's third hunt, and he was becoming more observant, I noticed, for before we started down the trail he tossed some fireweed seed plumes into the air to see which way the air was flowing. The previous day he had found fresh grizzly tracks, many fresh and old moose tracks, and one wolf track.

Binoculars hung inside our shirts to keep them warm so they wouldn't fog with our breath; rifles were slung over packboard corner posts.

The .30/06 shells in Terry's pants pocket clinked as he walked, and he stuffed a handkerchief among them. His rifle was a Remington Model 721 with a receiver-mounted peep sight; I carried the same caliber in a Winchester Model 70, with a Lyman 4X scope. The day before reaching our hunting grounds we had fired a few shots to check sights.

At each spot where we could scan waist-high willows, swampy sedge meadows, or openings in the dark spruces, we searched with binoculars. Gnarled spruce roots thrusting up like many-spiked antlers caught Terry's attention. He pointed. I grinned and whispered, "Roots." That wind-throw was an old friend—I had seen it annually for more than fifteen years.

We listened for sounds from the spruces, from the meadows, from the swamps. The area is ideal for a walking hunt, with little pockets of willows here, a meadow there, an open slope above. I hunt other areas where I climb above broad valleys and simply sit, mornings and evenings, waiting for moose to show. When a bull appears I make my stalk. But Deep Creek Valley calls for a slow, quiet, searching hunt.

We had walked nearly a mile when the sun slowly lifted above the 30-mile-distant, haze-blue, glacier-hung Kenai Mountains. The gray land brightened into the muted colors of an Alaskan fall—red fireweed and blueberry leaves, bearberry, yellowed birches and willows, and the soft yellows of frost-killed grass.

Two large animals had crossed a 300-yard-distant meadow, knocking frost and dew from the grass. Their path was clearly visible. A cow and calf moose? Or a cow with a bull?

A goshawk landed on a spruce branch overhead. With binoculars I looked into his fierce eyes. He tilted his head at us for a few moments, then silently took wing and disappeared.

We walked on, senses alert. We could almost feel the moose in a glade here, among the willows there, or in the shadow of the nearby spruces. We eagerly searched with binoculars and without, knowing that the first hour after sunrise is the magic one.

WE FELT THE cool dampness near the bottom of Deep Creek Valley and inhaled the musty rich odor of wet forest humus. A light mist hung over a swamp near the clear stream. Mice tracks and droppings showed in the freshly frozen mud at the stream bank. The water was inches deep at the 50-foot-wide crossing, belying the creek's name, and we stepped on the slippery rocks rapidly to keep our rubber-bottomed leather-topped pacs dry. I nearly stepped on an 18-inch Dolly Varden, its belly and sides brilliant red in spawning colors. It fled upstream, tossing spray with its frantically sculling tail.

We splashed 200 yards through a muskeg swamp, trying to walk quietly. When footing was again solid we sat on a log, using binoculars to search openings on the ridge that held our camp.

TWENTY TWO YEARS ago, when I first knew the then-remote Deep Creek Valley, it was a moose hunter's paradise. A few local hunters penetrated the area, and no one ever seriously hunted moose there without connecting. In 1959, within 2 miles of where Terry and I sat, during a November above-timberline hunt, I counted from one point fifty-one moose in the snow, scattered across Ptarmigan Head in the Caribou Hills like raisins in a rice pudding: forty-five of them were bulls.

Today there are fewer moose, for there are more hunters, and spruce has been taking over once-important browse areas. The moose herd on the Kenai Peninsula peaked in the 1960s, as did many moose herds in Alaska.

A faint breeze stirred, and in moments the valley bottom mist was gone. I swept binoculars across a meadow 200 yards downwind, and suddenly saw a cow moose, standing like a pointer, mule-like ears up, staring our way. She had caught our scent from that stirring of air.

"Don't move. There's a cow. She might have a bull with her," I softly warned.

My arms tired, and I slowly lowered binoculars and watched her with naked eyes. She abruptly turned and trotted into the spruce forest alone.

We moved on. At a swampy clearing I looked at a spot where I once killed a small bull. We stood next to a tree, our silhouettes broken, and glassed the clearing for 5 minutes. We saw flitting and twitting chickadees, and the twin white tailfeather flash of a junco, but no moose.

Three ravens flew over, wings swishing in the dense morning air. One clanged a bell-like note, then again. A red squirrel *chirred* beside the trail ahead; we watched for some time, but saw nothing that could have caused his alarm.

It was nearly 8 o'clock and dawn was 2 hours gone. We found a log in the sun, sat against it, and studied the broad valley with binoculars.

Half drowsing in the warmth, we watched quietly for nearly an hour. Terry tapped my leg and pointed upward. At first I saw nothing, then I saw a circling formation of high-flying wing-flashing brown cranes, circling and marshaling into formation for the long flight south. Their musical trumpeting drifted to us faintly.

I swept binoculars over an open grassy slope 500 yards away when suddenly a cow moose leaped into view through the 9X glasses. She was walking uphill, toward a dense spruce stand. In another moment she broke into a trot and swung her head to look at her back trail.

"I'll bet there's a bull following," I told Terry. Moments later a small bull, his clean 30-inch-wide antlers gleaming yellow, trotted into sight behind the cow. He frequently lowered his head, like a dog on a hot trail. The two disappeared into the trees.

"He's small. We could pack him out all right," I said. The farther from camp, the highway, or transportation, the smaller the moose I want. A half-ton of moose meat from a mature bull is a tremendous back-packing job. Alaska law requires that all meat of edible game animals must be utilized, and trophy hunters taking a big moose in the way-beyond may have to pay for an extra airplane charter, or an extra packer, to get the meat out.

We followed the pair, pushing through willows, wading the creek, climbing through head-high dead grass. We found their tracks and followed them briefly, then lost them in a dense stand of frost-killed grass.

Taking their general direction, we drifted on. Wind was from the side. Dead grass crackled under foot, and it was a relief to move into a spruce thicket and follow a game trail where we could move quietly, although visibility was only about 100 feet.

We stood in the shadow of spruces at the edge of a grassy meadow, watching the edges, listening. No moose. Two Canada jays flitted silently; a woodpecker hammered.

We had reached what I felt to be a reasonable limit for backpacking a moose, so we sat to wait. Perhaps the little bull would show himself. If not, we would return to camp to await the evening hunt. I seldom hunt moose during midday; it's usually futile.

We sat on a log and studied the area with binoculars. The sun was warm. The strain of listening and looking, of trying to move silently, plus the pre-dawn start, caught up with me. I dozed.

The silence was suddenly broken by a sharp crack, as a heavy animal stepped on a dead branch in a spruce-birch stand across the clearing, perhaps 200 yards away.

A few moments later, from the same place, we heard the loud unmistakable snort of a bull moose.

Then, silence.

SUDDENLY WIDE AWAKE, I was convinced we had heard the little bull. Perhaps an air current had carried him our scent. We started toward him quickly, in case another eddy confirmed our presence.

As we swiftly walked across the clearing I silently bolted a shell into the chamber, and we entered a stand of young birch and spruce. The waist-high brush made it difficult for Terry to see. I had hoped to put Terry into position to shoot his first bull: given time he was competent with the rifle he carried.

We were soon discovered. I looked up to see a cow moose staring at us from about 50 yards. I put binoculars on her quickly to make sure she carried no antlers, then stepped around a small birch to view the area behind her—and was astonished to see a huge bull moose near her, also staring at us. Two more cows stood near. The little bull we had seen earlier wasn't in sight; this was his great grandpa.

I was after winter meat, not a trophy. The bull carried a symmetrical rack that spread at least 60 inches. His antler tines were long and abundant, and the golden-yellow palms were wide.

The four moose were slightly uphill, silent, frozen. The .30/06 in my hands seemed a puny weapon for that huge, near-black, golden-antlered bull.

I stared at him for several seconds and forgot all reason. The grinding work of backpacking nearly half a ton of meat out of the hills was forgotten. My resolution to take only a small bull became meaningless. My hunting instinct was aroused. I wanted that big bull.

I slammed a bullet into his neck, and he went down as if I had broken it, which had been my intention. He floundered in the brush, hooves flailing high. I yank-slammed the bolt, ready for another shot, but fairly certain I wouldn't need it. Forgotten were the words of wisdom oldtime Alaskan guide Warren Tilman gave me twenty-five years ago. "Don't mess around with fancy shots on a moose. Shoot for the biggest part and you'll hit the lungs or the heart, and you'll have a dead moose."

The three cows stood, stunned momentarily, then they wheeled and crashed out of sight. Suddenly and incredibly the bull was up and walking swiftly to our right, mostly hidden by brush and trees. He stopped behind a thick spruce.

I stretched, trying to see, and in moments his huge yellow antlers appeared beside the tree, and then his entire head and neck came into sight. I drove another shot into his neck, and again he went down.

I turned to Terry. "Did you see him?"

I needn't have asked. His eyes were full of excitement.

"Quick, trade rifles," I said, handing him the scope-sighted Winchester and snatching the open-sighted Remington. If the bull got up again and ran, I'd have a better chance with open sights.

We stood watching where he had gone down, but saw no movement, and heard no sound.

We warily walked toward the tree and stepped around it. No bull. The ground was freshly torn, with much blood. The musky-sweet scent of a big bull moose in rut lay faintly on the air.

He had fled directly away from us, keeping the bushy spruce between us. Don't tell me moose aren't smart. He was so big that I didn't see how he could have left without our seeing him, but he did.

I wasn't concerned at first, for I had hit him twice in the neck. In my experience badly wounded moose seldom travel far. I expected to find him within a hundred yards. But a quick search along his probable route revealed no moose within 200 yards. We would have to trail him.

For about 50 feet his blood trail was clear, then dwindled to a speck every few feet—and then every 5 or 6 feet. I tore my handkerchief into strips and tied the strips along his line of travel.

Blood drops diminished to one every 10 feet or so, and we had to depend upon the animal's tracks, which often showed only when we lifted dead leaves from the ground. There were many fresh moose tracks, and it was difficult to stick with the one animal. We lost the spoor after 2 hours and 300 yards.

We left off the painfully slow trailing, sighted along our line of white handkerchief strips, and using them as a rough guide, strode off quietly and quickly, searching. I was sick over losing the wounded animal and deeply regretted shooting at him. I realized I had ignored my years of moose hunting experience, and the best advice I ever had on moose—to shoot for the chest.

We came to a clearing. I searched the edges with binoculars. Suddenly, I saw moving yellow-golden tips of big antlers. We walked 20 feet to a knoll and looked down 250 yards to where the big bull was bedded among some young spruce. Blood stained his neck, although he lay with his head up, looking about alertly.

I fired two more shots into him from a prone position, using the scope-sighted rifle, and his great head dropped for the last time.

When I lifted his many-pointed antlers we saw where I had hit his neck twice, but the rut-swollen muscles had stopped the bullets before they reached a vital area. He was musky-sweet with rutting odor, and we hastened to skin him and cool the meat. Many hunters swear a moose in rut is inedible, but I disagree. My experience with several dozen bulls killed by me or other hunters during the height of rut has shown that if they are skinned quickly, not allowing rut-perfumed hairs to touch the meat, and the meat is cooled quickly, then aged for about a week, there is no trace of off-taste or odor when the meat is cooked.

Before I began to dress him I looked sadly at his great collapsed body, lolling head, and awkward legs, and thought of the magnificence he had been when I first saw him. It is a terrible thing to love wild animals and yet have the need and desire to kill them. Logic, ethics, the biological soundness of the harvest, and sportsmanship had nothing to do with my feeling. I knew that the little bull we had seen would see to it that cows in the area would calve the following spring. But a dead animal is a sad sight, whether it be a fine Hereford steer or a great bull moose.

My family ate tender and mild moose meat that winter, and Terry and I relive our hunt each time we view the many-pointed, huge-palmed, 64-inch-spread antlers bolted to the side of our log home.

By Jerome B. Robinson

Hunting Caribou WITH THE CREES

DURING THE FIRST week of December 1994, an estimated quarter-million caribou crossed the height of land west of Quebec's remote Caniapiscau Reservoir and streamed into the valley of the LaGrande River, where five huge hydro-electric dams have been constructed over the past twenty years.

The caribou swarmed across the newly frozen reservoirs and crossed the graveled Caniapiscau Road that now probes the subarctic Taiga Forest for more than 400 miles east from the Cree Indian village of Chisasibi on James Bay.

In 1994 the road built to service the dams, powerhouses, and transmission facilities was opened to the public and nonresident hunters were given drive-in access to the winter range of Quebec's mightiest migratory caribou herd for the first time in history.

The Crees of Chisasibi retain exclusive outfitting rights to this territory as part of their settlement in the James Bay development agreement of 1975. When the Caniapiscau Road was opened to nonresidents in 1994, the Crees simultaneously opened Noochimi Camp, a comfortable, modern drive-in hunting and fishing lodge that offers a unique guided winter caribou hunt on snowmobiles and snowshoes from November 15 through February 15.

In January 1995, my friend Jim and I left New Hampshire to drive the 1,400 miles to Noochimi Camp. Eight days later I returned with a winter's supply of excellent caribou meat weighing down the truck and a head filled with memories of the most unusual hunt I have ever experienced.

For the Crees, hunts like this are not just routine, they're ritual.

SAM TAPIATIC, a leader of the James Bay Crees, pointed off across the snow-covered hills toward a sweeping bend in the broad LaForge River, a tributary of the LaGrande, about 100 miles east of the hydro-electric dam called LG4 in central Quebec.

"I camped with my family on that river bend to hunt and trap in 1960," he told us. "We had to travel upstream by canoe for two months to get to this place from our village. Now we can drive here in 5 or 6 hours.

"This was my family's hunting ground," Sam continued. "We came up the river every year in late summer and hunted geese and fished until freeze-up. When the first snows came we would pack our belongings on handmade toboggans and pull them farther north to our winter trapping grounds in those hills over there. After spring breakup we would canoe down the river 300 miles to the trading post at Fort George on James Bay to sell our furs and visit with friends. We would be gone each year for nine months on trips like that.

"There were very few caribou here then," Sam continued. "My grandmother remembered seeing caribou only twice when she was a little girl but then they disappeared and didn't come back into this country until about twenty years ago. Now they come each winter in herds of thousands and thousands."

I considered the man who sat before me. Born in the bush on a trapline, raised as a primitive hunter and trapper, then shipped off to school and college, Sam had emerged to become one of the key negotiators on the James Bay hydro development contract that won more than $100 million for his people. Now Sam helps invest that money for the Cree community. The Noochimi Hunting and Fishing Camp is one of these investments.

"We have had to become modern very fast," Sam says. "But our greatest strength is still our ability to live off the land."

NEXT MORNING, IN a pale yellow artic dawn, we left the warmth and comfort of Noochimi Camp and drove east in two trucks. Ahead of us Sam and his friend Eddie Pashagumiskum (Rippling Water) towed a trailer with two snowmobiles and drag sleds.

For more than 100 miles we drove at 50 miles per hour on a ribbon of glare ice that was too cold to be slippery. "You can steer all right at this speed, but don't slam on your brakes," Sam advised over the CB radio.

We were heading out to Eddie's hunting territory, where there was a cabin and a big canvas tepee for storing furs and trapping equipment. Our hunt would be on the same land where Eddie's family had hunted and trapped for generations.

Caribou tracks crossed the road at countless places and you could see where they had been digging in the snow on the hillsides above the road.

"They feed on the steep hills where they can push the snow away, downhill from them," Sam explained. "They dig with their front feet

and push the snow away with their hind feet. They eat the moss that grows down there."

FROM EDDIE'S CAMP we roared north on the snowmobiles, Indians driving, clients riding the drag sleds. Jim and I wore heavy boots but Sam and Eddie wore the traditional Cree smoke-tanned moosehide moccasins with canvas tops that extended almost to their knees. A pair of heavy, knitted wool socks and duffel-cloth liners completed their footwear. On their hands they wore wool-lined moosehide gauntlets that extended almost to their elbows over leather work gloves. They wore duffel-cloth-lined parkas with fur-trimmed hoods over heavy sweaters.

The cold was intense. The air stung. Caribou tracks were everywhere. I peeked at them through a slit between my parka hood and face flap as we trundled and bounced over the thigh-deep snow.

The big herds that had moved into this area a month before had now dispersed into small bands that foraged separately among the countless moss-covered hills and valleys. At any time we would be within a few miles of a small roaming herd, but we would have to find it.

Once Eddie stopped on a little hill to have a look around while we waited for Sam and Jim to catch up. When they had not arrived after a few minutes we went back to look for them.

We found them in a perilous situation. They were stuck on ice that had supported Eddie's snowmobile but had broken when Sam followed. Sam's snowmobile had plunged through the surface ice into a foot-deep layer of slush. Water had come in on top of the solid ice below and saturated the snow beneath the surface.

Jim, on snowshoes, was dragging the sled away from the half-submerged snowmobile and Sam, in his moccasins, was chopping down Christmas-tree-sized spruce trees and dragging them out to the wreck. It was so cold that ice formed instantly wherever air and water met.

At first I gave their efforts little chance of success. Freeing the snowmobile without getting wet before it froze into the slush seemed impossible. But Sam and Eddie calmly set to work and, within a few minutes, had the snowmobile up

on the bed of spruce boughs they had laid beside the hole. They tipped the machine on its side and revved it up before the slush had a chance to freeze solid. Moments later the sled was reattached and we were off again as if nothing had happened.

"How did you keep your moccasins from getting wet?" I asked the Crees when we stopped to make a fire and have a cup of tea.

"We quickly jab our moccasins into the water, pull them out, and let the water freeze on the outside before it penetrates the leather," Sam replied. "When the moccasins have a skin of ice on the outside, they are waterproof. Now we must be careful not to warm them by the fire or they will thaw and get wet." He used a stick and began tapping the ice loose, exposing the dry leather and canvas beneath.

At 1 o'clock we spotted a herd of maybe twenty caribou resting and feeding on a hillside a mile away. We drove off in a wide circle to get downwind of them. Behind the cover of a little hill, we parked the snowmobiles and strapped on snowshoes. Sam and Jim went off in one direction while Eddie and I split off to the side in a flanking maneuver. Quietly, we snowshoed the last half-mile using the terrain and little spruce trees as cover.

When you approach them silently and slowly from downwind, migratory caribou do not spook. These probably had never seen a man before; when they saw us they merely stared in our direction. At 100 yards we were simply a curiosity.

For the Crees, hunting is a meat-gathering expedition, not a shooting sport. Respect is earned by the hunter who gets close to the animals without disturbing them and kills cleanly with a single, well-placed shot. The Crees take fat cows and young bulls, not trophy bulls with tough, dry meat. They were pleased when Jim and I dropped two fat cows.

"Best for eating," they said.

By the time we had the animals field-dressed, Sam had a fire going and a teapot filled with snow dangled on a pole above the blaze.

"It is important not to hurry," he said. "After killing it is time to drink some tea and eat some meat to make us warm and strong for the cold trip back."

We roasted the tenderloins and the hearts of two of the animals on pointed sticks and ate them bloody rare.

"Eat this with the meat for warmth," Sam said, handing us each a frozen lump of lard he had dug out of his packsack.

"Our children are taught in school not to eat fat, but our parents always told us we had to eat fat when we are out in extreme cold to keep us warm," Sam said.

The sun had sunk below the horizon and the light was quickly leaving the sky. " Should we get going?" I asked.

"We'll wait for the moonlight," Sam said. "I have no light on my snowmobile, and anyway, it will be easier to see than now."

I will always remember that hours-long trip home under the shining moon and stars, riding in a sled with a dead caribou in the brittle cold. I was cold, but not too uncomfortable, for the caribou meat and lard had warmed me from within.

Next morning a steady north wind drove the windchill factor to a shockingly low number; still, Sam and Eddie decided to bring their wives, Sarah and Mary Ann, as well as seven-year-old Steven along with us. Hunting is a family occupation. Every family member takes part and has responsibilities.

Halfway to Eddie's hunting territory, Sam spotted fresh ptarmigan tracks and stopped the truck. He and little Steven stepped deftly into simple Cree snowshoe bindings (twisted leather thongs that grip the toe and wrap once around the ankle), and plodded off into the bitter cold and deep snow, Sam with a shotgun and Steven with his air rifle. Steven followed one of the white birds as it scuttled off under the spruces and killed it with a head shot when it stopped to look back. His father gathered several more with the shotgun and, in a few minutes, both returned happily holding their birds.

We left the women and Steven in a little grove of spruces that protected the area against the wind beside a frozen lake while we went off on the snowmobiles to hunt. The women and little boy would go out with their axes and gather spruce boughs to carpet the ground and build a wind baffle, then build a fire.

We struck the fresh tracks of two small caribou herds almost immediately that morning and split to follow them. Once again, we took to the high ground to locate the animals, then went low and circled downwind, getting within half a mile on snowmobiles, then strapping on snowshoes for the stalk.

I went in through a band of spruces that followed a little creek and when I could peek out the other side, there were about a dozen caribou within 100 yards. My eye settled on a prime two-year-old bull with graceful antlers. I dropped it with a single shot, but as it fell one antler hit a tree and popped off.

"Lots of good meat here," Sam said. "You can't eat antlers."

We headed back to where we had left the women and Steven. A little while later Jim and Eddie came in, crusted with snow and moving stiffly from the cold, dragging another sleek young bull.

"Come by the fire and get warm," the women insisted. "Have some hot tea and some meat. There is warm bannock and sweet wild berry jam. This is the way a hunt should end."

The deep carpet of spruce boughs they had made kept our feet off the snow while the wind baffle reflected our heat. Skewered ptarmigan and split caribou hearts and kidneys roasted on sticks driven into the snow around the fire.

Steven, oblivious to the cold in sealskin mittens, fur hat, and smoke-tanned moccasins, was bubbling with laughter and sliding down the hill above the lake on a little toboggan his father had made from tamarack.

"This is the way we have always lived," Sam told us when we had finished eating and were warm again. "Our strength comes from the land. Now that there is a road here, we hope hunters from the south will come and join us and see that our land is not a wasteland, as some people say, but a rich region where Cree people know how to live comfortably."

He took a piece of caribou meat and held it in his hand and stared into the fire for a minute, then tucked the meat under the spruce boughs. I asked him to explain.

"When we take from the land, we always think about what the land has given us and put something back in gratitude," he said. "It is our way."

By John Barsness

TUKTU!

THE LURE OF A NORTHWEST TERRITORIES CARIBOU HUNT LIES NOT IN "MATCHING WITS" WITH A WILD CREATURE, BUT IN BEING THERE.

FLYING NORTH IN A twin Otter float plane out of Yellowknife, Northwest Territories, you can see a dirt road in the thin soil that covers the ancient fossil-free rock of the Precambrian Shield. Say goodbye. It is the last dirt road connected with what is loosely termed "civilization" until you reach Siberia.

Beyond the road, the world is yellow-green and silver-blue. The yellow is the just-turned leaves of birch; the green, the branches of spruce. The silver-blue is the lakes, the unending slow rivers that make the Territories seem almost entirely aquatic; a series of small islands and narrow ridges suspended on a vast Precambrian sea.

This is an illusion, for the forest receives only as much rain as the American Southwest. But because of the cold, the little moisture that falls doesn't evaporate. Near Yellowknife, there's enough soil atop the bedrock to grow trees.

Following an hour's travel by Twin Otter, the soil and forest disappear and the desert appears, the tundra of dwarf willow, alder, and huckleberry. In September, the tundra turns orange-red and purple, a bonsai version of a New England autumn.

We flew north, and as I pressed my forehead against the window like a six-year-old, I saw my first caribou. Bedded along a braided path in the tundra, its velvet antlers were as extravagant in this bonsai forest as saguaro cactus in the Arizona desert. As we neared the Arctic Circle, we saw white tents pitched on the edge of a lake. We landed here, and shook hands with our Inuit guides.

The camp was edged with a low electric fence intended to keep migrating caribou from trampling the tents at night. I stepped over the fence and climbed the hill behind camp. Anthony Oogak, the young Inuit who would guide me, walked along. We sat in the gravel and looked across the finger bay beyond the ridge. Anthony said, "Caribous." Through binoculars, I could see a bull that appeared to be carrying brown sails above his head.

I looked at Anthony. "How do you say 'caribou' in your language?"

"Tuktu," he said, the word clear and precise, like the rocks and water.

Anthony would be guiding both me and Chuck Dearth, a tall, lean sportsman from Wisconsin who had hunted musk ox with Anthony the winter before. At dawn, Chuck, Anthony, and I got into one of the yellow plywood boats on the beach, and Chuck pushed off. When we were settled, Anthony stood up beside the outboard and said, "Exits are at the front and sides. Please keep seatbelts fastened when the craft is in motion. Coffee, tea, or me?" He then grinned demonically, like a cheerleader on hallucinogens. I began to suspect that my first caribou hunt would not be exactly what I'd expected.

Anthony started the outboard, and we ran the length of Little Marten Lake. The sun shone, but there was fog on all the bays. We huddled under the cold breeze until Anthony slowed and gently steered the boat through the mouth of a bay, basalt boulders rising under us like small gray whales. Then he pointed and said, "Caribous." Chuck and I looked and saw them, ½-mile away, trotting through a field of basalt that could have been the remains of an Inuit Stonehenge.

Anthony eased the boat next to a shoreside boulder and said, "Quick, up the ridge." He jumped into the water with the bowline. "They will come to us." As we hurried up the red ridge I thought, *Too quick, too quick.* I am at heart a simple deer hunter, and had dreamed of hunting these most extravagant deer since my rifle collection consisted of a single-shot .22. After waiting thirty years for this hunt, to kill a caribou in the first half-hour would be too quick.

We sat down in a rockpile on top of the ridge. Twenty caribou trotted toward us in a loose line. I could see their paths below us, worn down to bedrock in the ankle-high forest, and thought of the hollowed stone steps of centuries-old Mexican cathedrals. I looked over Anthony's shoulder as he watched the herd through binoculars and felt his calm tension, that of a predator who has evolved along with the caribou for as long as those paths existed.

Anthony said, "Cows and little bulls," and the tension left his shoulders. We relaxed and let them come. As they passed, a long arrowshot away, I could hear the clicking of their ankle bones, and knew I'd heard something like it before. And then I recalled a college computer class: fifty keyboards hissing under the fingers of students seemingly as bent on survival as these caribou, headed for the treeline near Yellowknife to wait out the Arctic winter.

After the caribou passed, we climbed to the highest point on the ridge and waited for more. There was already somebody up there, two of the "stone men" that Inuits have built over the centuries. Were they intended to help the

Inuits navigate the tundra lakes? To keep them company while waiting for the coming of *tuktu*? Anthony did not know; maybe shamans had built them for some reason known only to the spirit world. We sat and waited.

That's how the migration is hunted. This was the first trickle; more caribou showed up every hour or so, funneling along narrow ridges by the big lake. We sat and waited and asked each other questions. Anthony was not taciturn. He and Chuck had gotten to know each other some during the muskox hunt, conducted near the Village of Gjoa Haven, where Anthony lives. This was a "settlement" of a few hundred Inuits on an island in the Arctic Ocean, just north of the mainland. Chuck told of Anthony's snowmobile breaking down one night on the way back to Gjoa Haven; Anthony had gotten out his snow-knife and built an *iglu* faster than Chuck could have put up a tent. They slept comfortably at 50 below, and were found the next morning by other guides.

I asked Anthony if he knew many of the old ways, and he said his family had lived as nomads until he was almost ten, hunting and fishing, living in *iglus* in winter and caribou-skin tents in summer. He was now thirty-two, and still kept a dog team because, as he said to Chuck, "Snow machines don't always work, hey?" His family, and the others that make up the few scattered Arctic Ocean settlements, had been the last group of Inuits to have had no contact with white people. They know other Inuits who've become dependent on government handouts; they still hunt and fish and trap for a living, but their lives now mix both old and new. Here in the tropical southern tundra, Anthony wore a black Pittsburgh Penguins T-shirt and nylon jacket, but in winter he wears clothes made of sealskin, caribou, and wolf, for modern technology hasn't yet matched those "natural fibers" for life at 50 below.

By noon the fog had burned off, and we had seen perhaps 100 caribou, but no big bulls. It was just before the rut, and the cows and young bulls were hanging together, while most

Hunting with Inuits

I have been lucky enough to hunt with a number of Native Americans from several tribes, but the Inuits of the Northwest Territories are closer to their hunting roots than any others, and have been shaped in many ways by their environment. Anthony Oogak, for instance, always craved fat, which is typical of people who work hard and live in a cold climate. Anthony would slice chunks of raw fat from the caribou he was butchering and chew through them with relish—and yet he weighed perhaps 140 pounds.

As Bob Lloyd put it, "Inuits only have one gear," which is not fast, but rather so steady that they move more quickly than you'd think. I never saw one of them really hurry or lose his patience; a hot temper is something you simply can't afford to have at 50 below. One hunter complained that Simon Takkiruq wasn't walking fast enough for him so, as Simon said, he "put it on the big sprocket," referring to snowmobile gearing. At the end of the next day, the hunter went to bed right after supper.

Anthony Oogak had an encyclopedic knowledge of the animals of the tundra, even though the area is 600 miles south of his real home. He would point out different plants and explain their purpose in Inuit medicine or diet, using their Inuit names. Like the languages of many hunter-gatherers, Inuit language is so precise that there are words for every variation, rather than modifiers of a single term. *Tuktu,* for instance, is only the generic term for caribou: a bull caribou is a *pingit,* as opposed to a bull *tuktu.*

I have heard civilized people say that primitive hunters are different from modern sport hunters in that they take no joy in the hunt, and treat it as if it were a trip to the supermarket. After hunting with Anthony and the others, I think I am safe in quoting another Inuit in Hugh Brody's fine book, *Living Arctic, Hunters of the Canadian North:* "Your way of life, down south as white people, is a way of life I myself would not want to live. We are people who are free to go hunting every day." — J. B.

older bulls remained in bachelor bands. Chuck and I were of one mind: we each had two tags and had never hunted caribou, so we would take the first mature bulls that came along. More than anything, I wanted a white-sided hide, and caribou meat. We ate a sandwich and Anthony said, "Caribous."

There were a dozen bulls 1 mile north of us, edging a little lake. Chuck asked Anthony if any were big. Anthony shrugged, unimpressed. I got out the spotting scope and let Anthony look through it. He jerked his head back and shook it. "They all look big in that," he said, then grinned ferociously again. Chuck and I decided we wanted the two biggest bulls, and Anthony took us to them, traveling in a long downwind loop along a beach covered with fresh grizzly tracks. By then the caribou had all bedded down in the noonday sun.

When we could see antlers over the curve of the hill, we got on our bellies and crawled. When we got to within 100 yards the herd stood, trotted up the ridge, and stopped. I picked out mine and shot. A tuft of hair puffed from behind its shoulder, and they all trotted again, but my bull stopped after a few steps, walked backward and sideways, and fell. The rest trotted and stopped again, and Chuck shot his. His bull dropped at the top of the hill, and we were caribou hunters.

We took a few photos, then helped in the process of Inuit caribou butchery. Anthony skinned the cape from Chuck's bull and the hide from mine before gutting either bull. He seemed to work slowly, but had both off in less than an hour, with no holes in either hide. The bellies had begun to bloat, which Anthony said kept the hide tight, making precise skinning easier. He gutted both bulls quickly, then sliced the shoulders from the ribs of my caribou, cut around the hip joints, and popped the hind legs free. Anthony asked me if I knew how to bone, and when I said yes, he turned me loose on the shoulders and hindquarters while he boned the filets and tenderloins from the rear half of the spine. Then he inserted the tip of his knife into the spine, between the lowest ribs, and separated the two vertebrae.

Caribou antlers are like snowflakes — no two sets are identical.

By then we had a pile of boned meat, a stripped-down rib cage, a hide, a cape, and two caribou skulls. Anthony placed the rib cage on the raw side of the hide, placed the boned meat inside the rib cage, then wrapped it up exactly as would a horse-packer mantying a hay-bale, tying the bundle in half-hitched loops of manila rope. Then Anthony hitched a nylon strap, with clips on each end, to the rope on either side of the hide pack, and had us hoist the pack to his head, using the strap as a tumpline. Chuck and I each packed an antlered skull, along with our rifles and packs, and divided up Anthony's rifle and pack. Anthony started off, a pack weighing half as much as he did atop his head, and said he'd come back later for the other meat if the grizzlies didn't get it first. I was impressed with his compact packing system and asked him where he'd gotten the nylon strap. "Off a duffel bag," he said.

That night I lay in my sleeping bag in the tent next to the guides' and fell asleep listening to their cassette deck playing the "Inuit Johnny Cash." I recognized the tunes, but not the words.

In the morning, Anthony and I climbed a ridge and found a big hole dug into its side. Anthony pointed to it and I looked closer, seeing ill-defined tracks in the sand and gravel. "Wolverine?" I asked.

"No," Anthony said, scornfully. "Where Inuit digs for oil." He looked at me solemnly for a moment, then laughed.

On the third day I found my second caribou, a big white-maned bull that got past us in a little valley while Chuck and I debated which of us deserved to kill it. Finally we had to chase after it, jogging across the tundra, shedding jackets and packs and other gear as we went. After jogging ½ mile, we got to within long, but sure, range of the bull. We walked slowly back along the chase route, picking up gear as

Caribou of the Northwest Territories

Many hunters are under the impression that barren-ground caribou are much larger than deer. They do have huge antlers, of course, and their skulls are much larger. Add to that the bulls' thick white mane, and the impression is that of an animal closer in size to an elk than a deer. But in terms of body weight, caribou are very close to an average mature mule deer, and I have killed several really big mule deer that were much heavier than any of the caribou I saw taken at Little Marten Lake. Any good open-country deer rifle works fine. I used a .280 with 160-grain Nosler Partition bullets, which worked well even at 300 yards. One teenage boy used a .22-250 and also took one of his bulls at 300 yards; the other hunters used rifles from .243 to .270 and no one had any problems.

The caribou of the Northwest Territories are classified as Central Barren Ground by the Boone and Crockett Club. It's a relatively new classification and standards are low; 70 percent of the bulls taken at Little Marten qualify for the record book. But because of the scoring system, long spindly antlers often score better than more interesting ones. Caribou antlers are like snowflakes: no two are exactly alike. You can watch herds go by for a week and never see two identical sets—nor will you ever see a pair that has every feature, including wide double shovels, many-pointed bez, and palmated tops. When choosing our bulls, Chuck and I focused primarily on the tops, which contain palms and points similar to miniature moose antlers, but all four of our bulls happened to have double shovels, which is common at Little Marten.

You are allowed to take back 100 pounds of boned meat, which is just about all the prime meat on two caribou. The ribs and less tender cuts go to local Indians in Yellowknife. I brought back the maximum, because the meat of caribou taken before the rut tastes very much like prime elk—which is as good as venison gets.

You may have heard that caribou are innocent, or stupid, or naive, or however you want to put it. These caribou are, since many have never seen humans. There were two bowhunters in camp. One killed his two bulls in three days; the other got one bull and unsuccessfully held out for a bigger second one. The lure of a caribou hunt in the Northwest Territories is not in "matching wits" with a wild creature, but in being there. — *J. B.*

we went along, eating lunch when we came to the packs, and letting the bull bloat to Anthony's satisfaction. Then Anthony and I went back and sat in the sun, skinning and butchering my bull, while Chuck went hunting. We were just about done when Chuck came back, and Anthony asked if I would like to share an Inuit treat.

I shrugged and said sure. Anthony walked over to my bull's skull and cut out an eye, digging his knife deep into the socket to get the mass of fat behind the eyeball. Then he bit into the eye with his incisors, pulled on the other end, and sliced off the fat between his teeth with his skinning knife, chewing and grinning like a madman. "Best part," he said.

Chuck nodded. "They like musk-ox eyes, too."

Anthony held the eye toward me. "Want some?" he asked, stone-faced.

I looked at him. I have eaten many Native American dishes in my life—boiled porcupine, serviceberry mush, fried buffalo guts—and never disliked one, although none proved to be as much to my liking as, say, shrimp scampi. So I nodded, and Anthony sliced off a piece, being sure to include both fat and eyeball.

I chewed, and remembered what a Florida

friend once told me about eating armadillo; people say they taste like chicken, but the more you chew them, the more they taste like armadillo. The same can be said about caribou eye. It is not bad, but it's nothing special, consisting mostly of raw fat. The salty fluid of the eye actually improves the taste, if not the texture.

"You can spit it out if you want," Anthony said, quite solemnly and solicitously. I swallowed. He offered more, grinning again. I shook my head. He tilted his head and looked at me, smiling his mildest smile. "You know, if my parents hadn't told me how good eyes taste, I probably wouldn't like 'em either."

I had both my caribou, but continued along. Any hunter not addicted to MTV can watch caribou trot across the tundra all day, and it was just as fascinating to watch Anthony butcher and pack. Chuck killed his second bull in a steady rain and wanted a full-body mount. Anthony skinned the bull, with the hooves and cape intact, in 45 minutes. He made a tiny mistake near one of the hooves, and cursed once quietly. He never hurried, even in the rain. Sitting and boning the meat, I asked him how many caribou he skinned and butchered each year. He thought for a moment, then replied, "Oh, about 100."

Anthony said that this was the time of year when they killed caribou up at Gjoa Haven, too, but mostly cows and calves are taken there, since their hides make the best clothing. The bull hides are too thick for everyday clothing, but they make good winter sleeping robes. I said that's what I would do with mine; sleep under it on cold nights. Anthony looked up and smiled, asking how cold it gets "down there" in Montana. He had been to Edmonton once, to the world's largest mall, and it had been too damned hot. I said it sometimes reached 40 below, and he was impressed. Then we packed up the meat in the skin and walked out in the rain, hooves dangling from Anthony's pack.

Anthony never butchered the same way twice. Sometimes he kept the thin muscle of the belly intact, "sewing" the meat inside the ribs with a green willow. He told me about the women in his village who can sew water-tight winter boots, called *mukluks,* using tiny stitches to connect sealskin soles to caribou hide. Then he would heave his pack with the duffel-bag strap over his Pittsburgh Penguins T-shirt and walk 3 miles with half a caribou on his back. The only possession Anthony seemed slightly covetous of was my spotting scope, which he always wanted to look through, despite his joke about it making the bulls look too big. Otherwise, he had everything he needed to hunt right there in his pack.

Before long, the camp was filled with caribou antlers and hanging bags of meat, and it began to feel very much like an Inuit village. Toward the end of the hunt, when almost all of the hunters in camp had killed their caribou and were now fishing for grayling and lake trout, Anthony gave Chuck and me a couple of caribou-antler rings that he'd carved while watching us fish, our initials on each ring. I gave him my spotting scope in return, and still think I got the better end of the deal.

BY THE LAST evening in camp we were all pretty relaxed, and I witnessed one of the stranger multi-cultural events I'd seen in a lifetime spent wandering the wilder edges of North America: a Texan teaching an Inuit to shoot a bow. Drew Mouton had killed his two bulls earlier in the week, and now showed Simon Takkiruq how to draw and aim a compound. On the third arrow, Simon dead-centered a cardboard box, 65 yards away. We all shouted, and Simon and Anthony said they just might have to try bowhunting sometime, on musk ox. As they wandered back toward their tent, they talked about the best way to carry a compound bow on a dog sled. Across the still lake came the faint howl of a wolf, and then from the tent came the voice of the Inuit Johnny Cash, in clear precise rhythms telling of how he walked the line. The next day we white hunters would fly south, toward a dirt road and Edmonton; in a week, Simon and Anthony would fly north, toward Gjoa Haven and civilization.

By David E. Petzal

Hunting in a HARD LAND

THE TUNDRA OF NORTHERN QUEBEC IS UNCHANGING AND INDIFFERENT TO MAN; IT IS A PLACE OF EERIE BEAUTY AND SOLITUDE.

TWENTY-FIVE THOUSAND years ago, moving at the rate of a few inches a year, a wall of ice well over 15,000 feet high crushed its way across what is now northern Quebec, grinding the rock beneath it under the weight of unimaginable tons of frozen water. Then, as the earth warmed, the glacier retreated, leaving the land beneath leveled. Over more thousands of years, wind and unceasing rain scored furrows in the rock, and filled the furrows with water.

It is now a part of the planet where few things can live. Moss and lichens grow there, lending their greens and reds and oranges to the gray of rock and sky. There are cranberries and blueberries, and in the hollows where the wind is not so fierce, clumps of spruces huddle. The hollows are marshy, and there are grass bogs that quake at a footstep; the roots grow in the water beneath them, not in soil.

The animals who call this land home have adapted to some of the worst weather in the world. It changes over minutes, not hours, and can go from bright sunlight to rain to blinding sleet and back to sunlight in 5 minutes. In winter, the cold is appalling; it is enough to freeze rapids to a depth of 7 feet.

The list of creatures who can live here year-

round is short: Canada jays (called whiskey jacks), martens, black bears, wolves—and the animal that brings thousands of hunters to this desolation each fall, the caribou.

Caribou are circumpolar. In this hemisphere they inhabit Greenland, the islands of the Arctic Ocean, Alaska, and almost all of Canada. There are five species: the Barren Ground, the Woodland, the Mountain, the Central Canada Barren Ground, and the Quebec-Labrador. The variety that trots over the broken rock and bogs of northern Quebec, ankle bones clicking, is the Quebec-Labrador.

It is a stocky beast that stands about 50 inches at the shoulder (sizes vary considerably by species) and weighs 250 to 300 pounds for a good-sized bull. The long, loose body hair is hollow and brittle, and provides both superb insulation and buoyancy. A caribou is hot in cold wind that makes your eyes tear, and can outswim, I am told, a good man in a canoe.

The coats range in color from near-black to gray, and the big bulls have a pronounced white mane. Both sexes have antlers, and those of the bulls can be spectacular, high and wide, with shovels (palmations) and points.

The caribou's main predator is the wolf, and after a slump, the wolf is doing quite nicely in Quebec. *Le loup* is a formidable predator, but the caribou is formidable prey. It can run at 30 mph for short distances, but its most effective means of covering ground is a trot that eats up miles and which the caribou can maintain hour after hour. Wolves constantly shadow the herds and bands of caribou, looking for the lame, the young, and the sick. No wolf is going to run its paws off without the guarantee of a meal at the end of the chase, and so they watch and appraise with the eyes of a track coach.

Caribou season starts at the beginning of August and stops—for all practical purposes—at the end of September. It's not so much a question of season length as of weather; by the time October comes, you can find yourself stranded on the tundra, your plane unable to penetrate the snow, rain, and fog.

There are at present perhaps half a dozen well-established outfitters taking clients up to caribou country, and they have the operation running with military precision. Each year, the outfitters' association selects a motel near the Montreal airport. From there, they send hunters, guns, duffels, and archery tackle on a 2½-hour plane ride to Schefferville, which is the northernmost Quebec town to have an airport of any size. From Schefferville, the hunters break down into groups of six to eight and fly to their outfitters' camps in floatplanes for hunts that last five or six days. Then they reverse the process and return to Montreal laden—hopefully—

with meat and antlers. The process goes on virtually nonstop for eight weeks.

Typically, you'll live in a four-man A-wall tent with a heater and gas lantern. The tents are solid; they have to be, or the wind would tear them to rags in a day. Your day starts at a civilized hour with breakfast at 6:30 and a leisurely process of making your way to the hunting ground, either by foot or, more commonly, by boat. Two hunters go with a guide who is intimately familiar with the ground he hunts and the habits of the caribou passing through. He will take you to a high spot, and there you will sit, and look. Eventually you'll see a promising bull, and the guide will conduct you on a merry trot over the broken rock, the moss-and-slime-covered boulders, and through mud and bog, so that you may intercept the caribou.

It sounds simple, and it is, until you consider that you may sit for 3 or 4 hours in a slashing 30-mile-per-hour wind, and that you will be pelted with freezing rain every 10 minutes or so, and that the caribou may get your wind and trot off before you're set to shoot, and that your heart may explode while you are extracting your boots from knee-deep muck.

There is a prevailing myth that caribou are dumb, and that shooting one is a question of sitting on the nearest rock while the migration pours by, picking the Boone and Crockett head of your choice out of the mob, and squeezing the trigger. This may happen. However, it is far more likely that you will see the creatures in twos or threes, or in herds of a dozen, and that you will have to stalk them for some very tough miles, all the while being careful of the wind, and being careful that they do not see you—they have excellent eyesight. Then you may get a shot, or you may not.

The guides themselves are worth a trip to Canada because they are consummate woodsmen, and watching them at work is a privilege. The guide with whom I hunted this past September is named Maurice Boivin. He is a forty-eight-year-old Montagnais Indian who began hunting on his own as a ten-year-old. "My father showed me how to do it, and then said, 'Now *you* do it.' I was scared to death, but I learned." Maurice speaks the Quebec version of French and pretty decent English.

Each morning, we'd leave camp and travel for half an hour by Zodiac boat, and after disembarking, we would have a brisk uphill march o'er bog and boulder to the top of what was called "Maurice's Mountain," a 500-foot-high rise that gave an excellent view of the surrounding tundra. Maurice would go off on one side and I on the other, where I would glass for caribou, recite Milton's *Paradise Lost,* and think about Carol Alt.

As I was muttering Milton into my beard, I looked to my left and saw Maurice trotting toward me with a look on his face that I have seen mirrored by many guides. The look says something like this: *Oh, this is a big one and I know where he's going if we can just get there ahead of him and I hope the wind doesn't shift and this character doesn't fall on his face in the muskeg.*

The Disappearing Floatplane

The subarctic tundra did not really become accessible until the development of the floatplane in the 1920s. Today, these workhorses of the North are a vanishing breed, because they can be used only between June, when the fishing camps open, and October, when the hunting ends. The short flying season barely allows their owners to break even, and, combined with hard times in the aviation industry, has ended the manufacture of new floatplanes.

This has made the existing planes priceless, for they are irreplaceable. Flying at low speeds (75 mph or so, ground speed) and at low altitude (treetop to 2,000 feet, usually at 500) their pilots routinely carry huge loads under conditions that would keep less intrepid souls in the airport drinking coffee. — D. E. P.

And so I bade adieu to Milton and Carol Alt, put on my pack, and trotted after Maurice, down off the mountain and into a spruce-infested bog.

As we came up the far side of the bog, onto what passes for dry land, Maurice slowed to a walk. His hands were in constant motion, fluttering in a kind of sign language directed at me, at the caribou, at Fate, and at who knows who else. We eased up out of the draw and Maurice pointed west. The big caribou and a lady friend were about 250 yards in that direction, but we were unable to see them, or they us.

Moving a half-step at a time, I saw a patch of white 200 yards away. It was the shoulder mane of a big, iron-gray bull. His head was down, browsing, and the wind was in my face. I needed to move another 6 feet to get a shot. Whatever forces Maurice had invoked were on my side. I fired, offhand, and he went down.

IF YOU'RE HUNTING with a rifle, don't need to bring a cannon. I had a 7mm Weatherby magnum, and it was too much gun. A .270 would have been more like it. The average shot was on the order of 200-300 yards, so you do need something flat-shooting, but you don't need ton upon ton of muzzle energy. You may use whatever scope you like, but it must have caps for the lenses.

Bowhunters headed for the tundra have my deepest sympathy. Launching an arrow in constant high wind is something I was glad I was not faced with. If you do not use plastic vanes, you'll have to dope your feathers so they don't wilt.

It's hard for me to overdo this business of wind and water. From the moment we hit camp, we were told: "Don't walk out of your tent without your rainsuit," and it was good advice. I found it was best to put the rainpants on in the morning and never take them off, and keep the jacket in the top of my daypack. Not only does raingear keep the water off, but it helps to break the force of the wind, and it is much better to sit down on a clump of wet moss with rainpants on than without. Do not bring your leather boots, and I'm not even crazy about rubber-bottom pacs for this country. The proper footwear is 16-inch-high all-rubber boots.

This is not easy country. It is not the stuff of which picture postcards are made. It is somber, harsh, and uninhabitable by man. It will make you feel small and insignificant, and it will be there, unchanged and unspoiled, until the next ice wall looms out of the Arctic and begins its ages-long advance to the south.

Horned Game

If such a thing as prestige attaches to big game, then wild sheep are our most prestigious creatures. The difficulty of the country they inhabit and the sheer cost of staging a hunt for them place these animals in a class by themselves. A so-called Grand Slam of the wild sheep—collecting Dall, Stone, bighorn, and desert rams—is one of the supreme achievements in North American big-game hunting.

There are two types of people who should hunt mountain goats: those who are in superlative physical condition, and those who are not in superhuman shape but who have put their affairs in order and are at peace with God. Mountain goats live above wild sheep, and above oxygen. Hunting them is unique, unforgettable, and seldom repeated.

Antelope are Everyman's exotic game. There are plenty of them, and the hunts are not costly. Antelope live on more or less flat land, are not the brightest of creatures, and are cursed with too much curiosity. But they really can see you from miles away, and they really can run 60 mph if you spook them. This tends to even things out.

Buffalo are not off-brand cattle; they are true wild animals, and are the best-tasting game I have ever sunk a fang into. The buffalo's tongue, which is particularly prized, is four feet long, purple, and looks like a prop from a horror movie. At present, buffalo meat is hip and trendy because unlike beef, it contains almost no fat and no antibiotics or steroids. I love it anyway.

By Keith McCafferty

The MEDICINE TREE

IT WAS 100 TO 1 THAT HE WOULD DRAW THE PERMIT. BUT NOW, AS TIME RAN OUT, THAT LOOKED LIKE THE EASY PART.

EXCEPT FOR THE COLorful streamers people had thrown into the upper branches, it was just another Ponderosa pine. On the uphill side of the trunk was a small plaque noting its religious significance to the Salish and Kootenai Indian tribes. Joe Gutkoski, who had been hunting the country for 50 years, had advised us before the trip to curry the favor of the spirits by scattering seeds for the birds that brightened its branches. I thought we had done him one better by bringing rocks we had carried down from a 10,000-foot peak earlier in the fall.

"That's that," Kevin said, placing his stone under the plaque. "Let's go hunting."

Faith, Hope, and Charity were the names of the lakes posted at the trailhead. The map I carried called them Spud, Legend, and Fish Lakes, but then mine was an old map, printed when there wasn't much call for the names of remote Montana lakes to reflect the beauty of their settings.

We pitched our tent at the lowest jewel on the chain, Hope Lake, which we reached after a six-hour hike on the 15th of September. It was set in the cup of a headwall where rugged cliffs fell away in slopes of emerald grass. On the upper slopes of grass were two tan spots. I raised my binoculars.

"Rams," I said to my brother.

Kevin fiddled with the focus on his spotting scope. "The old man was right," he said. "The medicine must be working because that one with a chip out of his horn isn't half bad."

An hour later, having run out of cover, we stood 150 yards from the rams, the biggest of which regarded us incuriously over the tip of his broomed-off horn. The smaller ram had his head down, grazing.

So this is what it's going to be like, I thought, *just walk up to one and shoot him.*

I lowered my rifle. "I'm just not made that way," I said to Kevin.

"I'm not, either," he said, "but what did you expect? You give out two permits for a herd of a hundred animals." He stuffed the spotting scope back in his pack. "We're just backpackers as far as they're concerned."

Well, I told myself, *I'll just find the biggest one I can for Dad's living-room wall, and we'll shoot it and pack out of here.* I'd been on enough hard hunts. Why should I care if the mountains finally offered me an easy target?

But I did care, and that night when the rain came down on the tent, for the first time in my life I wondered if I would have the heart to pull the trigger.

In the morning it was still raining, and as the day grew cold the sky turned pink at the horizon, frowned with billowing clouds, and spit a torrent of hail. We took shelter in a grove of spruce and built a fire. Visibility was 30 feet. That night it began to snow. It didn't stop for 12 hours. We came out on the afternoon of the 19th, having never seen another sheep.

Had the spirits of the medicine tree given us their blessing, I wondered, *or a curse?*

A MONTH LATER we were back. The rams were starting their long migration from the alpine lake basins to wintering grounds on the round-shouldered mountains above the East Fork of the Bitterroot River. It was wide-open, heartbreaking country where a sheep could spot you at a mile and put a half-day's hike between you in five minutes. It was country that gave sheep the advantage if they decided to take it.

The first bunch we encountered didn't. They allowed us to close to 100 yards before an immature ram rose nervously from his bed, then canted his head to look at us as he picked his way to the top of the ridge. The ewes followed, pausing to punch their muzzles into the grass as they walked. A second bunch moved off at longer range, establishing a pattern of excitability that we noted throughout the day. Sheep that ranged farthest from the access spooked at the greatest distance, whereas the ones closest to the road seemed nearly tame.

"Here's the sheep hunter," Kevin said into the microphone of his video camera late that afternoon.

"And here," he said, panning the camera from my embarrassed smile to the cluster of rams that were clopping down the gravel of the old East Fork road, "come the sheep."

I had beaten 100-to-1 odds to I draw the most coveted hunting tag in North America. It was a tag that, on the open market, would fetch more than $200,000, as the one permit the state auctioned off annually did. But that night as we sat by our fire, I thought seriously of throwing it into the flames.

I had always considered fair chase to be a definition of ethical hunting, a call for hunters to restrict their pursuit to wild animals on unfenced lands and to voluntarily limit the technical advantages they possess to give game a reasonable chance of escape. The test of a true hunter was not how much game he killed but how many mornings he rose undaunted to climb the mountain that had sent him home with an empty pack.

Now it was apparent that as long as I slowly approached the sheep from below, then laid my rifle over my pack at 300 yards or so, I could kill any ram in the Bitterroots, and it would be staring at me, chewing its cud, when I touched the trigger. Fair chase was not a concept game managers considered when they designed trophy hunts that permitted so few animals to be harvested that they had little reason to fear humans.

We, too, sat silently as we looked deep into the fire, hoping, and not hoping, to find bigger rams in the morning.

But the great rams remained somewhere above us along the corridor of their migration. They were in a vast sea of timber, lost to both eyesight and temptation. After a week of hunting, we paid our respects to the old pine tree and drove home.

"I slowly crawled over the lip of the ridge, heart beating against the hard ground."

"AS A MEAT hunter," Gutkoski said as we sat in his den poring over maps of the Bitterroots, "I always take the easiest animal. Ancient man didn't wait to throw his spear until the animals ran, and by God I'm not going to, either."

He was 71 years old. He still hunted alone, still packed an elk out of the mountains nearly every fall. But even Gutkoski had held his arrow a month before when a young cow elk inquired of him with her nose at 20 feet.

"She was too pretty to shoot," he said. But I suspected the real reason was that she was the first elk he had hunted that didn't bolt from man's presence.

I told him that I had asked for guidance from the spirits at the medicine tree but received no sign. I had offered shining stones, and someone, I added laughingly, had placed a child's troll doll with fuchsia hair under an exposed root.

"Well that won't do any good," he said. "Offer food, and maybe you'll get your answer."

So I baked an Irish soda bread laced with caraway seeds, and when I returned to the Bitterroots the week before Thanksgiving, I scattered crusts to the Stellar's jays.

I was alone this trip, which adds gravity to any day afield, but even so, the country's mood had changed. It was winter now. Though the snow had melted from the stems of the brown grass, the trails the sheep made held a skiff of white. Those solemn hillsides with their lacy white trails dipping and rising toward the distant teeth of Bitterroots invited no casual visitor.

The sheep near the road had vanished. I hunted the whole of the day, hiking until my thighs burned and started to quiver, then resting and pushing on. It was as if the sheep had never been there, and it occurred to me that for all my reservations about this hunt, I had now been 17 days in these mountains and had yet to see a really mature ram.

NOW I HAD two days left. For the first time I felt the press of time, felt the weight of the day's end when the hills are barren and the freezer is empty.

That night I oiled my rifle by the light of the fire. The light glinted off the barrel, off the brass of the cartridges I fed through the magazine to make sure the bolt was operating smoothly. I had become a hunter again without knowing when it had happened, without questioning why.

In the morning I was 1,200 feet above the road before the horizons began to pale. Even at a mile, even in the poor light, I knew the ram I was looking at was big. He was feeding with a dozen sheep in a fold of the open mountain above me. To reach him without being seen, I would have to detour below to my right, then gain a ridge that climbed steadily up to the elevation of the sheep. By keeping to the timbered side of the ridge, I could get above and work down on them. I marked a lone pine tree as the place where I could begin the final stalk.

It took me an hour to reach the tree. I dropped my pack there, forcing myself to rest until my pulse settled down. Then I slowly crawled over the lip of the ridge, pulling myself forward with my elbows, my heart beating against the hard ground.

As more and more of the slope opened to sight below me, I began to worry that the sheep had moved somewhere else. Then, at the periphery of vision, I saw a ewe. She was much farther to my left than I had marked the sheep as being before, but country has a way of changing when you are in it and not looking through binoculars. She was up in an instant, the ram rising to his feet behind her. Now the rest of the band stutter-stepped out of a depression below and bunched, then cantered off. I swung the rifle with the big ram, but he was flanked too closely by other sheep to chance a shot. When they reached the bottom of the draw the lead ewe hesitated, then changed direction. A gap opened on either side of the ram. I never felt the gun go off. You never do.

The ram lay still. When the last sheep had disappeared over the crest of the far ridge, I walked back to the tree and got my pack. I slipped my arms into the straps and trudged slowly down the hill. He was all horn. They bulked dark against the grass, their rippled backs battered flat from fighting other rams. I counted nine age rings, and it was all I could do to lift the head off the earth. By the time I had packed the horns and cape off the mountain, plus the four quarters, it was after dark.

The medicine tree was outlined against the night sky, and I stood underneath it until my sweat cooled and I began to shiver. The rocks Kevin and I had placed beside a root had disappeared, and I wondered about that. But it was just a tree, for all I tried to romanticize it. It couldn't give me answers to my questions.

By Bill Burrows

RECORD SHEEP BOWHUNT

TAKING ANY SHEEP WITH ONLY A BOW AND ARROW IS THE HUNTING ACHIEVEMENT OF A LIFETIME ... BUT THIS GIANT DALL RAM WAS A WORLD RECORD TROPHY.

IT WAS THE KIND OF day best spent in a tent. Freezing rain drizzled relentlessly on the drab tans and browns of an Arctic autumn. The clouds and fog made it just as difficult to see our tent 1,000 feet below as it did to see my quarry, a fairly decent full-curl Dall sheep. Another 100 yards of skinning my cold, wet hands on the cold wet rocks lay between me and easy shooting range.

The ram had practically walked into our laps. My partner, Dave Dunkin, and I had spotted him while cleaning the breakfast dishes in the creek. I covered the last few yards to a point about 90 yards from the unsuspecting animal. As I squeezed the trigger, I thought to myself that this would have been a good situation for a bowhunter. The ram, and my desire to ever shoot another animal with a rifle, died simultaneously. Now, here we were in the middle of a 20-day backpack trip in the Arctic National Wildlife Range of Alaska. My ram was down and out of the way. For the rest of the hunt we could concentrate on Dave's quest for a bowkilled Dall sheep. Five years he had been trying. This year he would succeed.

Dave and I both live and work in Fairbanks in the interior of Alaska. When we started hunting sheep together in 1972, Dave was thirty, married, and managing the service

station he now co-owns. I was nineteen, single, and just beginning a career in broadcasting. We had hunted the north fork of the Koyukuk near Mt. Doonerak. When we first hunted there, it was a sheep-hunters' paradise. But the two rams we brought out stirred some interest. The resulting pressure had noticeably lessened the quality of the sheep hunting. It was time to explore new horizons.

I consulted the local office of the Department of Fish and Game. The man I talked to made a few suggestions, one of which really perked up my ears. But I was skeptical since I had no idea there were any sheep that far north.

"Oh sure. The Arctic National Wildlife Range is full of sheep. In fact, in the Hulahula drainage alone there are more than 1,200."

The Hulahula River is one of several in the range that start off at the Continental Divide and flow north to the Arctic Ocean, which is the northern boundary of the refuge. The 8.9 million-acre wildlife range was set up in 1960 to "protect the unique wildlife and recreation value" of the area. Within its boundaries are found a full spectrum of ecosystems from the shores of the Arctic Ocean over the Continental Divide down to the northern fringes of the Yukon Basin. There is also a healthy population of Dall sheep, which happens to be entirely huntable.

The fish and game man couldn't be too specific; showing hunters where to find the big trophies isn't the purpose of the Department's wildlife studies. But he could give me some good general directions to an area he liked. In fact, he was so confident of his advice that he issued a challenge:

"If you go where I showed you for a week or more and you *don't* get a ram . . . well, all I can say is, you're not very good sheep hunters!"

We're not very good sheep hunters. On that 1976 hunt in the Treels sheep country of the Arctic, Dave and I spent seventeen days discovering why this beautiful corner of the world was set aside as a refuge. We saw more sheep, bear, and blue sky than I thought possible on a single trip. We also did not fire a single shot with bow or gun. Nevertheless, we accomplished one thing; we were now familiar with a good location for next year's hunt.

Getting to the Hulahula River from Fairbanks (or, for that matter, from anywhere else) is expensive, uncertain, and hair-raising. In 1977 there was no direct flight to Kaktovik, Barter Island, our jumping-off place. It was necessary to fly the milk run through Barrow and Deadhorse, changing planes once in order to reach our destination. It even took two planes out of Kaktovik to transport us to the river bank where leg power would take over. I felt as if I had been through a review of aviation history in reverse when it was over, having flown in a 737, a twin Otter turboprop, a Cessna 180, and a Piper Super Cub. It was thrilling but there still remained 10 miles of backpacking before we would start hunting, and within those 10 miles would be the biggest thrill yet!

It was the second day of the pack-in and we were taking a rest stop. Three miles more and we would be at our intended campsite. My sweat-soaked T-shirt was just beginning to feel cold when I heard a *thump thump* sound. It sounded distant.

"What was that?" I asked Dave. We were both facing downhill.

"I dunno. Might be gunfire." A few moments later I heard it again.

"Get your rifle, Bill."

I jerked around to ask him why, thinking sheep. But what I saw straight up the mountainside was a little too big, brown, and hairy to be a sheep. Playfully flipping over boulders, 50 yards away, stood a good-sized grizzly. He flipped over another boulder which went *thump, thump.* But this time I didn't hear it since my heart was also going *thump, thump.* I reached for my rifle as Dave pulled out his .357 revolver. At the second of my working the bolt, our visitor switched his attention from the rocks to us. Exactly on cue, Dave and I chorused a yell.

Yaaaah!

The bear stood motionless for a very long moment. He couldn't smell us but he could sure hear us. Finally, dropping to all fours, the grizzly turned tail and pumped up the mountain. He covered in two minutes what would have taken me two hours. I did manage to shoot a few feet of film before he was out of range. For some reason, however, that piece of film turned out rather fuzzy and jiggly.

Two hours later we were setting up camp.

DURING THE FIRST week of our stay we accomplished a lot. We established a comfortable home, explored some of the areas we had missed the year before, and generally reacquainted ourselves with the rigors of climbing and camp life. This is a very important part of our hunting trips. We always bring along everything necessary to insure a comfortable camp, and we also try to allow plenty of time to enjoy it. Some backpackers believe in roughing it in order to keep their packs light. Sure, these individuals have an easier time of it on the way in, but once they get there, life can be pretty miserable. (Of course, being miserable has its appeal to some.) I've known some sheep hunters to go on a fifteen-day trip with under 45 pounds. On this trip, which lasted twenty days, my pack tipped the scales at just under 80. And that's a lot of work, but I think it's worth it.

It was during this break-in period that I managed to get my sheep hunting out of the way, as described earlier. Another day was devoted to taking care of meat and trophy. That done, we were ready for some serious bow-hunting. On the morning of September 3, a day we shall both long remember, we hiked in the crisp fall sunshine toward a valley already familiar to us from last year's hunt.

The valley we were headed for was actually a number of valleys converging into one. At the head of it rose one of the highest mountains in the entire Brooks Range, which fathered a modest glacier and, in turn, a creek. Like many in Alaska, this creek had no name. So we gave it one: Dunkin Creek. Due to ancient glacial action, Dunkin Valley differed from the other valleys we had looked at. This valley was a rich collection of lush basins and rounded knolls between small outcroppings of rock. It looked sheepy.

The only access to Dunkin Valley lay through a steep gorge. Down the middle of this gorge plunged a torrent of foam between flat slabs of rock. Climbing through this mess proved hazardous so we side-hilled up around to the right. In short order, we were strolling through the parklike terrain of the upper valley, the gorge forgotten. Sheepy though the valley looked, it wasn't until late in the day that our glassing produced anything other than patches of snow and light-colored rocks. It was after three and the lazy part of the day had turned to feeding time; suddenly the valley was alive with sheep. The most approachable bunch was just below the glacier.

"Looks like about forty of them," said Dave, peering through our spotting scope. That was bad news. Generally that many sheep in one group would almost have to be ewes and lambs. And generally, at this time of the year, the rams wouldn't be caught dead hanging out with ewes and lambs. But six years of sheep hunting has taught me that such generalities don't always hold true.

"Let me see," I said, hunkering down behind the eyepiece. After a few minutes of eyestrain I rolled over with a verdict. "I think that bunch down by the creek might have horns." Dave took another look.

"Maybe. Let's get closer."

AND SO WE did, being careful not to get so wrapped up in looking at the sheep at the head of the valley that we might overlook something in the basins we were passing. It didn't take long to establish that the sheep we thought were rams really *were* rams. But we still had a long way to go and it was getting late. We were just about to call it a day when Dave dropped to a crouch and motioned for me to do the same.

"There are two of them ... right up there." He pointed up to our left to a basin completely in shadow. Slipping out of my pack and digging for scope and binoculars, I asked the expected question.

"Where?"

Dave didn't answer right away; he was too busy with his binoculars. So I scrambled over to him and immediately saw the two sheep. Almost as immediately I determined that they were rams. They were so close that I really didn't need the spotting scope. But I set it up anyway for a closer scrutiny. For just a moment, the upper ram raised his head from his feeding for a few seconds. When he did, I got the first and last good look at his horns that we would get for awhile. That one glimpse, though, was all I needed.

"The upper one is absolutely huge," I told Dave. "Let's go get him!"

But it wasn't quite that simple.

Figuring the main valley as running east to west with the glacier at the west end, the two rams were on the east side of a small offshoot basin. The whitecapped mountain at its head fed a small creek that dumped into Dunkin Creek almost at our feet. In order to cross that convergence and have a chance at the two rams, we would have to show ourselves to the forty sheep below the glacier. As we pondered this problem, the rams fed a little higher up the mountainside. Now we couldn't cross without spooking them either. Not only that, but we couldn't go back. All we *could* do now was wait.

Mountainsides never look like what they really are when viewed from across a valley or from below. Feeding uphill, our two rams proved that point by disappearing straight into the side of the mountain! There must be some sort of ravine. Whatever it was, we grabbed the opportunity and made the crossing, looping around so the larger group couldn't see us. Within moments we were climbing the shale slide with nothing between us and the sheep but the swell of the mountain. An impossible situation was now very probable.

With adrenaline flowing, we climbed like grizzlies, not even conscious of our straining lungs and muscles. Reaching a predetermined point we figured to be above the rams, we stopped for a quick rest. We then began to inch our way across the face of the mountain, scanning the horizon. This was nerve-racking since the rams were on the move. Naturally we would have preferred to stalk stationary animals, but the lateness of the day gave us no choice; it would be dark before they bedded down again.

Suddenly Dave froze, crouched, and took a step back. He motioned to a spot ahead and a little below. At first, I didn't see anything. Then, I saw a big white worm crawling up the mountain. A moment later there were two big white worms. What I was seeing was a couple of inches of the rams' backs peeking over the swell of the mountain. They were 80 yards away, heads down, moving up and slightly away. Dave and I crawled over to each other. There wasn't much to say.

"I'll stay here," I whispered. "Go ahead, you can do it."

As I wedged myself between two boulders out of sight of the whole show, Dave crawled ever so slowly forward through lichen-covered rocks. There was no cover anywhere. If it were not for the fact that the two rams were in a slight depression, we would not have a chance. Even so, it was very tight. Fifteen to twenty minutes went by during which Dave progressed about 25 yards. I found that out by taking a quick peek, but that wasn't enough. Then impatience got the best of me. I decided to get a better look.

MOVING AS SLOWLY as I knew how, I rose from a sitting position to a half-crouch, scanning the mountainside as I did. I couldn't see a thing. *Where are they?* I said to myself, *They should be right over* ... suddenly, I spotted Dave as he flattened and, simultaneously, I saw one of the rams, the smaller one. But it wasn't a sheep's back I was looking at; it was a ram's head! If I was the cause of Dave missing a chance at that big ram, not only would I never forgive myself, but I was sure Dave would shoot me! For some reason, however, that ram didn't spook, although I'm sure he saw me. He just didn't identify me as a threat. Cocking his head back slightly, facing uphill to my right, his right eye stared hypnotically into mine for what I am sure was a solid 15 minutes. I never even blinked. My right leg turned blue, my hands froze to the rocks and both eyes shrivelled up like prunes, but I never moved a muscle.

Finally, just when I began to think that the motionless sheep head was a rock, it disappeared below the horizon as the ram resumed feeding.

Six o'clock was rapidly approaching, which meant the Arctic sun would soon complete its shallow slide towards the horizon. Dave looked back my way and shook his head. Apparently he couldn't get any closer. And he wasn't in position for a decent shot. Again we waited.

Once more fate took a turn in our favor. The rams suddenly tired of available fodder and took a few quick steps deeper into the ravine, presumably toward the second course of the evening meal. Whatever their reasons, it gave Dave the chance he needed. In a matter of seconds he gained another few yards. Having just noticed that he had forgotten his armguard and shooting glove, Dave now paused to peel off his wool shirt. It would hurt but at least his sleeve wouldn't deflect the string.

Dave tells me that he never did get a clear view of the big ram's head. He only knew that the one he would try for was bigger than his companion. From the kneeling position, 40 yards from the upper two-thirds of white body he could see, Dave drew his 65-pound Jennings Compound. He looked as solid as I have ever seen him in front of a target. He held for a few seconds then let fly with perfect form and followthrough. Instantly, I heard a loud *chunk.* Then, for the first time since we first spotted him, I saw most of the ram's body as he bucked straight up into the air and dropped from view. My glimpse of the great ram was so momentary that I thought to myself: *Did I really see what I thought I saw?*

Immediately, *four* other rams now ran up the far side of the gully not more than 50 yards from Dave, stopped, and looked back. Dave turned to me, still kneeling, and pointed to where the ram had disappeared, shrugging his shoulders as he did. At first I thought he had missed. I called out in a loud whisper.

"Where is he? Did you get him?" I was confused. Was our ram one of the four now nonchalantly feeding beyond the ravine?

"I don't know," Dave answered. "I think he's down there somewhere."

I LOOKED AGAIN at the four rams feeding as if nothing had happened. Suddenly I *knew* our ram was down; those other four would not still be hanging around if something weren't wrong. I have seen this sort of behavior before. I scrambled back to our packs for my movie camera. The scene was unchanged when I returned.

Enough time had passed, so we started

forward to see what we could see. In only a few yards we spotted the dead ram, not more than 10 feet from where he had been hit. We later found that Dave's arrow had punctured his heart. I ran ahead and recorded Dave's approach. As I swung the camera down and zoomed in on the dead ram I let out a gasp.

"My God ... "

Lying before us was the most impressive Dall I had ever seen. His body was huge, at least 50 pounds heavier than my ram. And his horns were simply enormous. It was not their length that took my breath away, it was their incredible mass. They were as thick as my arm with the mass carried all the way out. The bulk of the early growth rings swept far below the jawline.

Dave was still staring. I set my camera down and dug out a steel tape. Whipping it around the longer horn I found it to be 41 inches. The other was broomed back pretty badly, but it looked as if it would have been several inches longer in its original state. First measurement of a base was past 13, which for a Brooks Range ram was impressive.

Thrilled as we were, it was time to cut the back-thumping and get to work. We figured there might be 2½ to 3 hours of usable light left. (Remember, this is the land of the midnight sun.) For some reason we never even thought about coming back for the meat the next day. Instead, we just cut him up, loaded everything into our packs and took off down the mountain, floating with thoughts of Dave's accomplishment. It was 8 o'clock and 4 miles to camp.

I have read somewhere that the body has no memory of pain. Maybe this is why our ordeal doesn't seem so bad ... in retrospect. I do remember openly speculating on the possibility of our demise as we waded liquid ice down the middle of that gorge in total darkness. A twisted ankle would have been fatal. As long as I live, packing that sheep down the mountain 4 miles in the dark will surely stand alone as the stupidest thing I have ever done ... right up there with the time we did nearly the same thing in 1972. The important thing is, we made it, pulling into camp sometime after midnight. We stripped off wet clothes in front of the tent and tossed them into the darkness in a kind of euphoric delirium. Hot soup and warm sleeping bags brought us back from the edge.

Dave and I knew we had ourselves some kind of trophy, but we never seriously thought it would do much more than make the Pope and Young record book. Ninety days after it was taken, Dave finally got around to having his ram measured. Pope and Young officials in Anchorage scored the head at 163⅖, beating the existing World Record by one eighth of a point! But don't expect to see Dave's trophy in any record book. Even though five Pope and Young officials measured the head and even though Pope and Young headquarters has approved that score, Pope and Young has thrown up a final hurdle that a Fairbanks bowhunter who values his trophy would naturally refuse to attempt. Dave has decided not to ship his trophy to Salt Lake City, as required, to be measured again by the competition judges. The risk of loss or damage to a once-in-a-lifetime ram—not to mention the expense—just isn't worth it. Besides, just having bagged a ram with a bow and arrow, never mind how big it is, is enough of an accomplishment.

THIS HARSH COUNTRY OFFERS TROPHY REWARDS—IF YOU CAN HANDLE THE TRIP.

By Jack Wendling

Bighorn Ram OF A LIFETIME

A WIDELY READ OUTdoor writer once opined that "any hunter can get a sheep with two or three days' effort." Most assuredly this sage outdoorsman had not been humbled by Idaho's Bighorn Crags.

The Bighorn Crags are more than a collection of rocky spires. There are deep canyons with awesome expanses of slide rock interspersed with ragged granite spines. Moreover, there is deadfall timber from a sweeping fire of decades ago to impede cross-country travel. It all comes together as an agonizing country for backpacker and horseman alike.

The Bighorn Crags are located on the east side, high above the lower reaches of the famed Middle Fork of the Salmon River, a popular summertime whitewater rafting stream. The Crags are included in the roadless Idaho Primitive Area, and stream names like Waterfall and Roaring are indicative of the steepness and nature of the country. Road access to Hoodoo Meadows and Crags Campground trailheads is via Salmon City or Challis. Either way it's forty-plus miles off the blacktop. Of importance to the big-game hunter is that the Crags are home to an historic and viable herd of bighorn sheep.

Over the past seventeen years, I have given the Crags seventy-odd days and nights in pursuit of sheep. My intrusions into this inhospitable landscape were a near-annual feature before Idaho sheep hunting went to permits-only in the late 1960s. The Crags have kept beckoning, even though I am aware that they demand self-imposed hardship and privation as a toll for the intrusion. There are no free rides for the casual or comfort-loving hunter in the Crags.

In 1978, I was successful in the Idaho drawing for 100 sheep permits from 1,250 applicants. This was my first since Idaho adopted permit-only sheep hunting. My good fortune wasn't the result of prayer or clean living, but I would have tried either if I had an inkling that it would help.

At this time a hunter is limited to one Idaho ram, ¾-curl or better, in his lifetime. If the hunter is unsuccessful, there is a three-year waiting period before applying again. Seasons have been lengthened since the start of the permit system, but the take is nearly stable, probably due to lack of hunter experience and inability to utilize the added days. Couple this with the harshness of the Crags, and the odds are solidly with the sheep.

My son Scott, a first-year veterinary school student, and I arrived at Hoodoo Meadows, road's end and trailhead for the southern Crags, three days ahead of the opening. Scott, agape on viewing the Crags panorama from the high-line trail, remarked, "I never knew anything like this existed." I knew it, and I still find the Crags awesome. This is no country to hunt alone; accidents can happen. The Forest Service suggests parties of three. Anyway, the Crags experience is well worth sharing with friends.

It was our intention to set up camp in Jack Creek to have access to the basins above Wilson Creek. This was a new approach, and the unpredictability of the Crags didn't let us down. What was planned as a two-day, two-trip camp setup became three with an overnight siwash on the back trail of the first trip. The distance, steepness, and absence of a trail into

Jack Creek made the trip infinitely slower than anticipated.

OUR CAMP GEAR was of the backpack variety fitted into cantle packs to avoid the need for packhorses. With the proper selection of gear, the cantle packs permit riding while packing. But grain for the horses, hide salt, and food for ten days, coupled with the nature of the country, made a second trip with the expendables a necessity.

Horses are of mixed value for a Crags sheep hunt. They quickly become a liability in the big rock slides, and horsemen will ultimately revert to backpack and footwork when the hunting gets serious. The availability of grazing is unpredictable, varying from luxurious to nonexistent. Likewise, water can be a problem in terms of accessibility. Nevertheless, horses add a measure of mobility to a hunt when weather alters the patterns of the sheep.

Our second trip to our Jack Creek campsite came on opening day. Before dropping down to our campsite from the Wilson Creek ridge, we agreed to tie the horses and check out the access to the high basins further out. After 2 miles of slides and rock outcroppings, we broke over a saddle leading to a steep basin. We immediately spotted about a dozen ewes and lambs on the near side of the basin.

Continued glassing identified three rams bedded down to the far side and lower in the basin. The rams had a well-chosen bed site on a slide that was difficult to approach, and offered ready escape over or around a rock spine. Stories that rams do not inhabit the same basin with ewes have no credibility. While togetherness is not to be expected, proximity is not unlikely.

We were without a spotting scope, as this was to have been a quick scouting foray before going to camp. The rams were ½ mile away, but through 8X binoculars we felt confident that all were legal, ¾-curl or better. It was late in the day and the rams appeared settled for the night, so we backtracked to the horses and on to camp with plans for a serious stalk early the next day. But the Crags conjured up a surprise.

Scott and I left camp at early light under scuddy clouds and spitting rain driven by blustery winds. By the time we reached the saddle leading into the basin, we were met by intermittent snow. The rams were gone.

Visibility was restricted, and at times we were forced to retreat under our ponchos as the mixed rain and snow increased. A check of the adjacent canyons was also unproductive. The weather pattern was to persist, with the addition of fog below the ridges, for the next six days. The only sheep present were a scattering of ewes far down the mountain.

Sheep hunting takes a lot of sitting, looking, and looking again. Stationary sheep are difficult to spot, blending well with their environment. I don't buy stories that sheep hunters shouldn't wear red. I've had a band of ewes bed down on a slide with me, only a rope's throw away, while I've sat motionless, hardly breathing, wearing a red jacket and cap. Sheep are color blind. But reflective clothing is out.

Sheep may seek shade in hot weather or even enter timber to bed behind the bole of a big conifer. Ewes and lambs are more nomadic, traveling between basins, crossing to adjacent drainages, and drifting up and down the slopes. Rams are sedentary by comparison.

Rams are disposed to take up residence in one basin until it's time to migrate to lower elevations and winter range. Rams may well choose basins closer to their wintering area. The basin preferred by the rams will have forage, water, and talus slides, the latter for beds. Mature rams are gregarious, and a band may well be composed of animals of the same age. These rams were kicked out of the ewe bands as juveniles to begin their association. Comradeship persists, as the younger animals lack the size and strength to compete with their elders at breeding time.

A band of mixed-age rams suggests a less than optimum sheep population. I have seen seven same-age rams together in the Crags and heard a fellow hunter tell of seeing thirteen.

A Crags ram will pass the legal ¾-curl at four and one-half years, determined by counting the winter-stress growth rings. At this time the horns will show slight flare at the tips, which aids in determining legal size.

For all the accumulated observations of

sheep behavior and habitat from prior hunts, the sheep were not cooperating; but then neither were the Crags. After a couple of days of searching the basins and side canyons while contending with various forms of precipitation and fog, a change was in order if rams were to be found. We suspected that the rams had gone below the fog in the canyon. It was agreed to pull back to the trailhead, take the trail down Wilson Creek, and hunt up from below.

But the Crags coughed up a new surprise. This time it was tiny bloodsucking flies that buried their heads in the chest and lower centerline of our horses, causing intense swelling and tenderness. We were fortunate to have some effective repellent, but there was small hope that the horses could tolerate a girth for several days. So we continued to search above the fog for the rams while the horses recuperated.

FINALLY, THE HORSES looked able and we packed up and out for the trailhead at the Meadows. We had a better day for the trip out, but it was short-lived. Thirty minutes after arriving back at our rig late in the day, high winds and freezing rain made the scene, and heavy, wet snow came within an hour.

Brief early fall storms are to be expected in the Crags, but this one was the exception. We had snow and fog at the Meadows for four days, with conditions worsening, if anything. Wet snow on slab rock makes shod horses about as agile as a bear on roller skates. Consequently, the trail down into Wilson Creek was impossible, short of dire emergency.

Again, the Crags temporarily bested our intentions, as the day for Scott to return to school was imminent. Reluctantly we loaded up to head home in yet another snow squall. On the way, we found the weather unseasonable statewide. My thoughts were nevertheless on a rematch with the Crags in about a week.

Once the Idaho weather pattern had returned to normal, I was fretting to go back, but the Crags are no place for a lone hunter. Scott had returned to school, so I had to wait till my frequent hunting partner, Tom Lancaster, was ready to keep me company.

The weather back at Hoodoo Meadows was like Indian summer. Tom and I took the low trail into Wilson Creek hoping to find the rams low as a result of the earlier storm and the lateness of the season. We glassed the lower basins for two days but found only numerous ewes and lambs. The rams had to have gone high again. We broke camp and returned topside to think about the situation.

After resting the horses and hashing out the probable movement of the rams, we took the highline trail out and broke off cross-country to the Jack Creek campsite, which Scott and I had pioneered. An early start had us set up by midafternoon. With reasonable daylight left, we thought to check out the basin I knew to be frequented by rams. Tom stripped down to a pack frame with our jackets, ponchos, candy bars, and spotting scope. We tied the horses long in good grass to keep them overnight, if need be. I had my featherweight rifle, binoculars, canteen, and camera. This was to be a scouting foray, but nevertheless we prepared for an overnight siwash.

We arrived at our objective in good time and eased behind an upthrust rock formation to check out the basin. We immediately sighted a small group of ewes and lambs down in the basin to the near side. Glassing the far side I picked up two respectable rams above the ewes and about half a mile distant. I called to Tom to set up the spotting scope and we determined that both rams were legal.

Tom was anxious to try a sneak on the larger of the two rams. I chose more caution. "Scott and I saw three rams when we were in here. I'd like to know where the third one is so we don't blunder into him." We continued our watch on the two rams while trying to locate a third.

The third ram failed to show. What appeared as the better of the two in sight moved behind a rock spine and did not reappear for some minutes. With the thought that the better ram could have bedded behind the rocks or joined the unlocated third ram, we dropped below the ridge to swing behind the spine where, hopefully, I could get a shot at reasonable range.

The stalk took more time than anticipated and we arrived opposite the landmark we had chosen, apprehensive that the ram could have moved away. I took the lead and cautiously moved over the rim of the basin and down to where I could see the near slope and bottom of the basin. No rams. Moving to the side to better see through the scattered Alpine fir in the bottom, I spotted a ram unsuccessfully pushing his attentions on a ewe and acting hostile to two juvenile rams. Could this be the third ram? The two seen earlier on the side slope were still not in view.

I sat down to study the amorous ram and concluded that he was not the one we wanted. His horns lacked flare at the tips. Getting to my feet, I continued down into the basin slowly, a step at a time, searching among the trees and rocks. Suddenly, on stepping beyond sight of the top of a fir that had previously blocked my view, I spotted a ram standing broadside on a ledge 125 yards down and to my right.

I dropped to a sitting position, put the crosshairs on his horns to check the curl, and was moving onto his vitals when he spotted me and dug out down the ledge. I put the crosshairs between his shoulder blades and squeezed. There was no time to compensate for the bullet going high on a downhill shot. He was hit squarely in the back of the head, slid off the ledge and came to rest 20 feet down on a slide. It was 4:30 P.M., October 16, the forty-fifth day of the Idaho bighorn season and my twenty-first day in the Crags.

Tom was elated. I was pleased beyond words, but there was the thought that this was the end of my sheep hunting in Idaho.

My one-in-a-lifetime ram wasn't the broomed-off, full-curl patriarch with which I had hoped to conclude my Idaho sheep hunting. Could it be that the Crags were taking a parting shot at my ego?

We loaded the head and cape on the pack frame and left the field-dressed carcass for the next day. By the time we had scrambled out of the basin and back to the ridge, the sun was gone. The way to camp would take us across several steep and crumbly rock outcroppings and was no place to be moving about in the dark. We didn't stop for a breather on gaining the ridge, but put on a rush for camp.

Nevertheless, darkness caught up with us. We were past the rocks, and the trees were thinning ahead, so I knew we were close. I called ahead to Tom, "I think we're too high. Camp is below us." Without answering, Tom let go with a sorry-sounding whinny. Tom's pinto gelding replied in kind from below, and turning, Tom said, "You're right." Being on good terms with your horse has its benefits. In a matter of minutes we were unloading our gear at camp.

The next day we returned to the carcass, boned the meat, and made the final climb out of the basin. At the saddle, I had a last long look at the basin, and the tortured ridges and canyons beyond. Truly, this was country to test the persistence and determination of a hunter.

A day later the cross-country trek to the trail was no less effort than before as we led and cajoled our horses out of Jack Creek. When we finally cut the trail leading to road's end, Tom's comment was, "Back on the super slab." Uneventful hours later we arrived at trailhead and road's end under beautiful mild fall skies. Now that the hunt was over, the Crags were showing the congenial side of their character. But the Crags follow Murphy's Law, and an aspiring sheep hunter should expect the worst, because it will happen.

With permit-only Idaho sheep hunting (and an application for sheep voiding application for any other controlled-hunt species) many hunters do not develop familiarity with sheep behavior and the country. More than a few sheep hunts are terminated in three to four days; one day in to camp, the second to develop sore feet and rubbery legs while seeing no sheep, and the third to get back to the vehicle and home. This pattern may well be the norm for first-time hunters in the Crags.

Preparation, perseverance, and acceptance of the vagaries of the Crags are the key to success and survival. Otherwise, the Crags will have you asking why you are there ... and the hunt will be over.

Borrowing the words of an East Indian sage, "Joy lies in the attempt, in the suffering involved, not in the victory itself." If you buy that philosophy, you're a candidate for a Crags hunt. Good luck!

By Bill McRae

HIGH ON GOATS

THESE SURE-FOOTED ALPINE CREATURES EPITOMIZE THE SPIRIT OF THE MOUNTAINS AND LEAVE YOU FEELING THAT YOU'VE BEEN TO THE EDGE OF THE EARTH AND BACK.

BARRETT WYNN asked me how good I was at judging goat horns, and although I've photographed hundreds of big billies, I had to admit I'm not very good at judging horn size. It was just campfire talk at the time, but now, as I watched the big billy picking his way across a rock slide at the base of the cliff below us, it kept running through my mind.

A few minutes earlier I had passed up the goat at 50 yards, and even at 150 yards he would be an easy target. Besides, a strange thing was happening—the farther he walked, the better he looked. I brought the reticle of the Leupold 4X compact to rest just behind the billy's shoulder as if somehow it would help make up my mind.

"Barrett, those horns have to go at least 10 inches. What do you think?"

"You're probably right, but it will be marginal. Remember there are a lot of goats here and we have plenty of time to hunt."

I slung the rifle and with binoculars spent the next half hour watching in awe as the goat left the rock slide and picked his way up a near vertical face on the far side of the basin. Finally, in a spot where you couldn't imagine seeing a living thing that didn't have wings, he lay down and, like some heraldic monarch, surveyed the world below.

Mountain goats are strange creatures, but then, as my wife would tell you, so are the men who photograph and hunt them. I admit to having an obsession with everything alpine. It is a love affair with the mountains and all that they embrace—cliffs, waterfalls, lakes nestled in glacial cirques, meadows full of wildflowers, the evergreen forest that clings tenaciously to the slopes, and the windswept tundra. What's more, though I am fascinated by the wild creatures that inhabit the high country, I am especially intrigued by goats. Why? I don't know for sure. They are not as majestic as a bighorn nor as fierce as a grizzly. But there is something about them, a detachment, a cold indifference to foul weather and their giddy environment that somehow epitomizes the spirit of the mountains. I like goats because when I return from living among them I feel I've really been someplace special, like to the edge of the earth and back.

That was why I was hunting goats with outfitter Barrett Wynn in the rugged Cassiar Mountains of northwestern British Columbia. We hoped for a record-book billy, but mostly I wanted to savor again the wonderful world of the Rocky Mountain goat. This general region (which includes adjacent areas of southeastern Alaska) accounts for the majority of record-class heads. Here goats not only grow bigger but are more numerous than anywhere else.

Previous to this hunt most of my experience with goats had been in the Rockies of Montana and southern Alberta. And while these in the Cassiars seemed to have similar habits, I did notice one striking difference—goats tended to bunch together in much larger groups. We saw herds of as many as thirty and although the rut was still months away, the bunches invariably included large billies. One goat-hunting enthusiast that I met in the small town of Atlin, British Columbia, where Barrett has his headquarters, told me he once counted sixty goats on one mountainside.

I have a firm belief that there is no such thing as an easy goat hunt. It always involves a lot of hard work coupled with a sense of danger and high adventure. This pack trip was no exception and involved well over 100 miles of horse travel in the most pristine of wildernesses. No well-marked Forest Service trails here!

While we operated out of a couple of commodious base camps, we spike-camped most of the time, and as is always the case with goat hunting, there were some considerable forays on foot. Our party consisted of outfitter Barrett Wynn; guide, wrangler, and all-around mountain man Dee Verge; and myself.

The hunt was scheduled for the first fourteen days of August. It was on the third day that I passed up that billy. Next morning we were up at 5 and were in the saddle headed into the high country an hour later. About a mile above camp we ran into a young mountain caribou bull that acted as if he had never seen men or horses before. He ran along parallel to us, sometimes as close as 50 yards, for about half a mile and once he actually ran in a full circle around us. He seemed torn between curiosity and fear. Fear finally won and he ran up a steep boulder-strewn mountainside with unbelievable ease.

We located one lone goat feeding near the head of a large basin, and since solitary goats tend to be large, mature billies, Barrett set up his zoom spotting scope for a closer look.

"That goat has the longest, heaviest horn I've ever seen."

"Horn?" I asked.

"Yeah, take a look."

No doubt the billy was record class so far as his one good horn went, but the other was broken off with only a short stump remaining.

We glassed another cirque, finding nothing, then heavy clouds rolled in from the coast to end the day's hunting.

A couple of days earlier when the air had been very clear we had seen large numbers of goats on the north face of a mountain range about 10 miles away. Even with the spotting scope turned up to 36 power, they were little more than white specks against the gray and green of the mountain. We couldn't tell much about the composition of the herds but some appeared larger than the others–probably billies.

Barrett suggested that we could move and hunt the area. It meant leaving a mountain that I knew had trophy goats but it would give me a chance to see new country.

By the time we broke camp, packed everything, and loaded the horses, it had begun to rain. The country was so rough that it would have been impossible to go directly to the other mountain, so instead we would have to take a circuitous route via one of the base camps, a distance of about 20 miles.

It was a very wet pack train that pulled into base camp at 5:30 P.M. The camp, with its large well-equipped cook tent and individual 10 x 12 sleeping tents with plywood floors and woodstoves, somehow seemed much more luxurious than when I had stayed there five days earlier.

By morning the rain had stopped and we set out again. Horse travel in this country is such that if one didn't have a sense of adventure it could be considered an ordeal. We rode for miles through spruce and pine forests laced with muskeg and thick stands of willows higher than a rider's head. We skirted placid lakes with moose feeding in them, and forded fast-flowing rivers at the bottom of steep canyons. When we finally started to climb up into the mountains where we had seen the goats, things didn't improve much. Willows, dwarf birches, and a tree that the locals called ground balsam all seemed to grow in an impenetrable tangle near the ground.

The mountain range was a series of peaks connected by high ridges. Our face (where the goats had been) was made up of numerous cirques and basins rimmed with great limestone cliffs. Timber ran up the slopes on finger ridges interspersed with open chutes where avalanches had thundered down in winters past. It was classic goat country, and while we had been able to see the entire side of the range from 10 miles away, now we could see only small parts at any given time and would have to search for the goats.

Early the next morning we rode over the mountain by way of a ridge that went up around the edge of the basin where we were camped. The top and back side of the range, unlike the face, consisted of rolling alpine tundra. There were, of course, deep cuts and steep slopes, but for the most part travel was easy.

An abundance of sign indicated what we had already suspected—that the goats were using the cliffs for refuge and as bedding areas but coming out on top to feed.

The next hour was spent glassing. We located a distant band of stone sheep, and on other mountains far to the south more herds of goats. The thing that intrigues me most about the Cassiars is how this vast land seems to roll on forever, range after mountain range.

We mounted up and rode along just below the crest of the ridge, stopping to peek into each new basin as we came to it. About 8 A.M. I spotted a goat feeding above some cliffs about 700 yards away. A quick check with binoculars showed it to be a billy, and he looked big!

A lot has been made about the difficulty of telling the sexes apart, but for those who have spent a lot of time with goats it's quite simple. The billies look masculine while the females look feminine. More specifically, the billies have a blockier build and they are heavier and deeper in the chest. Though the horns of both are approximately the same length, a nanny's horns are invariably slimmer and more delicate looking.

Also, nannies are apt to be accompanied by kids, but the old saw about billies never being found with nannies and kids except in the rut didn't seem to hold true in the Cassiars.

In any event, after I spotted the goat it was decided that Dee would stay with the horses and Barrett would accompany me on the stalk.

The billy had dropped out of sight into a draw so the first part of the stalk was easy. Then at about 200 yards we again caught sight of him and had to proceed with caution. We left our day packs, taking only the spotting scope, my binoculars, and my Brown Precision .270 rifle. Eventually we crawled up behind some small boulders to within 125 yards of what turned out to be five goats, all billies, and all very large!

It was a goat hunters dream but also a dilemma in picking the best goat. We knew that there wouldn't be a 3/4-inch difference in horn length between the best and the poorest, yet those few fractions of an inch could mean the difference between a record-book head and one that was merely a good trophy. A difference of as little as 1/4 inch in base circumference would also make a considerable difference in the final score.

The problem is how to detect such small differences in the field. Frankly I don't know.

Both Barrett and I ruled put two of the billies as being inferior and with rising excitement we must have spent 15 minutes studying the other three. They hadn't seen us but were feeding closer to the edge of the cliffs and would soon be dropping over the edge to bed down.

Mortally wounded goats have a habit of falling off cliffs and breaking their horns and when studying the face of the mountain earlier I had seen many places where retrieving an animal would be virtually impossible. We had to make a decision soon.

"I think the farthest billy has slightly longer horns," Barrett whispered. "I'd suggest that you take him."

Actually I had been eyeing the billy nearest us. With a gulp I decided to go with Barrett's advice.

To shoot I had to raise up from behind the rock and when I did the goats saw me. Those nearest bolted and the one I was to take started for the cliffs, quartering away and to the right. The first shot dropped him and a second round administered the coup de grace. Off in the middle of nowhere, I had taken a trophy goat.

We knew that Dee would hear the shots and bring up the horses so while we waited I dug out my steel tape and we measured and rough-scored the goat's horns. They were both 10 3/8 inches long and had 5 7/8-inch bases. All the figures, less differences, added up to 51 2/8 points. Sixty days later an official Boone and Crockett measurer scored the head at 51 even, which puts it well up in the record book.

The billy was ten-and-a-half years old and appeared huge. We guessed that he must have weighed about 300 pounds. However, he hadn't seemed to be any heavier than the goats he was with.

That night in spike camp we roasted goat ribs over an open fire. The meat didn't taste bad but it was really tough. Other cuts were to make some fine stew later on, but just then I didn't care. The trip was a great success, and in goat hunting that means total good luck.

By Lloyd Bare

Hunt the WHITE BUFFALO

IF RUGGED TERRAIN IS YOUR IDEA OF A HUNT, THEN THIS ANIMAL SHOULD BE YOUR QUARRY.

WHY IS THE ROCKY Mountain goat considered a second-class citizen? His neighbors the sheep are generally classed as the most sought-after trophy in North America, while the goat is usually taken as a secondary trophy on a sheep or caribou hunt.

Called "white buffalo" by the early settlers, this animal is unique. It has no close relatives anywhere in the world, and though we refer to it as a mountain goat, it is not related to either the Asian or the domestic goat.

This beautiful, pure-white animal inhabits the rugged peaks at the very top of the North American mountain ranges, while sheep prefer the high, grassy basins. Often, sheep will come down and cross to other ranges, but the goat seldom leaves the alpine environment. Compared to the lively and wary rams, goats are phlegmatic. While most animals will run at the sight of a predator, goats will usually walk off and climb slowly out of danger. They can walk and climb where no other animal possibly can, moving with ease on cliffs and ledges where there is no apparent path or foothold.

The short, sharp, curving black horns found on Mountain goats are for protection, but they are rarely used to fight other goats. The well-known sheep and goat authority Dr. Valerius Geist points out a very good reason for this: "Sheep are well known for their fighting ability, but with their massive, rounded horns they do each other very little damage. In comparison, the goats would surely kill or seriously harm each other fighting with the sharp weapons they possess. Instead, they are only used to fight off the few predators that would dare attempt to make a meal of them or their young."

Goat hunting means climbing—sometimes until you are certain that your lungs will burst or your legs will turn to jelly. In many areas, sturdy mountain horses may be used to reach the treeline from camp each day or, in a few spots, to ride up to some of the high rims. However, in most good goat hunting areas it is simply a matter of putting one foot in front of the other, with an overweight pack on your back.

When horses are used, it is wise to dismount often and scan the countryside with binoculars, checking the bluffs and crags below, above, or across from your position. Like sheep hunting, going after goats involves a great deal of sitting and glassing. In the absence of snow, goats will be easily sighted after the hunter learns to ignore the many white rocks that are found in their lofty domain.

Regardless of the location, or whether horses are used, the goat hunter will find himself making a tough and often long stalk. This means much pre-season work to get into shape. Flatlanders will still have problems with the lack of oxygen atop a goat mountain, but at least some vigorous preparation will prove beneficial. After the first couple of days, the prepared hunter should be better able to cope with the thin air.

It is hard to make general statements about stalking goats, as each hunt will be unique. Most hunters want to get above the game if possible. With sheep this is often easy, but with the goat it is often impossible. More often than not, the stalk will be a sidehill approach or from below—almost unheard of with other animals. Goats can be approached from below for two simple reasons—their lack of fear and their phlegmatic nature. This doesn't mean that the stalk will be easy. Indeed, it may be long and hard, and in spots, even dangerous. But the rugged terrain is ideal for making stalks with the hunter remaining out of sight.

Although the wind may swirl and change direction in the lofty goat domain, it normally remains steady for quite some time, so there is not much chance of the quarry getting the hunter's scent if care is taken. The noise made by loose rocks during the stalk is not a problem, as the goats are used to hearing falling rocks.

Going down the mountains can be much worse than climbing them. When climbing, you can usually see what is ahead. Descending is something else. Often you have no way of telling what you're heading toward, and it is easy to get rimmed out. Stay with the guide; he knows the area.

I learned this lesson the hard way. In northern British Columbia, my guide and I had left the horses at the treeline and climbed the back side of a range looking for sheep. Finding none, we topped out and found a goat in the rugged crags below. After making a short stalk and taking the beautiful billy, Dale said, "Now we can load up and go back over the top to get the horses." I looked down and saw the creek that our spike camp was located on and asked, "Couldn't I go down to the creek and back to camp on foot while you climb over the top to get the horses?" I didn't want to do any more climbing than was absolutely necessary!

Dale replied, "Okay, but stay to the right. I think there's a waterfall on the left."

We separated and soon he was out of sight. Needless to say, I ran into difficulties. I was rimmed out several times by assorted cliffs and waterfalls. I couldn't have gone back up and followed the guide had I wanted to, because in several places I had to drop down a few inches more than I could reach for a handhold to get back up. I had never been so terrified. By persistence and good luck I finally reached the bottom. Then and there I vowed never again to leave my guide just for the sake of a little less climbing!

Mountain goats have very brittle horns, and the hunter must stalk them wisely so the goat won't fall off a ledge or otherwise take a tumble that could result in his horns being broken. This may not be an easy task, but why take the shot if the trophy might be ruined by a fall? The cape can also be scarred badly enough to make the hunter wish he had waited until the goat moved to a better location.

The hunter should make sure he will be able to get to his trophy after the shot. He must remember he is hunting in very rugged terrain and should closely examine every possible means of approach before firing. A trophy isn't worth much if the hunter can't get to it. In fact, to the true hunter, a trophy left on the mountain is far worse than no trophy at all.

This problem is complicated by the fact that a goat can absorb a lot of punishment. This is especially true when it has spotted the hunter, which happens quite frequently. A billy can even take a solid hit and just walk off as though nothing had happened.

I recall a trip where I took a shot at a fine old goat from about 100 yards. I was using a .300 magnum cartridge, and at the first shot the old monarch just stood there peering up at me. You would have thought I was throwing rocks at him.

I DIDN'T SEE how I could have missed, but nevertheless, I took a deep breath and squeezed off another round. Again, it looked as though someone had slipped blanks into my rifle. At the third shot I could see a red spot on his white coat. He stood still a few minutes more, then his knees buckled and he fell off the ledge he had been standing on. Examination of the trophy revealed that all three slugs had entered his lungs and could have been covered with a small saucer.

While I would not hesitate to go after sheep with a .243 or 6mm, these calibers are not reliable for hunting goats. The hunter should use nothing less than a .270 with a 130-grain slug. A stalk can normally be made to quite short range, but the long shot is always a possibility, so a flat-shooting caliber is a good idea. My own preference is the 7mm magnum or .300 magnum.

WEIGHT IN A goat-hunting rifle is very important; you don't want too much of it. A heavy rifle, in addition to weighing you down generally, can pull you off balance when climbing sidehill. Also remember that you'll run a good chance of shooting from some strange positions, and that a hard-kicking rifle can be a real hazard when fired sharply uphill. You have to compromise between weight and recoil. As a rule of thumb, any rifle that weighs more than 9 pounds is too heavy. As for kick, you'll have to be your own judge.

Goats have always been difficult for me to estimate. There is not much difference between an average 9-incher and a real trophy of over 10. First, you will want to determine if the goat is a billy or nanny. The nanny may have horns that are as long or longer, but they are not as heavy and will not score well.

Normally, a goat found alone in August or September will be an old billy. Goats found together are usually nannies with kids or young billies. Also, a nanny's horns will usually hook backward more sharply than a billy's, which have a more gentle slope.

Many times an old billy's coat will have a yellower cast to it than a nanny's or young goat's. This is not always the case, however, so take a good look at the horns. Often the hunter will have plenty of time to look the trophy over, and this is a big help. The length of the horns can be compared to either the ears or face; if the horns appear to be more than twice as long as the ears, the trophy is a definite possibility. If they are obviously much more than twice the ear length, the animal is no doubt an excellent trophy.

An average 8- or 9-inch billy will have horns that seem to be about three-fourths the length of his face. If they appear to be more than seven-eighths as long as his face, he is very good and may approach the 11 inches or over that make for a trophy to be celebrated in song and story. A full, long beard is another good indication of an old billy, but this can be misleading, as I found out on one trip. I took a goat that had a magnificent beard and full long chaps to go along with a huge body. I really thought I had something until I measured his 9-inch horns.

Besides your usual hunting clothes and

other gear, good optical equipment in the form of binoculars and a spotting scope is necessary. The binoculars should be lightweight and of good quality so as not to tire your eyes when using them over a long day's hunt. I have found Bushnell's Custom Compacts to be very good. They are extremely light and you don't notice the weight after a long day of carrying them. They are also of high optical quality. In addition, a good spotting scope will save much needless climbing.

Goats make excellent subjects for the photographer/hunter. This is due to their phlegmatic nature, which allows a close approach. They will also stand still for a photographer much better than sheep or other more wary game. The country they inhabit is very beautiful and their white coats really stand out against most backgrounds.

For the hunter wanting an average coat, there are plenty of good locations. Almost anywhere in sheep country across northern British Columbia is good, as are many areas in Alaska. Horses can be used in most of the British Columbia areas, but less so in Alaska.

The serious trophy hunter who would like to take a Boone and Crockett head should try a different approach. The Alaska panhandle coastal area ranges offer an excellent chance for a record goat. Goats have not been hunted much in this area, since most think of this as bear country. In fact, it is difficult to find an outfitter set up for goat hunts here. Arrangements can be made, however. The mountains are very rugged and rise steeply out of the ocean. There are many fine goats here, and I predict the next world record will come from this area.

For similar reasons, the eastern side of these same coastal mountains is an excellent choice. Here, you are in British Columbia, and the area extends from the west side of the Cassiars to the coast. Again, the area is extremely rough and horses are usually not used. If the hunter is in good shape and wants to tackle the rough terrain, either of these areas should provide a good chance at a truly outstanding trophy.

Sheep hunting is hard work. Goat hunting is hard work, and then some. Not only do you have to operate in rougher country, but at higher altitude as well. You may think yourself in great shape, but get up around 12,000-plus feet where the goats gambol, and the word "shape" will take on a whole new meaning. Whether you get a recordbook trophy, or just an average head, you'll have earned it.

By John Barsness

An Ancient LONELINESS

THE UTTER EMPTINESS THAT ANTELOPE CALL HOME CAN BECOME A STRANGE ADDICTION.

I KNOW ELK HUNTERS who set up their wall tents before bow season, then leave them in the woods through November so they can live and hunt from their elk camps every chance they get, on into rifle season. I know whitetail hunters who eat and breathe for the week they spend at deer camp each fall. And I

know far-gone mountain men whose idea of heaven is a scrap of nylon pitched at timberline, up among very old mule deer and bighorn sheep.

But hardly anyone dreams of antelope camp. Instead of a week spent in the wild, away from the FAX machine or assembly line, pronghorn hunts have traditionally meant a couple of days spent at a motel or in a motor home. That way, you don't miss Monday Night Football.

My first antelope camp was discovered almost by accident. I was in my mid-twenties, working as a chain hand on an oil rig along the North Dakota border, and only had a "long change" to hunt—the better part of three days. Until then I'd hunted antelope out of ranch houses and pickup campers, but all the ranchers I knew lived 300 miles away. There wasn't time to visit them, so my backpacking tent and a bag of charcoal went into the old 4x4, and I headed into the biggest chunk of Bureau of Land Management country on the map.

There had been a few motor homes towing meat trailers when I turned off the asphalt, but after 30 miles of gravel roads they'd been left behind. Another 10 miles of dusty two-tracks led into a piece of higher country that looked very much like a fertile section of the moon. Once in a while a windmill or four-strand barbed-wire fence interrupted the sage and rabbitbrush, but mostly the terrain was sand: low tan flats, rounded gray buttes, squared red mesas, and multi-colored sandstone mushrooms; every variation of the irregular geometry of the badlands.

I had no plan, just a desire to get away from human noise, so I kept driving, even when the two-tracks faded into traces across hard sand. After a long time, when I noticed the sun was headed down, I stopped and got out.

I was on a rise of uneroded ground, tufts of grama grass waving in a breeze that felt cleaner than sea air. Beyond the rise there were more low badlands, rising in the distance like the mud-daubed huts of an African village.

Then something more concrete appeared: a particle of white moving against the badlands. I ran back to the 4x4 for the binoculars, and focused on a doe pronghorn trotting across the sand. Tomorrow was opening day, so I set up the little tent, cooked a deerburger on a few coals, and watched the dark blue shadow of the earth rise in the sky as the sun went down.

In the morning I woke to light on the walls of the tent. The badlands seemed to be the place to go, so I drank a glass of apple juice, stuck a candy bar in my pocket, and walked there, the .243 on my shoulder. I hiked up the first red-gray knob and looked around. Perhaps 3 miles away was the dust of another vehicle on what passed for a real road, and then I heard a very distant shot, so far away I wasn't quite sure what it was.

The hill was the beginning of a ridge. A game trail followed the shoulders of the ridge and I followed the trail, finding deer and coyote tracks dried in the clay, nearly as hard as dinosaur prints. In one patch of sage I jumped a desert cottontail.

A flat draw paralleled the ridge, and at each hill I'd carefully edge around its shoulder and glass. After ½ mile I found seven antelope, does and fawns and one average buck. They were within long range, but it looked like the back of the ridge would bring me much closer. So I walked there, following the fossil trail, and crawled over the ridge on all fours, up behind a low sage. The antelope were now within 100 yards, looking very orange in the early light, moving slowly as they fed on rabbitbrush. It was still cool, and as I bellied forward on the hard sand I felt a long way from the lazy heat of the wide cattle pastures where I'd hunted antelope before. There were no fences or windmills, just barren land. It felt very lonely, much lonelier than any elk ridge I've ever climbed, especially after the rifle made its odd sound in the long silence and the buck fell and the rest of the antelope ran.

That ancient loneliness turned out to be quite addictive, though over the years it's become harder to find. More hunters have come into this corner of the desert, and while most of them stick to plainly tracked roads, some bring all-terrain vehicles and ride into the edges of the rougher hills. They don't kill many antelope, but they push them back. I still hunt this country with my wife, Eileen, but now we bring pack-frames to haul our antelope out of the far

side of the Wall is a little unroaded valley, in which lies one of the few natural ponds in this northern desert, fed by an alkaline spring that grows cattails and geese. The pond always has fresh pronghorn tracks around it.

On the way to the Wall we found a desert tragedy: four rabbit feet and a white cotton tall. No tracks were set in the hard sand to tell us if it was the work of a coyote or golden eagle. We crossed a dry wash, and over the hill found a single doe pronghorn, which Sean turned down, wanting a buck. Eileen stalked and shot it at 75 yards. After field-dressing the doe, we draped it belly-up over a tall sage to cool, tying orange ribbon on the sagebrush to mark the place and keep birds away.

canyons, the same packframes we use for bigger game in the mountains. It's tougher, but we still find our loneliness.

Four years after we started these long treks to the empty places, we took Eileen's son Sean along. He lived, for the most part, with his father near the Idaho border, and though he'd hunted for three years, he didn't yet have the combination of patience and quickness needed to kill a timber deer, let alone an elk. He was discouraged, so we took him out where the deer and the antelope play, setting up camp at the high end of a long ridge overlooking the edge of the badlands.

We dug a pit in the sand, built a fire, and cooked elk steaks. The sky turned slate and the three-quarter moon singled out the buttes as if they were cut from gray paper. Even in the moonlight, we saw more stars than you ever might, the horizons wide as oceans and far from city lights. The Milky Way was not just a flat line but something nearly tactile, like flakes of mica suspended in black ice. We ate our steaks and heard coyotes, and told Sean about the antelope we'd find and where we'd find them.

The next morning the moon was down and the sun well up when we left camp, our daypacks full of lunch and water on our packframes. We headed across a series of washes toward the long low line of red clay we call the China Wall, 2 miles from camp. On the other

Then we crossed the Wall at the gap near the east end. From there we could see the cattails of the desert pond emerging at the end of the low ridge that bisects the valley. We sat and glassed and ate lunch, but saw only a long migrating line of sandhill cranes, miles to the south and a mile up, looking like the dissected spine of a rattlesnake moving across the sky. Then we poked around the edges of the ridge and looked into each side draw, the little flats where antelope like to hide. Nothing.

It was less than 2 hours from sunset when we crossed the ridge to look at the other side. As soon as I raised my binoculars over the top I saw antelope—a line almost as long as the flock of cranes—emerging from a draw across the valley like elk from timber. I ducked, and we trotted behind the crest of the ridge until we could drop into a wash that ran like a 6-foot tunnel through the sagebrush. We followed the draw around pools of mud that showed tracks of jackrabbits and sage grouse. The wash wound back and forth; sometimes we passed within yards of where we'd been 3 minutes before. Every so often we climbed the sandstone wall and knelt in the sage to find the antelope. They kept moving toward the pond.

Finally the wash curved away from their

path, 1/2 mile from the herd. We crawled to the top of a low ridge and could see another deep wash, winding just below us to the edge of the far badlands, where the antelope walked slowly, feeding in the orange light. We decided Eileen would take Sean on the final stalk—the fewer people the better—while I stayed on the ridge to give signals. We watched until the herd passed behind a low gray knob. Eileen and Sean jumped up and ran down to the wash.

I could do nothing but watch, like a director at the opening night of his play. I could see Eileen stopping, her palm turned back to Sean, then peeking over the edge of the wash to watch the antelope. I could see the antelope stringing out from behind the gray butte, and counted them as if I were counting sheep—not to induce sleep, but to keep myself from rushing down the hill to the wash.

Then Sean and Eileen disappeared and I couldn't see them until their orange vests appeared at the last swing of the wash, along the sage flat under the far badlands. The first antelope were directly in front of Sean and Eileen, almost too close. I watched through the binoculars as Sean eased his chest into the side of the wash and rested his .270 on a low sage. Then I watched all forty-one antelope walk slowly by, unshot, two bucks at the rear. I wanted to scream.

And then a trailing buck, the largest yet, came out from behind the gray butte. I watched and waited, biting down on my neckerchief. The buck walked along the same path the herd had taken, and when he walked directly in front of Sean and Eileen his hind legs suddenly collapsed, and then his front, and the sound of the shot came back from the far hills. I looked through the binoculars to see the orange vests crawling out of the wash, Eileen motioning Sean to walk ahead, rifle ready in case the buck got up again.

By the time we returned through the gap in the Wall it was more night than day, the moon just risen. I had the hindquarters and Sean had the front. Eileen carried the rifles and packs. In that half-light we stumbled down washes and

up hills, leaving my vest on Eileen's doe as we passed to keep coyotes away until the next day. Halfway through the hike Sean began to fade, and I left him and his mother behind; she knew the way and I'd come back to help if they needed it.

They didn't. The moon rose higher, its pale ivory light making the buttes look very much like astronauts' photos of that other desert, a quarter-million miles above, though gravity was far more powerful here. As I climbed up the last slope to camp my steps grew very short, and after I'd lowered the tailgate of the pickup and eased the hindquarters down, I turned on the headlights to show Eileen and Sean the way, then walked back to the end of the ridge and shouted. They were in the last draw below camp.

That was six years ago. Since then we've started hunting a week after opening day. More ranches are charging pronghorn hunters, which means more pronghorn hunters are pushing into "our" public hills. Despite their numbers, they mostly hunt only the first couple of days, from motels and motor homes. By the time we show up, the hills are empty of all but the antelope and the loneliness. Since then Sean has killed deer and elk, served in the Persian Gulf, and sailed around the world, but when he comes home he always talks about the night we packed out his first buck by moonlight, and how it felt to be in antelope camp.

It is a land of sand and sagebrush and wind.

By Keith McCafferty

A DIFFERENT *Kind of Hunt*

WHEN PURSUING ANTELOPE IN THE MISSOURI BREAKS, YOU MUST FIRST CONQUER THE GUMBO … BEFORE IT CONQUERS YOU.

WHEN YOU DRIVE northeast from my home, the lodgepole forest spreads into open plain. Sweetgrass whorls up the sides of brown hills. The currents of the Yellowstone River, and then the Musselshell where the bridge crosses at Harlowtown, die into whispers. This is a land of vast silences. In 500 miles you'll slow for a dozen one-horse towns: Two Dot, Winnet, and Judith Gap, feed stores, taverns, gas pumps, school yards. Horses dot the shade under the cottonwoods in dry streambeds. A small boy, dropped at the ranch gate by his school bus, climbs the fence and drives himself home in an old flatbed pickup.

It is homesteaders' country, and for a few years in the 1920s, the Northern Pacific Railroad bamboozled cornbelt farmers into thinking they might reap riches under the sage. Then the rain stopped and the dreams rose in dust. The chinked log cabins still stand, their roofs buckled like the backs of old horses, yokes and rusted plows swallowed in the thistles. Cattle came and some of them stayed. But it is not cattle country, really, not a good country for any of man's agriculture, and today much of it lies fallow under the wings of hawks, the hooves of antelope, and the stately, moving shadows of clouds.

It is the antelope that bring my brother and me here in the fall. We have a camp up in the Breaks, at the head of a coulee that runs between parallel ridges before reaching the north bank of the Missouri River. The ridges are sharply peaked like the spines of small mountains and swept bare by the wind; it is 4 miles between the spines and 10 down to the river's bank. This is the amphitheater of a hunt whose terms are dictated, not by man nor animal, but by the color of the sky. For the earth here is suncracked clay that turns to gumbo when it rains. Radial tires pick up the mud until it swallows the axles; bias tires hold their line a little better. But when you are this far from nowhere and raindrops kiss the earth, the place you cut your motor is one with which you will long be familiar.

Last October it snowed up here, then melted, just a few days before our trip. We drove in after dark, when the mud had stiffened, pitched our tent under the stars, and congratulated ourselves for coming. We figured if it was cold enough to freeze the gumbo at night, we'd always be able to get out first thing in the morning. It did not occur to us that the treads of boots pick up gumbo in the same manner as the treads of tires, or that if the weather changed, we might have to eat our antelope right down to their hocks before finding a way back home.

Of course, that was if we could shoot an antelope. It had never been a problem before, although the hunting was far from easy. There was an old stock pond in a crook of the ridge a quarter mile below camp, where the bands paused to drink, and sometimes you could catch them there in the evening. There was always an off chance of bushwacking antelope that filed through gaps in the ridges as they travelled from one coulee to the next. But for the most part, hunting here was done from long range. You saw the antelope and they saw you. One man remained in sight while the other made a detour to stalk down on them from the folds and cracks in the coulee. It was nothing to hike 6 miles to stalk an antelope, and customary to find it gone when you arrived, for these bands, though lightly hunted, were as spooky as any I have encountered.

This was the kind of work that ate inches from your waist and added years to your heart, but at the end of it you had your horns. So it had been before. So it seemed to be the next morning. For a while. Then the sun lifted a sheen from the earth, still saturated from the early snow, and we began to slip on the slick surface.

Kevin said, "Well, nobody ever said antelope hunting was supposed to be easy."

"If this is as bad as it gets, we'll manage," I told him. But this was not as bad as it got. That was still a couple of hours down the trail, at the end of which we sat on a rock to scrape the gumbo off our boots. This was a pointless exercise, for a man could no longer take six steps in the stuff before accumulating a load the size of a snowshoe. But a breather was called for, and we had strategy to consider.

Across the coulee, on a bench of grass just underneath the rock face of the far ridge, thirty antelope flickered tan and white in the heat mirage through the lens of our binoculars. They were about 3 miles away, knew perfectly well where we were, and held a commanding position.

"One of us could stalk them from here, get down in that gulley, the other one keep their attention." I shrugged my shoulders. "Maybe it would work."

"Not a chance," Kevin said.

"Well, we could work our way down the coulee on this side and they'll figure we've left the country. Then when we get out of sight below, we can cross over, work up the far side from behind the ridge, and come down on them from above."

"You're talking 6 or 7 miles in this snot," Kevin said. As he kicked his foot, several pounds of gumbo splatted to the ground, the tread mark of his boot still cast in the mud.

"Do you have a better suggestion?"

That afternoon, after we had completed our circle and lay panting on a pass in the ridge—only to find that the antelope had fed their way back across the coulee to stand no more than 100 yards from the rock we had argued upon—he came up with one.

"I feel a road hunt coming on. Do you feel a road hunt coming on?" he said. I surely did, and we slogged back across to camp and lifted our aching legs into the truck. Kevin thought he could skid the rig out to a cinder road 3 miles away, where an antelope might stand still long enough for one of us to make a short stalk. We made it as far as the cinder road, and a little bit farther. But a quarter mile west on the road a hunter's truck was stalled in gumbo. We had to back the rig all the way to the two-track we'd followed from camp. Well, we would just hunt the other direction. But that passage, too, was blocked. A four-stall horse trailer had jackknifed sideways. A splattered pickup was mired in mud. Two men stood ankle-deep, one of them running gumbo streaks through his hair with his fingers, then disgustedly wiping them on his jeans.

"Do you think there's a way we could help you?" Kevin called out.

"How are you at riding a horse 40 miles?" The man who spat these words said thanks, but no thanks, and turned to the fellow who'd had his hand in his hair. "You know, we oughta just go and shoot that son-of-a-bitch Joe. I got about half a mind to do just that, tellin' us this is an all-weather road. You know what I mean?" Kevin put the rig in reverse and we fishtailed back up to our camp. I set up the spotting scope and there were our antelope, all the way across the coulee and down about 3 miles. They might as well have been in Wyoming.

"Well, now we know why nobody lives here," I said.

That night the weather went soft on us. It started to mist, and sometime after we had turned in I heard the first drop of rain. It tapped on the canvas for a while, and we tried not to notice. Finally, Kevin's voice rose from the dark. "Should we pack up and try to swim out, or go on ahead and die here?"

"Die here," I told him, "I'd just as soon die right here."

Three days later, neither the question nor my answer seemed to be facetious. The rain had come back again to darken our night and the two-track down to the cinder road was impassable. We had eaten the last of our dinners and spread our provisions under the cook tarp outside the tent: three fruit rollups I had stolen from my daughter and forgotten I'd had, two packets of hot chocolate, two packets of hot cereal, a quart of old cider that was starting to kick.

"It's turning into a different kind of hunt, isn't it?" Kevin said. He had bent to sketch an antelope in the mud and was sectioning steaks off its backbone with the point of a stick.

It took the better part of a day under these conditions to stalk animals that might have been approached in a couple of hours over hard ground. We concentrated instead on catching them as they moved through passes in the ridge. The day before we had guessed wrong, twice, the antelope crossing out of range as they fed out of our coulee. For two nights we had spent the last hour of light at the pond down the hill, and that is where we turned our muddy boots on this evening in growing despair.

There was a gnawing in my belly now every time we came up on a rise and looked down to see nothing. It was not physical hunger, but a sickness of feeling that farmers must get when the sky comes up clear in the morning and the crops need rain, that the Indians must have felt when the buffalo were late.

We almost didn't catch them. When we came over the ridgeline, they were stringing out below us in a canter. I pulled the rifle out of recoil as a doe dropped from the herd and rolled into the wash. And they were running then, and Kevin was running, too, scrambling back up the ridge to try and glimpse them as they turned the corner and ran out from below. I heard his rifle crack twice.

A few minutes later I buried my fingers in the the thick, brittle coat of the antelope. There had been a buck with the band, and a good head, too, but I had instinctively centered on the fattest doe. I could smell the sage in her hair. When I was dressing her out, Kevin came down out of the pass dragging a doe. "I figure we're set up through Christmas," he said. "Maybe the ground will be hard enough to drive out by then."

And so the hunt, if not our adventure, came to an end. We packed the antelope back up to camp, scraped fat off the kidneys, and sauteed steaks in the skillet by the light of the fire. We drank the hard cider. The coyotes started up and we howled with them.

Then the clouds rolled in, purple and billowing. They struck the stars from the sky and stilled the chorus on the hill. "God will have his way with this country," Kevin murmured into his beard, and I stirred from my chair to get a bucket out of the tent to catch us some water. We went to bed listening to rain pang its bottom, and drifted off to sleep with the rhythm of the land.

The Buffalo Commons

The country my brother and I were stranded in on our antelope hunt is among the most sparsely populated in America. It is land opened by the 1862 Homesteader's Act, and its history is boom or bust. Agricultural subsidies and the energy crisis brought it back to life for the last time in the 1970s, with fencepost to fencepost cultivation and oil, natural gas, and coal exploration. But extractive agriculture and the "here today, gone tomorrow" nature of the fuels industry has left many communities grasping for a means to survive. Citizens have turned to get-rich-quick schemes in order to hold on to their homes. Legalized gambling and garbage dumps serving Eastern cities are being seriously pursued.

Some people think there is another way. Among them are Frank and Deborah Popper, New Jersey academics who have been preaching the concept of a "Big Open" or "Buffalo Commons" for several years. They and other environmentalists hope for an end to grain subsidies and cattle grazing. They envision a network of parks across the prairie states owned by private conservation organizations, by Indians, and by the government, which they hope will aggregate land for wildlife refuges as more farms and communities disappear. They see a prairie filled with bison, elk, antelope, and deer, an American Serengeti that will draw tourists. Some residents who were initially opposed to their ideas (in one central-Montana town, angry citizens threatened to turn loose a buffalo in the hotel lobby where the Poppers were planning to speak), are beginning to change their minds. Perhaps a radical shift in direction is the only way they can hold on to their homeland. The movement is gaining momentum.

What does this bode for hunters? An increase in game populations, for one thing. Ranchers who run struggling cattle and grain operations would be encouraged to raise buffalo instead and to go into the outfitting business.

Larger public land holdings could mean more hunting opportunity. At the same time, some radical environmentalists do not want the ranchers to change their occupations so much as to leave altogether, and do not look upon hunting as an ethical means of game management.

I think hunters should be guardedly optimistic about the concept of a "Buffalo Commons." But they should air their concerns at the meetings the Poppers and other proponents of this concept sponsor in depressed communities throughout the Plains. Hunters should get in on the ground floor now. Because every time a farmer falls to pay his mortgage, their dream comes a little closer to reality. — K. M.

By Ross Seyfried

GHOSTS *of the Wind*

With incredible speed and eyesight, antelope seem invincible. But if you know their weaknesses, you can get so close you may have to step back.

A WHILE AGO I HAD A discussion with another antelope "hunter" who was proud of his ability to zap the animals standing so far away they were in next week. He asked me how long my shots were so I thought over the last nine antelope I had taken or guided hunters to. I figured with a pencil for a moment, looked the fellow square in the eye, and said, "Six hundred and fifty-five yards." Then I added, "That was the total range for all of them."

We know that antelope can run like bats out of hell; that they can see you before you leave New Jersey to come to Wyoming. We know that they stand out there in the open, begging you to screw up ... but if you know how, you can get close enough to see their eyelashes.

To do this, you have to use their weaknesses, and believe me, they do have weaknesses. Antelope are wild and wary, but they are very, very curious. They are also bullheaded and predictable. During the rut, the bucks lose their brains altogether. And if you look closely, that "flat" prairie is not nearly as bald as it seems. It will hide a lot of antelope ... and antelope hunters.

To collect those nine antelope, I used all of their weaknesses against them, often in combination. Take "curious," for example. I was guiding a fellow I'll call "B" on the open plains of Texas. The ground was smooth, except for a scattering of 3-foot-tall yucca bushes. We spotted a big buck all by himself, and we wanted the monster very badly.

A rolling hill gave us cover to walk to within 500 yards, a range where many would make the classic mistake and try a shot. But when a man points a rifle at a 12-inch target over a quarter mile away in a stiff Texas wind, the odds are not particularly inviting. We opted to get closer—much closer.

We began the stalk by sneaking from yucca to yucca . . . and it almost worked. When we were somewhere between 300 and 400 yards, the buck jerked to attention and riveted his eight-power eyes on us, but as often happens, he did not run.

He was curious! I was wearing a white T-shirt, and for the moment this fellow was puzzling on the flash of white. We settled quietly behind the yucca and let him stare. I pulled my shirt off and very gently moved it to the top of the yucca, hooked it on a spine, and left it to flap in the breeze.

We retreated, using the same cover, until we were again out of sight behind the hill. Then we sprinted to our right, almost 90 degrees, and stalked again, using a different route. When B took a rest on my shoulder, 80 yards from the buck, the outcome was not in question. The antelope was stamping his hoof, still staring, and moving toward the shirt.

You can take advantage of their curiosity by looking like another quadruped. Two hunters work best, with the one in front bending over while the fellow in back hooks his hand in the leader's belt and rests his head on his leading arm. I have pulled this stunt when there was absolutely nothing to hide behind. If there's a trick to it, it's to not move deliberately. Move randomly; stop to "graze" or even bed down. Proceed in an arc that brings you closer without ever giving them the feeling you are headed their way.

This four-legged approach works best on single bucks or very small bands, but if you want to get close to a herd or to antelope that have been spooked, stealth is the answer.

Begin from the highest ground you can find and search every hill and fold. The name of the game is to see them before they see you, and remember, when you're looking through binoculars, you're only leveling the playing field. They see everything you see, and probably see it better.

After you spot a band, there's no rush. Study every angle, looking for cover that will let you stalk in close. Surprisingly, antelope regularly get into places like ravines, where they can't see out, so take careful note of how the land lies. And be patient.

I REMEMBER ONE great Montana buck that moved with a harem of about 30 does. I was on a ridge 2 miles away when I spotted them. A move to a second, smaller hill cut the distance to about 500 yards. They were in a very shallow draw, and the wind was blowing, but little else seemed to be in my favor. I watched them for an hour, memorizing every sagebrush and waiting for them to move into the depression.

When the odds seemed best, I started. I moved sage to sage, rock to rock, until I reached a large clump of brush about 100 yards from the band. Beyond was a 5-foot rock that shielded my crawl. From the base of the rock I peeked over the top and found myself in a situation that a lifetime of hunting had never before presented. I was going to have to stalk backward to get a shot. I slithered 10 yards to the rear, and when I squeezed the trigger, the buck was still only 15 steps away.

Fine, you say, but what happens when antelope are spooked by other hunters or are generally on the move? Then I use the fact that they're predictable. Antelope will often return to within a reasonable distance of where their run started. Watch from afar and note their direction. They will run hard for a way, slow to a trot, and then alternately walk and trot for miles.

Even if they don't circle, they may well tell you exactly where they're going because they're bullheaded, and when they make up their minds to go somewhere, very little will deter them. At times like this, use a vehicle to move way in front of them. Find a ridge, bush, or gully that will hide an ambush, and be careful! Once they've been stirred up, they're no longer curious, and anything out of place will put them on a dead run again.

Even disturbed antelope will quickly return to old habits. They water in the same places at similar times. They have preferred places to cross fences and patches of feed they'll return to time after time. If you fail today, look again tomorrow; odds are better than ever they'll be back.

Over two hunting seasons, I made five different stalks on one buck in the same little valley. The first evening, I blundered into him, and he got away. The next time, I had him dead to rights when a doe chose to run past me, over the top of my buck, and pull him out of my clutches. A friend managed to miss him once, shooting over him because we were too close.

The fourth encounter ended when a puff of wind from a dust devil put him on the run. Finally, a year later, needing a change of luck, I took a young lady after this old wide-horned fellow. We found him in his valley and slithered down a gully, crawled behind an old cottonwood log, held our breath, and peeked over the top. He had moved, but because he was curious, he just had to look back. We collected him at 175 yards.

DISTURBED ANTELOPE WILL seek quiet, and this causes them to end up in unusual places. When they vanish, a clever hunter will look in the nooks and crannies: a little meadow hidden by a bend in a creek; a small pasture behind a ranch house. Be sure to look in the deep holes and bowls, and if there is a patch of timber way up high where an antelope "would never go," be sure to have a peek. I've found them snuggled up to elk.

Because antelope are curious, they can be decoyed. (I advise against taking a realistic decoy onto public land, but on controlled private land, with the right kind of decoy, it seems perfectly safe.)

My decoy only vaguely resembles an antelope. "He" was cut from 3-inch-thick Styrofoam. The paint is more brown than an antelope but duplicates the basic color pattern, and he wears pathetic little horns that resemble those of a yearling buck. I would not hesitate to paint on a hunter-orange stripe or spot to fend off an idiot with a rifle, because I believe that color is invisible to antelope.

Only a moron could mistake it for the real thing, but it does fool antelope, and I use it in two ways: first, as stalking cover, staying behind it when I must move in open view. Once, with another hunter, I used my plastic friend to move right through the middle of a scattered band of more than 100 antelope. We passed within 50 yards of two different bucks and made it all the way to the small ridge that screened the doe we were after. She was the oldest, wildest, and cleverest antelope I've ever hunted. Our stalk through the herd, over almost flat ground without a hint of cover, was one of the most exciting hunts I've ever made. The old lady won and perhaps still survives to lead her band, and that's how it should be.

The second way is as a decoy, and because bucks lose all their sense when they breed, fake antelope are absolute poison during the rut. Bucks defend their does very vigorously, especially from an interloper who looks like a peanut yearling. In this situation it's absolutely necessary to begin the decoy-stalk before the antelope have seen you or your vehicle. Once they're aware that something foreign is in their world, they won't play. I like to find a buck with as few does as possible and move in on him from afar. When the ground cover falls, I show the decoy gradually. The does will remain wary, but a buck's reaction will range from a curious approach to a savage attack.

Once I showed the top edge of the decoy to a big old buck who had only a single doe and her fawn in his possession. He came to immediate attention but didn't move. I made a couple of bleats that lit his fuse. He came in so fast, there was barely time to take the safety off and shoot. I dropped him at 15 feet.

Antelope are wonderful, and they're different. They prefer places where the road signs read HAT SIX or BAR 7; where folks have names like Jake, Slim, Curly, or Needles. These folks guard their elk and mule deer fiercely, but they'll generally let you take on their antelope if you ask them. And if you're interested in hunting, you'll find there are few animals finer.

By Jim Merritt

The LAST BUFFALO HUNT

IN A SLAUGHTER NEVER EQUALED, THE GREAT HERDS VANISHED, AND WITH THE BISON, THE PLAINS INDIAN SAW HIS WAY OF LIFE DIE. BUT THERE WAS TO BE ONE FINAL RIDE WITH THE LANCE AND BOW...

ON THE RANGE THE routine seldom varied for the buffalo hunter. Rising at dawn, he shook off the Dakota cold, then joined the other hunters in the outfit for a breakfast of bacon, sourdough bread, and coffee. There was no need to hurry. Wait for the animals to eat their fill, and many in the herd would be at rest, making even easier targets.

The October sun had burned off most of the frost by the time the hunter set out, carrying about 40 pounds of gear, including a .45-caliber Sharps rifle, 100 cartridges in two belts slung across his shoulders, and a leather scabbard containing a honing steel and a pair of knives for ripping and skinning. He worked alone and usually on foot, a stealthy approach being easier without a horse. As he neared the top of a rise, he dropped to his knees and elbows and crawled into position to view the herd spread out below him. About 10,000 buffalo, he guessed, were scattered in small groups across the undulant prairie. In the distance he could hear the familiar boom of Sharps from the other outfits working on this bright, Indian summer morning of 1883.

In the draw below him. a group of about fifty animals fed contentedly on the yellow grass. With the barrel of the big Sharps propped on a weathered buffalo skull, he estimated the distance at 150 yards. Selecting an old cow on the periphery of the herd, he took aim behind the shoulder, and squeezed off a shot. The cow shuddered on the bullet's impact but remained standing. Then blood began pumping from her nostrils, and when she dropped, the hunter knew he had shot true. The hunter had to immobilize the animal with a lung shot to keep it from running off and stampeding the herd.

Some of the others in the herd looked up at the report, and when one of them moved toward the fallen cow the hunter took aim at his second target. For the next hour he picked them off one by one. Finally, he hit a young bull in the leg. He fired again and managed to down it as it limped away, but the rest of the herd was at last alert to danger and began moving out of range. He might have pursued but elected not to. Several dozen dead buffalo lay

in the short grass, and it would take the better part of the day to skin them out.

They would return in several days with a wagon to collect the hides. A few years before, when the herds had numbered in the hundreds of thousands, a hunter could work out of a single camp for months, and the hides might be left out on the range for most of the season. But a herd of this size could be wiped out in a matter of weeks. Moreover, this herd was on the move, pushed east by the relentless shooting toward the Sioux reservations along the Grand and Moreau Rivers, and the hunter would have to keep moving with it.

IN THE DECADES following the Civil War, the numbers of professional buffalo hunters who plied their bloody trade on the great prairies of the West grew to many thousands. Buffalo had been killed in great numbers earlier by such men, but the coming of railroads like the Kansas Pacific and the Atcheson, Topeka and Santa Fe provided an efficient way of transporting buffalo hides east, and once the rails had penetrated the plains, the slaughter began in earnest.

In the early 1870s the southern prairies had still been so thick with buffalo as to defy description. Each spring, massed in herds that might be 20 miles wide and 60 miles deep, they followed the ripening grasses north, moving out of Texas and the Indian Territory and into the phalanx of hunters spread across western Kansas into Colorado. At the height of the killing as many as 20,000 hunters may have been waiting for them. The hunters generally took only the hide, leaving the carcass—which on an old bull might weigh 1,500 pounds—to rot.

Mountains of pressed buffalo robes, meanwhile, crowded the freight docks of towns like Dodge City and Wichita. A good hunter could average sixty buffalo a day and might kill 3,000 in a single season. In the wake of the hunters came others to gather up the bleached bones, which were stacked by the railroad tracks in piles up to a half mile long, to be carried east for crushing into fertilizer.

By 1879 the southern herds were gone—vanished, in a wink of time from a landscape they had dominated since the end of the last Ice Age 10,000 years before. The hunters shrugged in disbelief at their own bloody efficiency, then moved into the remaining buffalo country north of the Platte.

Railroads opened up the Montana and Dakota ranges to wholesale slaughter, just as they had in the south. When the Northern Pacific pushed up the Yellowstone River in 1881, the towns of Glendive and Miles City sprang into existence as centers for the northern hunt. A

typical hunter working out of Miles City might have one partner and two additional hunters hired at $50 a month each. His outfit would consist of a pair of wagons and eight draft horses, two saddle horses, two tents, a field stove, three Sharps rifles, and enough powder, lead, primers, shells, knives, and provisions to last from October to February, the season of the buffalo's winter pelage.

The first two years of concentrated hunting on the northern range were good indeed, but by the end of the third year the herds were vastly shrunken. The accounts of one New York jobber were typical, and reflected this decline: In the spring of 1881, he bought 26,000 robes and hides, and 45,000 in 1882; following the 1882-83 season, he shipped only 7,500. Hunters also noticed this precipitous drop, but many chose to ignore it. Hadn't they seen an estimated 75,000 head crossing the Yellowstone on its way toward Canada just that spring? This immense herd would return, they were certain, to supply the trade at least through another year. And so in the fall of 1883 the buffalo hunters prepared as usual for another season in the field.

PREOCCUPIED BY THE killing, the hunter did not notice the tiny figures crouched on buttes to the east. Under the high October sky, the Sioux scouts listened to the distant pop of rifles carried on the wind and watched the herd drift slowly in their direction. It had been less than a fortnight since the hunt had started, but already the herd had shrunk by nearly half. Still, the appearance now of even 5,000 buffalo was a source of wonder and astonishment—a vindication, perhaps, of Sitting Bull's prophesy that *Pte,* the buffalo, would return and that the white men would vanish from their land.

The Sioux had depended on the buffalo for as long as they could remember. It was their standing crop, sustaining them with food, clothing, and shelter. Meat from the succulent hump ribs filled their bellies in summer. Dried, mixed with berries and pounded into pemmican, it carried them through the snow months. Buffalo chips fueled their lodge fires. The dressed hides of buffalo covered their tipis and were fashioned by squaws into moccasins and leggins. Untreated, a fresh buffalo skin was impervious to water and could be made into kettles or stretched on a willow frame to create a bullboat. The matted wool of a buffalo robe was their mattress and winter blanket. The thick hide from a bull's neck, hardened with glue boiled from the hooves, made a war shield tough enough to turn an arrow. They used braided hair for rope and sinew for bowstrings. Ribs became knives and sled runners. From buffalo horn—boiled until supple, then cut into strips and bound together with rawhide—they crafted bows that could send an arrow clean through a bull.

The buffalo's central importance to the Sioux and other plains tribes was not lost on those responsible for controlling Indians on the frontier. By the 1870s the first tentative steps were taken to control the terrible slaughter. When the issue was debated in Congress in 1874, however, the Secretary of the Interior stated that he favored killing off the buffalo as a way of settling the Indian question once and for all. A bill to protect the buffalo passed anyway but died when President Grant refused to sign it. The following year the Texas legislature considered a similar bill and was advised by the regional military commander, General Phil Sheridan, that each hide hunter ought to receive a medal: "Let them kill, skin, and sell until the buffalo is exterminated, as it is the only way to bring lasting peace and allow civilization to advance."

Nor were the Indians flawless conservationists. But given their relatively small numbers, primitive weapons, and fondness for running buffalo on horseback—a more sporting and exciting, if vastly less efficient way of hunting them—Indians made little dent in the bison population. Blame for the buffalo's demise lay squarely with the *Wasichus,* or white eyes, overrunning their country.

For a while, the Sioux had succeeded in stemming the flow of whites through their land. In 1867 the great chief Red Cloud had soundly defeated the U.S. Army, closing off the Bozeman Trail through their hunting grounds along the Powder River. But eight years later, the discovery of gold in the Black Hills brought a new invasion and fresh conflict, culminating in the Custer debacle at the Little Big Horn.

Of all the Sioux leaders, none fought longer or more fiercely to preserve the old ways than Sitting Bull, the victor at the Little Big Horn. After the battle, he retreated with his followers into Canada. But the game proved scarce in the land of the Great White Mother, where settlers had done as thorough a job of killing off the buffalo as they had in the south. Sitting Bull's people grew hungry and weary of exile. So in the summer of 1881 he led them back across the border and surrendered at Ft. Buford on the Missouri.

The Army held Sitting Bull prisoner for two years before releasing him to the Standing Rock Reservation, where white officals hoped he would take up farming and become a model for the rest of the Sioux. (He didn't.) Soon after, in an act of cruel if naive irony, officers of the Northern Pacific invited him to speak at the dedication of their new railroad, whose construction had been directly responsible for the decimation of the buffalo on the northern plains. Accompanied by an Army interpreter, the most famous Indian in North America arrived in Bismarck and delivered a scorching diatribe in his native Lakota. "I hate the white people," he told the assembled. "You are all thieves and liars. You have taken away our land and made us outcasts." In place of these remarks, the interpreter substituted friendly platitudes. The crowd gave Sitting Bull a standing ovation.

Sitting Bull went home to Standing Rock, where the Sioux were reduced to living on government handouts of beef and flour. The White Father also delivered cattle on the hoof to the reservation; rather than slaughtering these animals conventionally, the Indians ran them on horseback, killing them with bow and arrow or with the few ancient trade guns the Army had allowed them to keep. Longhorns, however, proved a sorry substitute for buffalo, so when the scouts returned in the autumn of 1883 to tell of the herd approaching from the west, the news seemed too good to be true.

THE SIOUX HAD not seen buffalo since June of the previous year, when a large herd had appeared near the western border of the reservation. The Standing Rock agent, James McLaughlin, ordered rifles issued to the Indians and accompanied them on the hunt. McLaughlin described these events years later but made no mention of a hunt in October 1883, which suggests that Sitting Bull and the thousand warriors who accompanied him to meet the herd did so without agency permission.

A brief record of the hunt in the fall of 1883 is preserved in an account by William T. Hornaday, a naturalist and chief taxidermist at the Smithsonian Institution, who interviewed several white participants after it was over. (Hornaday became a tireless campaigner in the buffalo's behalf and played an important role in rescuing the animal from extinction.) Although no firsthand Sioux account of the last buffalo hunt exists, descriptions of similar hunts allow us to imagine it in all its ritual and excitement.

Once safely removed from agency headquarters, the hunters collected out on the prairie. They sat facing west, forming two horns of a crescent, in front of which was placed a painted stone as a kind of altar. A half-dozen scouts gathered around the stone and swore to Sitting Bull to report correctly on the numbers of buffalo they would see. The old headman sealed the oath by drawing on a pipe, then touching the earth with it and raising it to the sky in tribute to *Wakan Tanka,* the great spirit, and to the buffalo god *Tatanka.* Each scout took the pipe in his turn and repeated Sitting Bull's gestures.

The ceremony over, the warriors jumped to their feet and scrambled to their ponies. They could forget for a moment the humiliation of agency life and the likelihood that the buffalo they would soon encounter would be the last they would ever see. Finally the warriors broke away from the scouts and raced furiously back to camp.

The hunting party set out early the next morning, and it was not long before they met the scouts returning with their report. The herd was dwindling, and by the time the Sioux were upon it and had joined the white hunters in the fray it was down to perhaps 1,200 head—a little more than one animal for each warrior.

Since the Army had disarmed the Sioux years before, most of them reverted to bows and arrows in this final, furious melée. In two days they finished off the entire herd.

As the Sioux hunters prepared the meat for winter, the old man who had led them watched and ruminated. The historian Mari Sandoz pictures Sitting Bull alone in his lodge, "his pipe cold beside him, remembering the great Indian and buffalo country he was born into. It was just over on the Grand River there, the year before the fire boat, the *Yellowstone,* came smoking up the Missouri. Now all of it was gone, vanished like wind on the buffalo grass. True, he had known glory, much glory, but his broad face was hard as the walls of the upper Yellowstone when he thought about it, what is glory to a man who must see his people as he saw them now."

In their own camps, the white hunters talked about what they had seen. No lovers of Indians, they had felt nonetheless an unexpected sympathy for the Sioux in what was certainly their last buffalo hunt. There were more buffalo out there, they told themselves, but they were west of here and far out of range of the Sioux confined to their Dakota reservations. The professional hunters would not realize for another month that the buffalo they were talking about had been obliterated along the Canadian border by other white hunters and by half-starved Blackfeet and Assiniboins. The only survivors were a few strays that took refuge in the Missouri Breaks. Three years later, William Hornaday would scour these remote badlands and turn up 275 head—nearly half of all the buffalo left on earth.

Thanks largely to the efforts of Hornaday and other conservationists, buffalo would make a slow but steady comeback, from an estimated 635 in 1886 to perhaps 80,000 today. While encouraging, the latter figure still pales next to the 60 million that may once have roamed North America. The great herds that had sustained the Sioux and other plains tribes were gone forever, and with them any hope for a return to the old way of life. Sitting Bull spoke for all his people in his song:

A warrior
I have been.
Now
it is all over.
A hard time I have.

By Rick Bass

The GREAT UTAH Buffalo Hunt

SOMETIMES, ONLY THE HUNTED SCORE. THIS WAS ONE OF THOSE TIMES.

"A BUFFALO *WHAT?"* I screeched, incredulous.

Kirby licked the flap of the long white envelope before sealing it, and slapped it against the palm of his hand. "Permit," he said. "A buffalo permit."

I gave an involuntary shudder, and then another. I had honestly fooled myself into thinking that this year would be different. Every year he had to try something spastic—"a new experience," as he put it—something really unusual, like donkey hunting in the Grand Canyon, say, or Tasmanian devils in Australia, or maybe a Great Porcupine Stalk.

"What's wrong with deer, ducks, geese, and quail?" I asked, trying to quiet the spasmodic twitching that was flaring up in my left eyebrow. He invariably managed to drag me along on these new experiences. "For gosh sakes, shoot a turkey or even a pheasant if you feel like doing something really exotic this year," I said.

"You don't understand," he said, chagrined,

shaking his head sadly. "A buffalo hunt would be a new experience."

"That's what you said about fly rodding for piranhas," I groaned, subconsciously rubbing the pink, crescent-shaped scar on my wrist.

Kirby cleared his throat. "Oh yes, I forgot to tell you—the hunt is limited to black-powder guns only," he said craftily, walking out to the front door and placing the envelope in the mailbox. "I filled out an application for you, too."

I paused. He had done it again. No matter how bizarre the experience, he always trapped me. He knew I loved black-powder hunting like a mountain goat loves rocks. "When is it?" I sighed, submitting to the inevitable.

"They're holding a special hunt in August—one of their herds has gotten too large to manage."

"Who is 'they?'"

"The Utah Division of Wildlife Resources," he mumbled, rubbing his mouth with his hand so that it could just as easily have passed for "The Texas Parks and Wildlife Department." I noticed that he was suddenly very busy studying his tennis shoes.

My toes curled. "Did you say, 'Utah?'"

He looked up, staring out the window, still not looking me in the eye. "Yeah, well, that's where they are," he said weakly, seemingly preoccupied with the actions of a mockingbird family in the mesquite tree out by the kitchen window. It was summertime in South Texas, and the birds were everywhere. "They've got one of the finest state wildlife management programs in the country," he said, still watching the bird family. "They've really worked wonders with their buffalo herds … "

I started toward the door, ready to withdraw my application. I did not want to leave Texas. I throw up when I travel. "Utah buffalo are out of style this year, Kirby," I told him. "Texas whitetails are in."

He sighed. "Black powder," he said to himself, but speaking plenty loud enough for me to hear. I stopped in midstride, my hand poised over the mail box. "Black powder,"' he said again—almost chanting it—and slowly, I lowered my hand.

"I've already called and made plane reservations—our tickets will be ready in a couple of days," he said as he left the room, an alligator-sized smirk covering his face.

THE SMALL TWIN-engine plane taxied around on the dirt road on which we had landed, throwing dust and gravel clouds in all directions, both props screaming in the dry desert air. The pilot gave us a curt wave—almost a salute—and said something to his co-pilot (they both laughed) before giving the plane full throttle and accelerating down the flat, dusty road. After maybe only a hundred yards the heat waves that were shimmering up from the rocks enveloped the plane, making it impossible to discern when it actually became airborne. In no time the plane was a small, noisy spot in the hot blue sky, and then it was nothing but a small, quiet spot, and then it was nothing at all. It was very quiet again.

I cleared my throat and looked around, still holding my backpack in one hand and my Hawken buffalo gun in the other. My immediate impression was that I had never been so hot in my life. For lack of anything better to do, I scuffed my foot in the dust, and a large orange-and-black grasshopper sprang up and soared away, clacking noisily. I squatted down to examine the side of a lone boulder and started when I focused on the pair of small black eyes that I suddenly found staring back at me with intense interest, peering over the top of the boulder, not 5 inches from my own eyes. I yelped, and the gray-green lizard blinked once and darted back off to wherever it had come from, scooting in and out of the sage, dancing across the sand like water on a hot iron.

KIRBY SHOULDERED HIS pack and took a deep breath before thumping his chest Tarzan-style and exhaling. "WAGHHH!" He took another breath and thumped himself again. "WAGHHH!" He turned to me. "That's what the mountain men used to say," he explained. "Wagh!" he repeated, loudly.

"Yes," I said standing back up, already dizzy from the heat "Waghhhh." I looked around in a 360-degree sweep. "Not a very big turnout, is there?"

"No, there's not. Isn't it great? They only issued five permits, and we got two of them." He, too, looked around. "We've got the whole place to ourselves."

"Lucky us," I said. My stomach was still in an uproar from the plane ride. I sat down on a rock, trying to figure out how best to break it to him. "Now Kirby, correct me if I'm wrong, and I very well could be." I paused and looked around for a stem of grass to pluck and chew on, but there was none—nothing but red rocks and heat. "But I've always heard that a buffalo is a plains creature."

He nodded. "So?"

If it had not been so hot I would have leaped up from my rock and gone for a stranglehold on his jugular, but instead I settled for trying to conserve energy. The tic in my eyebrow flared up again. "Kirby, there are no plains around here," I said quietly. "No buffalo either."

"Sure there are." He turned and pointed to the southwest. At the very edge of the horizon, at the end of a horrid stretch of desert, was a shining, sparkling blue break in the haze—the Henry Mountains.

I stood up and squinted. "Kirby, those mountains are 30 miles away," I said disbelievingly, looking at the mountains and then down at my pack and heavy rifle.

"Probably more like 100,"' he said. "Things look a lot closer in the desert." Then, realizing I had reached the end of my limits—my eyebrow was fluttering like a mad butterfly—he dangled the carrot in front of me once more. He reached in his pack and pulled out a tattered old nickel postcard. It showed a large, furry buffalo standing knee-deep in a foothill meadow, grazing contentedly, with tall trees and cliffs and patches of snow lingering in the background. A small blue stream was lazily snaking and gurgling its way through the meadow, and my Adam's apple bobbed twice as I snatched the card from him. I turned it over, but the writing on the back was indecipherable—it could just as easily have come from Yellowstone or the Tetons as from the Henry Mountains.

"Black powder," he reminded me. "Black powder."

I shouldered my pack. "Let's go."

We made good time, reaching the foothills by the end of the third day. Kirby kept me entertained the whole way with stories of the region—the real story behind Robber's Roost Canyon, and how the Dirty Devil River got its name, and even how to track Gila monsters. He had not told me there would be Gila monsters in the area.

"I tracked one for a week out here once when I was collecting for the university," he said, pointing to the thin, furrowed tracings in the sand. "Caught up with him just as he was bedding down for the night. It was about this time of day, and he was really sluggish, so I had no trouble capturing him. I put him in the pillowcase and then forgot about him until I was headed home the next day. I'll never forget the gas station. It was in Hanksville, Utah, and gas had just skyrocketed from 39 cents to 55 cents a gallon while I had been gone. Waghh! I was in the restroom, shaving, when I heard this horrendous commotion. The gas station owner had this huge Doberman Pinscher—a big black beast—and he—the dog, not the gas station attendant—had been snooting around in the back of the truck when the Gila monster worked out of the pillowcase and latched onto his tail.

"The dog, his name was Gonzo, yelped once and jumped out of the truck, knocking over the box containing a month's worth of *Sceloporus undulatuses.* The box broke open when it landed, and little gray lizards began skating across the hot cement like water striders on a pond, literally thousands of them racing all over the place—scampering into the office, out into the street, into people's yards, and up onto their front porches—and Gonzo went bonkers as they began to swarm under him. He took off down the street, howling, the Gila monster still clamped to his stub of a tail—they say they don't let go 'til they hear thunder—dragging and bouncing along behind him like a beaded orange-and-black kite streamer. A big 18-wheeler cattle truck that was driving past swerved to miss hitting Gonzo and plowed into my—well, at the time it was the university's—truck, flattening it like a soda can. A few of the smaller cattle spilled out of the truck and began their own stampede down Main Street, bawling and lowing and doing what cows do when they get scared. In no time at all the streets were covered with dead lizards and moon pies. I had to hitchhike home. Took me ten days to make it back to Laredo."

I CLEARED MY throat and wiped the sweat from my forehead. "Sounds like pretty wild country," I said, unable to think of anything else; I certainly had no Gila monster stories of my own to counter with. I grimaced as a droplet of sweat rolled into my eye. The orange sun ball was almost completely under the horizon, and my pocket thermometer showed that the temperature had plummeted to a balmy 110 degrees. "'Makes buffalo hunting seem tame," I said.

"It was an experience," he agreed. Suddenly he stopped and bent over, examining something that was under a clump of sage.

"What is it? A baby Gila monster?" I asked.

"Even better than that," he said, holding up a fist-sized chunk of compressed dried grass and weeds. "It's a buffalo chip," he said triumphantly. "Our first one." He licked his lips. "Wagh! It'll be hump ribs and fat tongue tomorrow," he crowed. "We'll camp here, right in the foothills," he said, and he set his pack down and immediately began searching for more buffalo dung.

That night we had a fire made of buffalo chips, just like in the movies. "Doesn't smell bad," I said as I cleaned my rifle for the tenth time. "In fact, I think it burns cleaner than wood," I said as I watched the faint, barely visible blue wisps of smoke spiral up into the clear, dark night sky. There was no moon, but there were so many stars out that the looming silhouette of the big peak we were camped under was well lit. From somewhere up on the peak a block of shale clattered down the slope. The last thing I remember hearing Kirby say as I dropped off to sleep was something about a big bull, as big as a Volkswagen, with hooves of steel, that was up on top knocking those rocks down.

I woke up sometime around 2 or 3 in the morning, shivering. The chips had burned bright and clear for a while, but they weren't much on staying power. I sat up and looked around. Kirby was gone. Groaning with stiffness I would not have had had I been sleeping in a South Texas bunkhouse while on a whitetail hunt, I stood up and stretched. Up on the mountain, a couple of rocks clattered down, and then a couple more, and then a whole slough of them came rumbling down, trailing a gray-white dust cloud in their wake that was almost eerie in the starlight. I sighed. "What are you doing?" I hissed, unconsciously respecting the night stillness as if I was in a library back in the city and not in the middle of the wildest, most desolate country in the North American continent.

"Scouting," Kirby whispered back, also respecting the silence, dislodging another rock that did not share our respect. "I know they're up here. I can hear them grunting and lowing. Listen."

I started to say something about his having had beans for supper but stopped. He was right. There was something up higher, something that was making herdlike noises: hooves clacking against rocks, mothers lowing for lost calves, and the like. I scrambled up the rocks to where he was kneeling, head down, one ear on the ground like the movie Indians used do to a set of railroad tracks whenever they wanted to tell if a train was coming.

"Big herd—ninety, maybe a hundred head," he said softly, still bent down, listening.

"Are you sure, Kimo-Sabe?"

He glowered at me and sat up, wiping the twigs and dust from his ear. "Lets go take a look at them,'" he said eagerly, and then, as if just remembering, added a hushed "wagh" for emphasis.

"Sure—why not?" I said, adding strength to the theory that there's one born every minute.

I will have to admit that Kirby was right on his guess of how many buffaloes were in the herd. Just as we reached the flat, grassy plateau midway up the slope, they caught our scent. They were bedded down in this same flat, grassy plateau. The meadow suddenly erupted as the great brown creatures screamed in alarm and began springing up out of the tall grass in all directions, bellowing angrily at having their sleep disturbed by two tourists from Texas. In seconds they had condensed into a noisy brown nucleus. There were, as Kirby said later (he counted them as they went by), ninety-three of them. And they all came storming at us, a wall of angry hooves and horns, eyes gleaming with red rage in the starlight.

I AM A good jumper. In life-threatening situations I can jump real well. This was one of them. I jumped up and grabbed an overhanging branch of the biggest pine near me—Kirby swore later that it was a 10-foot jump—and pulled myself up into the tree with 1 second, maybe 1½ seconds, to spare. Since Kirby is not half the jumper that I am, he dived behind a large boulder, escaping with an equal margin of safety, his yells for the cavalry drowned out by the roar of the stampede.

Five minutes later the last of the herd finished thundering past and rumbled on down the slope. I lowered myself down out of the tree, coughing at the dust that was still hanging thick and stepping around all the downed timber. The forest smelled like an aftershave lotion as sap oozed out of broken limbs and branches. From far off down the slope there came a brief, tinny crunching sound, as if ninety-three buffaloes had just run over some pots and pans, and then there was a brief ripping sound, as if the same ninety-three buffaloes had just tried to fit into a two-man pup tent all at the same time, and then there was silence as they rumbled on off out of earshot. Long after we stopped hearing them, we could still feel the earth trembling, as if it was laughing at some knee-slapping joke. The experience was over. I winced, thinking of my Hawken. It had taken them 150 years to do it, but the buffalo had finally scored a short, sweet revenge. I shrugged it off and flipped my boots off and checked them for pebbles, a habit I have started doing before any long hike, before putting them back on and starting down the trail in the direction the buffaloes had gone.

"C'mon," I said to Kirby, who was staring off at the horizon, glassy-eyed, his jaw sagging. Out to the east, there was a faint blue-silver cast where the sun would debut in another couple of hours. "C'mon," I repeated. "If we push hard, we can make Texas before whitetail season ends."

Kirby nodded. "Wagh," he said quietly, and started down the slope behind me.

I nodded, agreeing. "Wagh."

Other Game

Wild boar and black bear are among the most resourceful of our wild creatures. They can live on almost anything, and no other critter messes with them. Boars are highly alert, and an experienced black bear may just be the wariest of all our big game.

Javelina are—there is no other word—charming. These diminutive porkers are as much a part of the desert as cactus. They make a challenging hunt because they are shy and elusive, but I'd rather just watch them go about making a living in the land where everything stings, stabs, and bites.

Forget that Gentle Ben garbage. The big bears—grizzly and brown—are among the supremely dangerous animals on this earth. In the movies, they are presented as slow and lumbering, even when enraged. In reality, they are as quick as cats, and if something important is at stake, they will not back down. You will die or they will die. A few years ago I shared a jet boat with an Alaska guide who had nearly been killed by a grizzly two days before, and his eyes were still filled with the terror of it. He and his sport had taken a moose, but the bear got there first, and when they approached, it attacked. Both had the presence of mind not to run. They shot, and kept shooting, and it saved them. Whenever I think of the big bears, I think of that guide's eyes, and the .44 magnum revolver that never left his hip.

Consider this: A male mountain lion—say, 160 pounds—can kill a bull elk—700 to 1,000 pounds. That gives you some idea of what these creatures can accomplish. Solitary, secretive, and silent, mountain lions can live almost anywhere, and after being trapped nearly into extinction, they have rebounded in a major way. If you're ever inclined to find out how tough you really are, I suggest that you hunt one of these big cats on horseback, with a pack of hounds. You'll find out.

By Keith McCafferty

The HEART *of the* PACK

THE WORLD OF ORVEL FLETCHER, ONE OF THE LAST OF THE OLD-TIME LION HUNTERS, IS THE ESSENCE OF THE EARLY WEST—HARSH AND BEAUTIFUL—AS ACROSS A NEARLY BIBLICAL LANDSCAPE HE RUNS HIS PACK OF HOUNDS, WHOSE BLOODLINES GO BACK ALMOST A CENTURY.

FORTY DIRT-ROAD miles east of Trujillo, New Mexico, lies an upside-down world, a country of canyon spokes that radiate into an elevated prairie precisely in the middle of nowhere. The surrounding plateau is rich grassland, which grows poorer as it is fractured by these fingering canyons. And as the land becomes poor, so do those who own it; until, finally, the narrow, terminal mesas are worked by old Spaniards whose veins run with Indian blood.

Two of these men, one of whom lived without electricity in the house in which he was born, had lost over a period of years many head of sheep to a tom lion that left an outsized track. This lion was difficult to hunt because it was irregular in its comings, and for many months seemed to disappear from the face of the earth. Although in this country that was a reasonable explanation for the lion's absences, it always came back. And the last times its tracks were discovered in the dirt of a road, one or the other of the ranchers had called Orvel Fletcher over in Santa Fe.

Twice Fletcher made the three-hour trip. Twice he hauled a pack of hounds, and twice the tracks had looked fresher to the ranchers than they did to the big, spotted Walkers. So this time Fletcher did not try to raise my hopes. The information was that the tracks had been made after last night's rain, which as far as it could be trusted was good news. But it was already noon of a blustery March day: the Sangre de Cristo Mountains north of the capital were lost in clouds, the wind could have blown the scent, and it looked like more rain.

As for the ranchers, one was a tall, rail-thin man with prominent cheekbones below bushy white eyebrows and an aristocratic head of silver hair who stood beside the road, his arms cradling a cheap, silver-barreled, bolt-action rifle. The other man was smaller, darker, dressed in dirty dungarees, and unarmed. He wore a black glove over his left hand, and as we drove he one-handedly rolled tobacco into brown cigarette papers. Gnarled piñon trees leaned over the road and on the outside bends drooped over vertical cliffs of rimrock that footed far below onto the floor of a narrow canyon.

The tracks, crossing into long grass, looked cookie-cutter sharp in the crumbled earth.

"This is where the lion goes. This morning, no?" The tall man, Pete, pointed with a long, walnut-colored finger. He hunkered over the track.

Fletcher put his hands on his hips. Fletcher was a sober man when hunting, and often gazed into a middle distance with the preoccupied look of someone others wait on to determine a course of action. He ran his hand through his hair. His daughter had once told him he looked like an old farmer; and he was a big, weather-reddened man, broad of face and hands, and dressed as a farmer in a blue work-suit and a felt hat that had long before turned the dust-color of the country. Now he appeared to be looking at that country and sizing the situation in his mind, and then he turned, without a word, to unhook the smeared horizontal window of the truck camper and pull out a hound.

Fletcher's best dog, Judge, followed a finger to the track and raised his nose. Fletcher scowled. His hand disappeared back into the camper and collared a smallish, red bitch. He walked along the road edge and pointed to other tracks, called to the dogs and worked into the grass. The scent was better contained by the grass, and as soon as Judge opened, Fletcher called back for Ben. I felt around in the camper and pulled him away from the rest, which were pouring over each other to get out. The big white Walker tore down the road. All three hounds bawled. Fletcher yelled back once more, this time for us to follow in the truck, and then became smaller and smaller in our vision as the hounds worked through the grass to a scrub of trees and behind them along the rim, and out of sight.

AS SOON AS we heard the dogs, the ranchers began speaking Spanish, the excitement in the voices betraying the conviction that they, at least, felt we would catch this lion. Because I had come to know the individual hounds by their voices, I was not sure, and became less and less sure as their intermittent bawling carried across the scrub. But I felt a curious sense of satisfaction in having gained enough understanding of the dogs to draw any conclusion, however speculative or premature. I had followed Fletcher's pack for many dozens of miles on horseback and had learned many things about tracking lions. Foremost among them was that the point reached when the hounds began to run heads-up marked the beginning of the chase, but in a very real sense the end of the hunt.

And it was the hunting of lion that was rapidly disappearing in the modern West.

Years back—before so many roads veined the mountains and there were so many trucks that could negotiate snow—finding and working out a cold trail was prerequisite to chasing lion. According to Fletcher, and according to Walt Snyder, New Mexico's Chief of Game Management, those elements were largely lost when the horseback hunter became a passenger, driven until a fresh track was found in the snow. Snyder says nearly all of the sportsmen's kill of lion in his state can be attributed to the ease with which a hound trees a lion in winter, and the fact that it does not take a particularly good hound to do so.

Fletcher, whose hounds were bred out of a pack that was racing lions across hard ground shortly after the Spanish-American War, is fond of indicating the nondescript mutt which has the run of his household and telling you that "even this Daisy dog could catch the lion snow."

But here conditions were anything but favorable for his hot-nosed Walkers. Once out of the grass the land assumed a Biblical look, the earth already cracked and dry after the rain, its bald surface interrupted by the juniper and piñon and cane cholla and the yellow bars of sandstone rimrock. And there was a wind.

What worried me, however, was neither the country nor the weather. It was the hounds, Ben in particular, who we could hear now and then. It was because we heard him, not Judge or the bitch, that I knew we might not catch up to the tom. That he was striking most often indicated the tracks had been rained on, washing some of the scent from the ground even where the impressions remained visible. For Ben was the only hound in Fletcher's pack that consistently ran his nose up into the bushes to pick up wafers of scent underhanging the leaves. This idiosyncrasy periodically elevated Ben's importance over that of other young dogs.

Fletcher's choice of hounds in any situation was never by chance. In this case it was Ben for his elevated nose, Judge for overall excellence and experience, and the bitch with her beautiful, drawn-out bawl, because she was eager and would spur the other two to work harder on a cold trail.

By the time we caught up in the truck, by way of a spur road that was nothing more than two parallel shadows in the grass, the trail had warmed somewhat and Fletcher was scrambling along behind the dogs. He yelled for the rest of the pack. The four hounds in back tumbled from the tailgate and streaked silently toward the three, working the lion. Pete got out, gun in hand, to advance and was sharply called off by Fletcher. I had been in the same position several days before and explained to him that the dogs were put off by an unfamiliar presence.

"He sounded about half-mad."

"No," I said, "that's just Orvel."

THE FIRST DAY I hunted with Orvel Fletcher we climbed into the Jemez Mountains and, lipping out onto a mesa shaded by Ponderosa pine trees, looked down on Los Alamos where Robert Oppenheimer's team had developed the atomic bomb. The hounds found the tracks of a big tom lion, which had left urine-scented, scraped-up heaps of pine needles all along the overhang.

Fletcher leaned over his mule.

"Old. Snowed on them. Last snow was Thursday, I believe." He pointed down at one of the dogs. "See how Trigger gets the scent where the snow trapped it."

Fletcher got off his mule and walked around with his hands on his hips, pointing to the distorted impressions left by the tom and calling in to his dogs. The hounds worried the old trail. They punched their noses into the tracks and blew snow out their nostrils. The mules had sweated through their blankets and were enveloped in steam. The hounds opened, in mournful wails, and the picture's anachronistic qualities, oblivious to Fletcher but driven into relief by the nuclear-fission facility at the foot of the mountains, suddenly made me wonder how much longer we had for this sort of thing.

ALREADY HE IS one of the last oldtime Southwest houndsmen. His contemporaries—Ben Lilly; Clell and Dale Lee of Blue, Arizona; Jimmy Owens—are either dead or too old to hunt much anymore. His career has spanned thirty-five years, during which he estimates his dogs have treed 800 lions. Fletcher has probably caught more lions than any living man. As a guide he has been sought out by such prominent figures in the hunting world as Dr. Frank C. Hibben, publisher Otis Chandler, and the late Jack O'Connor. The hounds are descended from Lilly's pack, the bloodlines running back through almost a century of Walker/Plott crosses, which all hunted in the inhospitable, colorful,

rimrock canyons and mountains that still preserve some of their bones.

It is for them that Fletcher, almost sixty, still hunts the cats. For the pack no longer earns its keep the way it did when he ran forty hounds and ran bear, lion, and jaguar in three states and Mexico. Now Fletcher only takes out nine or ten clients a year for lion, a few for bear, another handful each fall for mountain game. Hard times and heartworm have reduced the pack to fourteen, as few hounds as he ever kept, and about all he can afford to feed.

And yet Fletcher refuses offers from former clients and other houndsmen of up to several thousand dollars for just one of his dogs. And nine out of ten pups are knocked on their heads at birth. The few which receive his favor are individually trained, a costly venture requiring many long drives into the mountains. One evening after we had returned from hunting and were pitching beaver carcasses to worn-out dogs, I asked him why he didn't raise a few hounds just to pay for the others.

He shook his head slowly. "Just could not do it," he said.

We went inside his trailer to eat. He thanked his wife, Chris, for dinner and shortly after sitting down stood up. "I never get full," he said. "I eat until I get tired." Then he pulled off his boots and sat back down, this time in a rocker next to a wood stove, and looked far away for several minutes, before inclining his head in my direction.

"Let me tell you why I won't sell a hound," he said. "I just lost a hound, several months back, a well-mannered dog." Fletcher paused, searching for the words. "The kind he never done anything wrong in his life. Lion slapped him off a cliff.

"And had a dog die this year eleven year old, I figured had been in on 300 lion. Why, they could buy that dog like they could buy me. Hound laid still for sixty stitches after a lion had laid open its scalp." Fletcher ran his finger through his own rusty hair. "So that a flap of skin hung over one eye. And never whined one time!"

Fletcher brought out an old '94 .30/30: no stock, just the action and barrel. There were deep pits bitten into the worn-silver steel. Jaguar teeth marks, Fletcher said. He explained that when the hounds close on a wounded animal and shooting is out of the question, the thing to do is stick the gun barrel in the jaws. To get its attention. If the lion has caught a dog, Fletcher will slap it with his hat. A bear, he grabs by the ears. Numerous encounters have left their scars. Fletcher's right leg alone bears the teeth and claw marks of bobcat, lion, and bear, and the welts of two accidental shootings.

Apart from the hazards of dealing with animals brought to bay, Fletcher has had two trees fall on him. He has spent days camped beside terrified hounds that found themselves stranded on narrow ledges. And once, to save a dog named Cougar, he trusted the end of the rope to total strangers as he descended a cliff.

But this readiness to wade into the center is more a houndsman's trademark than any stamp of individuality. What distinguishes

Fletcher is his skill at finding a cold trail, deciding whether it is worthwhile to follow, getting the hounds started in the right direction, and then controlling the balance of authority that shifts among the members of the pack, including himself, with respect to the condition of the track and hotness of pursuit.

DURING THE FIRST hour Fletcher followed the lion along the rim, the trail was very cold. The hounds had come to depend on his eyes, and Fletcher called them in to the rain-spattered prints. His voice lifted across the scrub. By the time we caught up, the initiative had changed: the dogs no longer echoed the houndsman. First Ben, and soon the others were leapfrogging ahead in the way that Walkers unravel a trail, not straddling the track but ranging out to shortcut their work. From the truck, we heard them with increasing and, as the afternoon lengthened, decreasing regularity.

My hopes, which had dropped with Ben's belling, stirred with the rejoinders of the other hounds, and now plummeted once more. We drove along the rim and at odd intervals cut the engine to listen. It was difficult to believe that the dogs had lost the tom, especially a tom that was on the prowl following a long contour of rimrock, freshening his old scrapes, moving quickly with little heed. The hounds didn't need anyone to direct traffic as long as this cat didn't cross a long expanse of rock or suddenly start minding its step when hunting deer.

It was more likely that the lion had dropped off the ledge into the climbing shadows along the canyon walls. We stopped beside an overlook with nothing to do except hope for the sound of the hounds.

Now, even the ranchers were beginning to feel the weight of the evening and passed hours. The tall rancher drummed his fingers against the window. The small man with the black glove over his hand removed it, and inspected a claw of fingers that extruded from a starburst of scar tissue over his palm. He said he had been out shooting coyotes, set the butt of his rifle on the ground, and placed the hand over the muzzle. Boom!

I thought about the day I felt a need to explain to Pete that when you hunted with Orvel Fletcher you learned by your mistakes. That Fletcher respected even misplaced effort, but sometimes got so caught up in hunting that he lost sight of the gulf of experience that separated him from almost anyone. I also wanted to tell them both that we had been part of something here that had some history behind it, then realized their leathered faces would register no comprehension because they were a part of that heritage. I was the outsider here with the privileged glimpse, a backlook through the wrong end of the scope into a somewhat dated, but still beautiful, harsh world of hounds deep through the heart and a houndsman whose blunt individuality and self-reliance were the very essence of the early West.

I had come to New Mexico to see a lion, but that didn't seem to be the point of it at all.

WE FINALLY PICKED up a distant baying and found the animated, white specks of the hounds at the bottom of the canyon. I remembered that Fletcher had told me he got "old vibes" when he heard faraway hounds. He heard the ghosts of hounds that had been dead for twenty years.

It was night by the time we reached him. The two ranchers sat smoking in the truck while Fletcher and I followed on the heels of the hounds, circling the paw marks of the lion in the beam of my flashlight. Fletcher was tired and regretted not having had time to haul the mules. With them, we could have started back on the trail in the morning.

"I hate to call them off now," he said. "If it hadn't rained they would be running that tom head up.

"Listen. That's Judge."

Fletcher stopped and placed his hands on his hips. His voice started low and rose as he called to the hounds: "Here Ben! Here Judge! Here Boy!" And rose to a whistle. "Here! Heh, heh, heh, heh, here!"

Abruptly, the music stopped. He turned and we walked back toward the truck in the cold, brittle air.

By Dan Sisson

FULL BOAR

TO EXPERIENCE A DEMANDING HUNT LACED WITH DANGER, THERE'S NOTHING LIKE GOING HOG WILD.

"HOW COME WE'VE never gone wild boar hunting, Grandpa?"

"Becuzzz ..." Grandpa drawled slowly, distinctively pronouncing each syllable, "pigs are not *indigenous* to Oregon."

"What's *that* mean?" I asked.

He chuckled. "That's what the dictionary's for, kid. It's sitting right there in the corner and all you have to do to unlock the mysteries of the English language is use it."

I reluctantly paged through the dictionary until I found the word. "It means 'native,'" I said.

Grandpa fairly beamed. "Good work, kid." I waited for some smart comment about the younger generation, but Grandpa surprised me by asking, "So when did this mania for boar hunting take hold of you? Haven't we been taking on enough of God's critters as it is?"

I shrugged. "I was just reading a story about wild boar hunting in Tennessee and I wondered if there was any such thing in Oregon."

"Nope!" Grandpa replied emphatically. "You go to California for that kind of hunting, kid—at least in this part of the world. And come to think of it, your Grandma and I have been thinking about going down to the Santa Cruz mountains to visit our friends the Wolfingers. It's a 14-hour drive, but if you want to go with us, we could probably find a way to go pig hunting. If I'm not mistaken, California has an open season all year long. I can't promise anything, kid, but I'll see what I can do."

I grinned. "I'd like that, Grandpa." So I left the proposed boar hunt in Grandpa's hands. Two weeks later he asked me if I could get permission to take a few extra vacation days at Thanksgiving. I got the okay from my principal and then we were off on my first big trip to California.

The roads were icy and the mountain passes filled with snow when we headed south. Within 7 hours, though, the snow had disappeared and the temperature had risen 25 degrees. I felt warm, or nearly warm, for the first time in a month.

After 10 hours the 6,000-foot passes had turned into 1,500-foot ridges and I was seeing hillsides of scrub oak and manzanita, some pine, and a lot of clay-colored rocky hills. Most of the hillsides were already brown.

Grandpa pointed out that the pigs feed in the early morning and late evening in groups of about fifteen to thirty animals, rooting around in patches of ground cover in search of roots and acorns. They even come into hayfields and damage crops.

Once we got to the Wolfingers' place we made plans to go hunting. It had been raining for several days before our arrival so the creeks were running everywhere, which wasn't to our advantage. During the dry season, pigs tend to concentrate day and night at the few watering holes to be found on low ground. But now they would be spread out in the forests where there was sufficient water for the first time since the beginning of an extended dry summer and fall.

Mr. Wolfinger knew a local guide named Ralph Nichols, who occasionally took hunters out. More important, Ralph knew where to find a big boar or two, or so Mr. Wolfinger said. He told us that Ralph would pick us up the next morning.

Ralph arrived in a battered pickup and I was a bit taken aback by his looks. Although he was not more than forty years old, he had gray hair and looked like something from another age. He kept pulling on his suspenders before speaking, and seemed hesitant about everything he did. I looked at Grandpa quizzically and when he saw my expression, his eyebrows raised a notch. Our guide looked like he had a screw loose.

When the distance closed to 40 yards the boar suddenly jumped up and began running toward the kid.

Despite our reservations we climbed into Ralph's pickup and headed into the mountains. We drove for an hour before Ralph slowed down and began squinting at every gully that had a trickle of water in it.

After another mile he pulled off the road and announced that we were nearing a place where there might be some pigs and that maybe it'd be a good idea to walk.

"The pickup'll scare 'em," he explained.

So we each grabbed a rifle and quietly walked to an area that obviously had been visited by pigs in the last day or two. Large 10x20-foot patches of forest ground cover looked raked and scratched over, and little cloven hoofprints appeared wherever the soil was muddy.

We sat for about 20 minutes in silence, listening for any sounds of pigs in the area. Eventually, we gave up, and Ralph gave us the sign to head back toward the truck.

We did the same thing three more times, and we could always see where wild pigs had been, but by the time we got there, they were long gone. The fourth time, however, as Ralph pulled off the road and into some bushes, two small pigs, about 20 pounds apiece, ran across the road. We figured we'd found a herd and our excitement mounted. Ralph grabbed his .243 and whispered that we didn't have time to get our rifles out because we had to "git on 'em 'mediately." So Grandpa and I left our rifles and canteens and everything in the pickup and followed Ralph as fast and as quietly as we could.

We reached a small flat covered with scrub oak and I watched Ralph study the ground intently. He pointed to a mass of tracks, but one in particular caught my eye. It was twice as big as any of the others and I could see it excited Ralph and Grandpa. Ralph pointed to it with his rifle barrel and matter-of-factly said, "Boar. Over 225 pounds."

The tracks headed up a draw, so we did too. At first the walking wasn't too bad for Grandpa, but as we continued, our path grew steeper and the sun got hotter. By 11 A.M. the temperature had reached the 80s, and Grandpa began to wilt.

It wasn't long before he said to me, "I think I'll go back to the pickup. We've been following these tracks for 3 hours and I'm tuckered out. But you go," he said. I protested, saying I didn't want to leave him, but he told me he could find the pickup easy enough and that I ought to stay with Ralph. It might be my only chance at a boar.

My respect for Ralph was increasing every minute. He may have been short on conversation, but he was long on tracking experience. He had a knack for following the pigs over loose rocks and hard clay soil—I knew I would have lost the trail hours ago.

By 2 o'clock there was evidence we were getting closer to the big boar. Every so often we'd find a sandy spot that looked smooth and pressed down. Ralph would trace the pig's outline with the rifle barrel and say, "He's gettin' tired."

As we walked, Ralph gave me his rifle to carry. It was an old bolt-action .243 and I wondered if it was a big enough gun for a boar, but in the excitement I didn't ask. I also didn't check the magazine to see if there were any shells in it. I just assumed it was full.

We hadn't gone 200 yards in a deepening forest when Ralph stopped and pointed. There, in a shady spot 60 yards away, was a boar facing away from us. He looked massive, with a huge neck and shoulders, and a snout that pointed off to one side.

Ralph motioned for me to get in front of him. He whispered, "Shoot him in the right shoulder." I lined up the sights and fired. The bullet made a solid *thwack* and the boar shuddered and began to sink downward. Ralph and I began walking toward him, thinking he was dead. But when the distance closed to 40 yards the boar suddenly jumped up and began running toward us. As he did he made a slight half circle and I gave him the second round in the left shoulder.

That slowed him down some, but he kept coming. I could see his lips curled back and a pair of gleaming tusks pointed at me. I fired a third shot, which hit him squarely in the chest and slowed him down—but he kept coming!

When I opened the bolt to ram the fourth bullet into the chamber, I realized the magazine was empty. I turned to look for Ralph, and saw him shinning up a tree. I was left standing there, facing the big boar. Two seconds later the boar lost his charge. His front legs buckled and he crashed on his side, less than 15 feet away.

Worried he might get up again, I moved back and began looking for a tree to climb myself. But when I heard Ralph congratulating me on some good shooting I realized the boar was down for good.

I looked at Ralph. There was no more hesitancy in his manner. He sure could move fast when he wanted to.

Ralph must have known I was on the verge of collapse, because he said the magic words: "Kid, you sit down here and keep an eye on that boar. I'll go get your Grandpa and the pickup and we'll haul that critter up with a winch. And I'll tell your Grandpa how you handled yourself. Yessir, that's a real HAWG! I'd say 250 pounds!"

As the sound of Ralph's footsteps faded in the distance, I sat down. I had to, because my knees were shaking too much for me to stand.

By Lionel Atwill

ALIEN ROOTER

When it comes to survival, no power beats pork power.

THE SECOND MOST populous big-game animal in the United States has this to say about his exalted status: *"OINK."*

That's right, oink; for number two is not the antelope, not the elk, not the black bear. The Avis of animals is the porker—a.k.a. piggy, piney-rooter, wild hog, feral oinker, razorback, Russian (or Eurasian) boar.

Call him what you will, the pig is pervasive. He is found in at least 23 states in numbers well exceeding 2 million. Fourteen of those states require licenses to hunt the hog; in California the piggy is so revered he has been classified as a big-game animal since 1956, subject to the attendant seasons and license requirements of his indigenous kin. Texas has at least 1 million hogs. Florida has the second-largest population, over half a million, and regulates hog hunting on public ground. In some years Floridians kill more hogs than deer.

The worldly pig

HOGS MAKE OUR other populous naturalized aliens—pheasants and brown trout—look as if they just stepped off the boat. Pigs were brought to the Hawaiian islands by Polynesians as early as 1000 A.D. Columbus was thought to have released eight swine in the West Indies on his second voyage to the New World in 1493. Forty-six years later Hernando DeSoto brought 13 of Columbus' porkers from Cuba to Florida, and throughout the rest of the 16th century Spanish explorers released hogs through the Southeast and Southwest.

Porkers were set free to roam because of their predilection for survival. Pigs are woods smart and gritty. Turn one loose on an island and he will probably survive to be hunted down by the next band of human castaways that washes ashore. That was the motivation behind the nautical custom of loosing hogs on islands around the globe, a custom DeSoto brought to the New World. There is an outside chance that the bloodline of DeSoto's pigs runs through wild hogs today; certainly, current wild hog populations can be traced to at least the 18th century.

If you ever have encountered feral hogs, you can see that wild streak. They neither look nor act like their barnyard kin. They are rangy, lean, and exceptionally keen of nose and ear—and their eyes are better than most hunters think.

Pigs can live in the mesquite scrub of South Texas, the swamps of Alabama, or the hills of New Hampshire. Prolific breeders, sows are also excellent mothers. "A sow may give birth to four to six piglets, but eight will survive," says a Texas biologist. Omnivorous, porkers are better at rooting out acorns than deer or turkeys are (after all, pigs are used to find truffles in Europe). They prey on snakes, birds, and the young of domestic and wild animals, and are so efficient in their eating that the remains of a pig kill are often no more than a wisp of hair and a track.

Their keen senses make pigs worthy game, and their lean bodies make them tasty cuisine. (Handle carefully, however; pigs can carry brucellosis, leptospirosis, salmonellosis, toxoplasmosis, balantidiasis, trichinosis, trichostrongylosis, and sarcoptic mange, all of which can infect man.)

Wild Blood

IT IS THE porker's fearsome reputation that holds a particular attraction, however, a reputation often underscored by taxidermists who mount hogs with tusks pulled two inches out of their jawbone so those potent scissors, which can reach 6 inches in length without dental enhancement, look like the fangs of the Devil.

Wild pigs grow large: 400-plus pounds is

No Easy Matter

Hog hunting strategies are as varied as the country in which the pigs live. In the swamps and thickets of the South, hunters often rely on dogs to bay up pigs. In the more open landscapes of Texas or California, glassing and careful stalking work. No matter where you hunt, however, a few general observations hold true.

1) In warm weather, hunt near food sources or water in the early morning and late afternoon when pigs are on the move. During the day, keep your eyes open in dense cover where porkers lay up.

2) As the weather cools, expect to see pigs feeding at any time of day.

3) When you spot feeding pigs, note what they are eating. Pigs are such efficient, smart diners that they will work an area repeatedly until all the food is gone. If, for example, they are feeding on a mast crop, continue to check that area and similar areas. Chances are good you will encounter them again.

4) Use enough gun or bow. Pigs have a stout shield of thick hide protecting their vitals. They do not go down easily. A 30 caliber or larger rifle is adequate; for a bow, use at least 55 pounds.

5) A pack of pork is particularly difficult to stalk. First, you must have the wind. Second, note their general direction of travel and try to intercept them rather than move straight in. Finally, if you are spotted, freeze. Often the pigs will calm down in a few minutes and resume their business, but remember that after such an alert, they will be more on their guard.

6) One general rule about safety: Before you pick a target, pick a tree. — L. A.

On the Wild Side

Professional wildlife photographer Weiman Meinzer is among those men who can't say enough, both good and bad, about feral hogs. His adventures range from the bizarre to the incredible, and he characterizes the animals as shrewd, anvil-tough, and hell-bent on revenge.

"They remind me of a grizzly bear," he said, "because they'll retrace their steps and wait on you."

Like the time he put a 500-grain muzzleloader slug into a big boar at 25 yards. Despite what Meinzer recalled as a perfect hit, the boar never faltered—it just clacked its sharp tusks and rumbled into heavy cover. Then the boar lay down so he faced the hunter and readied an ambush. Meinzer saw the waiting pig in time and added another 500 grains of lead. Game over.

Often, somebody or something on a pig hunt gets hurt. Dogs get cut, horses slashed, and hunters laid open. Wounded hogs don't want to simply survive, they want to get even.

Men so caught up in hog hunting recall how tough an adversary—physically and mentally—the wild pig can be. Most everything they say is true, too, from the way a big boar will backtrack and charge you from behind to the way an entire herd will go nocturnal at the first hint of hunting pressure. Somehow, these men may believe themselves better hunters for their ability to outwit—or outrun, when necessary—a big wild boar.

"What gets me is that they're so darned durable," Meinzer said in an almost reverent tone. "They are truly thinking animals, too, especially the big boars and sows that lead groups. You hit them one time [with hunting pressure], and you can kiss them goodbye."

Therein lies the difference between an obsessed hog hunter and the rest of us. Hit once, twice, or thrice, I have no intention of kissing a pig—goodbye or otherwise. — Doug Pike

not unheard of for a feral pig, and a porked-up domestic boar can top a ton. Most will fight if cornered. On occasion, one will charge without provocation. A bowhunting friend of mine shot a hog in Texas. When he tracked it down, two other pigs appeared and created such a jaw-popping, hoggish racket that my friend retreated up a tree. The two healthy hogs proceeded to eat their recently departed kin. That sort of story is not rare among hog hunters. Throw in the mystique of Russian or Eurasian wild boar lineage, and the porker's reputation for ferocity is secured.

How much of that "wild boar" blood exists in porkers running about the United States is a point of speculation. Allegedly, there is a true wild boar population on a game farm in New Hampshire and on a few ranches in Texas, but most of the feral spareribs in this country have only a touch of Eurasian boar in their parentage, if they have any at all. Those who sell hunts for pigs will often brand a rangy, black hog as a pure Eurasian or Russian boar. And given the lethal glint in such an animal's eye, most sports need no more convincing.

In truth, black and rangy does not turn a feral porker into a scimitar-toothed Cossack. According to a paper delivered by biologists John Mayer and I. Lehr Brisbin, Jr., at a symposium on feral hogs, "... the coloration in pure Eurasian wild boar consists of light brown to black bristles with cream to tan distal tips ... Feral hogs are variable in coat coloration patterns; common patterns include all black, all red/brown, all white, spotted, belted, and miscellaneous rare domestic patterns (e.g., blue or gray roans)."

How can one tell a feral pig from a Eurasian boar? Mayer and Brisbin's research has showed that the most dependable method relies on "seven cranial measurements in adult males and three cranial measurements in adult females." They noted, however, that, "... in general, Eurasian wild boar tended to have longer hind foot and snout lengths than either hybrids (wild boar and feral pig crosses) or feral hogs." When it comes to pigs, the nose knows.

By Christopher Michaels

Stalking the "Perilous" PECCARY

Often portrayed as the porcine version of Jack the Ripper, the javelina isn't dangerous or big, or even a true pig. Here's a realistic view of this fine little game animal.

DURING THE DAYS when Western pulp magazines were popular, the javelina often appeared in Southwestern desert stories as a villain. The stagecoach broke down, and the passengers, who were then forced to walk, were treed in thorny mesquites by a drove of slavering, vicious critters that kept them there nigh unto death. If the readers grew bored with that one, the editors could always count on the cowpoke who lost his horse and, afoot, was slashed to ribbons by bloodthirsty peccaries.

The truth is that the javelina, a fine little game animal and an unusual trophy, isn't dangerous, except possibly when cornered, or wounded and too closely approached. Nonetheless, the ferocity propaganda persists, and most hunters without javelina experience believe it, sometimes with amusing results.

For example, one fall at guide Jim Barbee's West Texas deer hunting camp, a young Indianan who'd tagged his buck was eager to collect a javelina with his handgun. Jim, an old friend, asked me along. We glassed several bands, and finally found an exceptionally large specimen, probably an old boar. (The sexes look alike. You've got to be certain a big one isn't an old sow with piglets, which can be born any time of the year, usually in pairs. Sows, for some reason, can't nurse more than two.)

Jim pointed out the boar from among pigs. There was no breeze. He explained that javelina's eyesight is extremely poor. "Go slow, and you can get close. If they look at you, stand still 'til they quit."

Uneasily the fellow started his stalk. Every few steps he paused and nervously looked back as if not sure he wanted a javelina after all. When he was still too far to shoot, the boar and several others became uneasy. When alarmed, javelinas raise the 4- to 6-inch bristles around their necks, and although adults average less than 40 pounds, they can suddenly look huge and ferocious.

INSTEAD OF WAITING for them to settle down, the fellow shot and missed. The herd exploded into every-which-way flight. Four ran straight at him, and he fled, dropping his gun, and yelling "Help!" at every bound. The more he yelled, the faster the spooked pigs ran, right on his heels, emitting low, evil-sounding grunts. At last they scattered for cover, but the fellow kept going another 50 yards.

I said, "How would you call it?"

Barbee, a droll sort, said, "No question at all. The guy won. Wish I'd bet."

Those javelinas were simply frightened. I've had spooked ones run past so close that they brushed my pants leg. Their sense of smell is acute, and so is their hearing, but they're gregarious, and don't always distinguish danger sounds from those of their band. So when they finally do get the message that something is wrong, they panic.

Their habits are quite predictable. They move about, feeding, until mid-morning, and again in late afternoon. They're sensitive to temperature, and in summer they move mostly at night. In fall and winter at 70 to 80 degrees, they bed down in shade near water, or in foothill country up in rimrocks. Because their coats are thin (I've seen several pigs with eartips destroyed by frostbite), they dislike winter wind, and avoid it by feeding on lee slopes or in protected canyons. On mild overcast days, hunters may see wandering javelinas at any hour. They habitually follow dry desert washes or brushy draws that lead up slopes, or go single-file along cattle trails. Wherever they go, they stipple the ground with their tracks.

Although javelinas eat numerous plants and roots, their staple is prickly pear cactus, which grows throughout their U.S. range in south and west Texas, southwestern New Mexico, and southeastern Arizona. A hunter who checks pear patches will eventually find his quarry. If a water source such as a cattle tank, windmill overflow, or desert seep is near, any band in the area will usually be within half a mile. They get much liquid from cactus, but must have water too.

Years ago one of my first javelinas, the largest I've taken—51 pounds field-dressed—was the result of finding water. An Arizona game warden friend and I were scouting east of Tucson. Near a motte of palo verde trees bordering an expanse of prickly pear, we found a rare desert seep. Javelinas don't wallow like domestic swine, but they do like to lie in such places. It was a welter of tracks.

Facing a light late-afternoon breeze, we slowly prowled the desert, looking for freshly-ripped prickly pear. Javelinas have a pair of intermeshing, self-sharpening canine teeth in each jaw. These do not curve outward, like the tusks of swine (javelinas are not true swine). The teeth are used to rip forage, like prickly pear branches and pads, and for defense. At most, these teeth are about 1½ inches long.

Soon we discovered freshly ripped pear, juice still dripping. Guns ready, we eased ahead. Suddenly javelinas were everywhere, munching away. I saw my partner raise his rifle to the left. Ahead of me, only 40 paces away, a big fellow stood broadside. I'd made a Texas hunt, my first, immediately prior, and been coached on shot placement. For a javelina mount you need the entire front end, including the shoulders. (Backstraps and hams furnish the best meat.) Their bulky vegetarian diet makes paunch shots messy, and taboo. Thus you need a broadside shot, and careful placement in the ribs, behind a foreleg. It's a small target.

We shot simultaneously. The pear came alive with the wildly scattering drove. My boar was down, but a rush of bolting animals at and around me put my hair momentarily on end. I admit I probably looked scared, until I heard my warden friend laughing.

Because of that experience, I can't resist relating one that followed. I really wanted live-javelina photos, and camera equipment was then too slow and poor for distant shots. The warden knew of a tame boar, owned by the Marshal of Tombstone. We visited him and he offered to take the boar out into the desert. It trotted happily around, then moved to me, thrust its head between my knees, and rubbed.

The Marshal said quietly, "Stand real still. He sometimes gets touchy with strangers. One feller tried to pet him and got slashed ten stitches worth."

The warden found my wild-eyed look and rigid stance hilarious. "Don't fret," he said. "I've stitched up hurt deer and elk. Only thing worries me is how to fix the big artery running down inside your leg." He doubled over with laughter.

To climax the episode, the boar withdrew and turned his hindquarters toward me. The bristles around the musk gland high on his rump flowered, and he let off a puff of what a Texan I know calls "javelina smoke." It smells something like skunk, but compared to javelina musk, skunk is Chanel No. 5!

The musk, naturalists believe, is for communication, and is a means of finding each other. It exudes from a skin gland, and it should be removed, with a patch of surrounding skin, so none gets on your hands and inadvertently on the meat.

Javelina is never fat, like pork. It's excellent. My wife roasts the hams, making small slits for several garlic cloves. Also, javelina hide makes beautiful, bristle-pocked leather for billfolds, belts, and loafers.

How you hunt this animal depends on location. In the south Texas brush country it's done from deer blinds or by glassing pear flats, prowling near tanks, or watching ranch roads for crossing bands. Shots are at short to medium range.

In western Texas, New Mexico, and Arizona the terrain is mountainous. Glassing open foothills and draws often presents long shots. I dislike these. Proper bullet placement on the small target is too chancy. The sportiest hunting, in my opinion, is the close stalk. Shooting with a camera, I've gotten within 10 feet.

Javelina are perfect for bow and handgun hunters. In Texas' Big Bend region I've hunted several times with a .22 magnum, which is legal there. I stuck to ranges of 25 yards or less, not trusting the caliber farther.

These hunts hold ample drama. During one, moving upwind along a dry wash, I smelled them before I saw them. (Hunters scouting washes or rimrocks should keep this in mind.) Presently six were in sight, coming single-file, noses high, testing, uneasy. I was on a bank several feet above them, and I let five pass. Although nervous, each raising bristles and starting to trot as it passed, none spotted me. I took the sixth, dropping it within 7 feet.

I suppose there's a possibility of getting slashed by hunting this close; I've seen dogs badly cut up when baying a group. However, the chance is remote, and working to get close is truly sporty because they don't always cooperate. Often they'll spook, even while you're still far off.

IF YOU WANT a special thrill, try a predator call. Why javelinas occasionally respond is unclear. Perhaps the squall sounds to them like a piglet in trouble. When they do rush toward a caller, they usually come ready to do battle.

A companion and I discovered this while hunkered in a wash trying to bring in a coyote. Suddenly there was a crackling of brush, a rush of movement, teeth popping, and we were surrounded by an agitated group that we didn't take time to count. We jumped up yelling and waving our arms, and they ran. I've heard numerous hunters scoff at the javelina as a game animal, but we thought that experience was fairly gamy.

By John Barsness

JOHN'S BEAR

BAIT AND DOGS ARE FORBIDDEN IN MONTANA, SO A YOUNG MAN AFTER HIS FIRST BRUIN NEEDS PATIENCE, ENERGY, AND OCCASIONAL ADVICE FROM DAD.

"HOW MANY DOES that make, son?" Melvin asked, as the cow elk and her new calf stood looking at us from across the aspen creekbottom.

"I believe sixty-six," John said. The cow was as sleek as any harbor seal in her new summer coat, the calf reminiscent of a dachshund on stilts as it tried to hide under its mother. We had seen sixty-six elk, but no black bears.

It was a normal day of spring bear hunting in Montana, where you cannot use bait or dogs. Many years, the hunting resembles astronomy, with the bears representing black holes—nothing appears where something should be. Once in a while, you'll find a track or a pile of freshly digested grass, and at such times you can almost feel the bear out there, like an undiscovered planet, subtly changing the orbits of the rest of the solar system along with the orbits of your eyes, which subtly change into dry glass after days of looking through binoculars for bears.

On the first day this lopsided elk/bear ratio didn't bother Melvin and John much at all, because in West Virginia they don't have many elk. It was interesting to listen to them talk as we searched perhaps 40 square miles of Montana with binoculars. They are two men who have spent their lives in the Allegheny Mountains hunting turkeys and deer. I answered whatever questions came my way, but the conversation moved mostly between father and son, as if they were a planet and moon, and I an asteroid outside their closed orbits. Even when Melvin bragged to me about John's recent degree in wildlife biology, it was as if he spoke to his son indirectly, through me.

John mentioned that he wanted a coyote hide to take home. Toward the end of the day, we eased down the ridge to the edge of a sage-brush draw, and were looking across the valley at blue mountains when I saw a big yellow coyote slipping through the sage below us.

"There's your coyote," I whispered, and John sat down quickly and shot. Limestone dust erupted from the hillside just above the coyote's back and it left suddenly, as coyotes are apt to do.

"Damn," John said quietly but hard, like a pitcher who'd just missed a called third strike.

"Shot just over him," Melvin said quietly. He paused, considering. "You have to remember that rifle's sighted 3 inches high, not right on like we do back home. And it was downhill."

John said, "But—"

"No buts about it," Melvin said, not sharply but firmly. Then he softened. "This isn't West Virginia. Be patient and you'll learn."

John looked at him, then nodded. "Yessir." His father's words seemed to firm him, much like a rational prayer.

I didn't speak for several moments, not wanting to push myself between their almost palpable connection. I finally said, "We'll see more coyotes."

"Yeah, but will we see a bear?" Melvin said, smiling. He was along not to hunt but to observe, though I sensed he wanted John's bear as much as John did. I smiled and shrugged; I'd warned them that Rocky Mountain bear hunting was chancy.

Soon after, the sun set and we walked back to my pickup. As the constellations appeared, Melvin talked about John's impending graduate work, chasing radio-collared wild turkeys in Mississippi. I hadn't seen a father and son so proud and accepting of each other in a long time, and wondered all the way down the mountain if they were so close because they hunted together, or if they hunted together because they were so close.

The second day also passed without a bear sighting. My plan was to sit across a valley from a big clearcut and glass for bears, but almost as soon as we sat down the clouds turned dark and we heard thunder. It didn't seem wise to sit under lodgepole pines during a thunderstorm, so we walked 4 miles out in the rain.

The next day we tried again. There were still no bears, but neither was there any rain. Melvin's bad knee was sore so he lagged behind, saying he'd do some bird watching. John and I sat down on the same hill we'd sat on the day before and started glassing.

"How many bears you usually see this time of year?" he finally asked.

I shrugged. "One every other day is a good average in this country. It's different than deer hunting, especially whitetails."

John nodded, almost smiling. "You sit on any stand back home and you'll see a dozen deer by sunrise. And you'll hear two or three gobblers on any ridge in spring."

"It's a biological principle: carnivores are scarcer. You might see only one bear this whole week."

I could tell he was thinking, even as he glassed. "It's just. . . ." He reorganized himself. "Dad spent so much to bring me out here, and I missed that coyote." He paused. "I haven't missed a deer in seven years."

I knew Melvin wasn't rich, and I'd also seen the way John had quickly pulled out his own money to pay for his bear tag. "Bears are bigger than coyotes. You won't miss. Just listen to us about where to aim, especially if it's a long shot. Your dad's hunted in Wyoming and he knows how to do it."

John glassed and thought, and then nodded once. Melvin walked up slowly, easing down to the ground beside us. "'No bears yet?" he said with an exaggerated frown. Even with the clowning, I could tell my West Virginia friends were beginning to doubt the existence of Rocky Mountain black bears.

"No," I said. "I'm going to check out another clearcut, over that way. Whistle if you see something." I grabbed my rifle and headed down a skidder trail, following it to the edge of a smaller clearcut. A mule deer doe fed in the timber along the far side, but that was my only sighting. As soon as I took the binoculars from my eyes I heard a loud whistle.

I ran back tip the skid trail to find John on his feet, waving. "There's a bear!" John tried to whisper, but across 100 yards, it emerged as a hoarse stage-shout.

Melvin sat behind the spotting scope. "He's got to be 250 pounds." I took a quick look through the scope. An average black bear—black, not brown or blond, and maybe 150 pounds—walked deliberately across the mile-wide clearcut. He didn't even break stride to sniff elk tracks. I shook my head; stalking moving black bears almost never works. That ambling walk traverses mountains much faster than any human can follow. But I thought we could intercept him.

"Melvin, you stay here and signal which way he goes. John, let's go." It was a half mile across the valley, and we took off with packs and rifles at a basic-training trot. The bear was headed toward a deep creek.

We were both breathing too hard 20 minutes later when we climbed the hill above the creek. John's eyes were as wide as an owl's as he eased slightly ahead of me, straining to locate the bear. When we reached the edge of the hill I plucked on his jacket. He twitched, then turned. "Take it slow," I whispered. "He could be anywhere."

We took three slow steps and looked across the creek. No bear. I looked across at Melvin through my binoculars. He pointed down at his his feet. We walked back across the valley.

"When you were halfway there, he turned and walked downhill into those trees," Melvin said, pointing to a stand of lodgepoles a mile across. I shrugged.

Successful hunters are wise enough to listen to the voice of experience.

John's mouth was twisted, as if he'd just bitten a lemon. "That was my chance."

Melvin smiled, lighting his pipe. "If you tried for 2 whole minutes, you just might learn some patience." John looked at him blankly, then laughed.

The next two days passed without a single bear sighting. On the last day we headed back to where we'd seen all the elk. Black bears like to eat elk calves, I reasoned, so why not try there? The ground had frozen hard during the previous cold, clear night—the kind of weather bears like. Late in the morning I leaned my elbows on my knees and glassed another mountainside.

"There's a bear," I said. It was grazing in a small natural meadow across a deep canyon, level with us. "He's brown, and he's big."

John and I quickly headed straight down the canyon, then climbed up the other side, edging the small stands of fir. It was steep and, by the time we climbed the slope, hot. I suspected the bear would be back in the cool timber by the time we arrived, and he was, the meadow seeming as empty as any burned-out slum. John started into the timber. "No," I whispered, grabbing him by the arm. "This isn't a traveling bear. He lives here." I pointed to the fresh coils of green droppings in the meadow. "We'll back away, downwind, then come back tonight and kill him."

John looked doubtful. I tried to sound as positive as Norman Vincent Peale. We left the deep canyon and hunted a long creekbottom that afternoon, seeing no bears or bear tracks. Two hours before dark, we returned to the canyon and glassed and waited.

The mountain's shadows moved across the bear's meadow like clear water filling a pool. John whispered that if he'd shot better, at least he'd go home with a coyote hide. Three elk moved into the meadow. Melvin suggested that they wouldn't be there if the bear was nearby. I shrugged.

Just as the sun touched the edge of the pines on the highest ridge, Melvin said, "You gonna shoot that bear, or not?" John and I brought our binoculars up like thirsty men about to drink. "No, not over there," scolded Melvin. "Right down there."

A large brown bear stood directly below us, looking downhill between tall lodgepoles. It was a long shot but the light was going fast. "Right here," I said to John, placing my daypack on a rock. "Rest your rifle here, and shoot him."

Melvin nodded. John lay down quickly, easing a cartridge into the chamber. "How far?"

Melvin shook his head. "It doesn't matter. Just aim at the bottom of his chest."

"What?" John turned his head quickly toward his father. "That's a long ways."

"Listen to your father," I said.

John looked at his father, not me, then turned and settled the rifle into his pack. His back rose as he breathed in, then held still, and the .300 jumped on the pack and the shot thudded into the canyon. The bear rolled once before it stopped bellydown against a tall sagebrush. It was lying there, its huge square head resting on one front paw, when we walked out of the timber a few minutes later. We finished skinning the bear in the last blue light of the canyon, then cut off the hind legs and boned the rest of the meat by flashlight, dividing the loads onto our three packs. We climbed out of the canyon by the light of a half-moon.

As I eased the heavy hide onto the tailgate of the pickup, Melvin said, "He was holdin' out on us, son, waiting until the last day to take us to his secret spot." He lit his pipe and the flame touched his tired, amused face.

John shook his head. "I just wish I could've shot better." The bullet had broken the bear's neck. Melvin had concentrated so hard on compensating for the steep angle that he hadn't noticed the slight breeze coming from the canyon.

"You made a decent shot," I said.

John shook his head. "It wasn't where I intended. It was luck."

"Let me tell you something, son," Melvin said firmly but quietly, pointing his pipe toward the bear hide. "You listened to the voice of experience, which is more than most young men will do. And you had a little luck, but not much. A little luck and a lot of hard work. When you get older, you'll learn to take your luck when it comes along, and be thankful for it. Especially on a night like this."

By the time he'd finished speaking his voice had grown stronger, developing into a cross between a sermon and a plea. It was as if Melvin were praying to luck and telling his own story. John didn't say anything. I just stood and let the last sweat of the climb evaporate into the dark light of the sky, and thought again of fathers and sons.

By Norman Strung

BERRY BEARS

'TIS THE SEASON WHEN WILD FRUITS RIPEN AND HANG HEAVY, AND THESE USUALLY UNPREDICTABLE CREATURES DO FOOLISH THINGS—ALL ON ACCOUNT OF A SWEET TOOTH.

I HAVE FOUND BLACK bears to be the most difficult game animals to hunt on the North American continent if you stalk them afoot. True, if you bait them or dog them they are relatively easy quarry, and I have no argument with those methods where they're legal. But in many states dogging and baiting are not legal, and given those restrictions, filling out a bear tag with any regularity amounts to a longer shot than picking a Super Bowl winner on the Fourth of July.

Unpredictability is the problem with hunting bears. Deer, turkey, elk, moose, and other big-game animals follow patterns of territoriality, migration, and daily activity that can be analyzed. Bears, on the other hand, are patternless. They feed almost continuously in the summer and fall, consuming anything edible, from ants to acorns. In their search for sustenance to see them through winter dormancy, they range far and wide. Their wanderings are aimless. You may find tracks or scat, but that's no guarantee their maker is nearby, or will ever pass that way again.

This haphazard lifestyle means most bears are taken as the result of a chance encounter: someone is in the woods with a bow or a rifle, usually after deer, and he bumps into the makings of a rug. A lucky break, and a reason for celebration, but not exactly bear hunting.

There is, however, one exception to the rule of unpredictability—berry time. When wild fruits ripen and hang heavy from branches and vines, bears forsake all other foods and glut themselves on the sweet berries. It's a phenomenon that both concentrates their numbers and finds them doing foolish things.

We live in a canyon out west and during the spring and summer, it's rare to see any signs of bears; they are roaming the backcountry and dispersed over its considerable landscape.

But when the hawthorns and chokecherries ripen along the creek bottom in autumn, the bears are drawn down from the mountains, seemingly ignorant of any human threat.

I have found scat 10 feet from my front door. A neighbor shot a bear on his front porch after it peered in the window at dinnertime. One evening, my wife saw our Labrador outside the gate and across the road. This is an absolute no-no to his training. She grabbed a switch, sneaked over the fence to reprimand him, then back-pedaled over the barbed wire when Chief barked behind her, and a 300-pound black bear reared up out of the raspberries. By comparing notes with our neighbors regarding color, cubs, and size, we've ascertained that as many as twelve bears have been working the canyon berry patches at the same time, geography that accounts for less than 3 square miles!

I should also point out that such behavior isn't unique to the West. A friend in northern Minnesota and another in Speculator, New York, have described similar activity during this period. Plainly put, if there are bears around, berry patches will draw them like a magnet and provide ample proof of their presence and eating habits, too. Tracks on trails leading to and from berry patches are one reliable sign, and broken limbs or branches on bushes are another. When bears feed heavily on berries, they often devastate a place. I have seen a raspberry patch the size of a house lot that looked like it lost a battle with a bulldozer.

But the real giveaway is scat. When bears have been dining on berries it will be the same color as the fruit and laced with seeds. Identifying the preferred berry is important, too. It's been my experience that bears are selective about the species of berry patch they'll raid. In the course of a season, they'll feed on raspberry, chokecherry, huckleberry, pin cherry, service berries, and rose hips, among others, but they seek out whichever of these fruits is ripest, probably because it has the highest sugar content.

If I were to pick a specific week for the height of the berry craze, it would be the one following the first frost. I base this, again, on a bear's sweet tooth. A light frost raises sugar content in fruits and vegetables; hence, the period from that freeze to when the fruits begin to dry on the vine rates as the time they are the most delectable. Hearkening back to our canyon community, that is precisely the time when bears knock on doors.

As to hunting tactics, the cardinal rule is always hunt into the wind, no matter how light the breeze. There is an Indian legend that says when an air-shot arrow falls to the earth, the deer will hear it, the eagle will see it, and the bear will smell it. I've found that quite true.

Several years ago I was hunting the berry patches near my home, when I heard a heavy limb snap ahead of me. It was a frosty morning, and a puff of condensed breath indicated the wind was my ally. I crept through the clawing hawthorns to the edge of a little park, and on the other side stood a big, jet-black sow with two long yearling cubs, raking berries into their mouths.

Although the cubs would surely be kicked off to fend for themselves later in the fall, shooting a sow with cubs at her side is illegal in Montana, so I played the part of an observer. Bears have notoriously bad eyesight, and that fact was obvious. Although I wore full camouflage, I also had on 400 square inches of blaze-orange vest. All three bears looked in my direction several times, but even though we were less than 50 yards apart, they never saw me.

Then convection, or some other quirk of the fickle wind, found my breath blowing toward the bears. My scent took about 30 seconds to reach them, and the effect was like a lightning bolt. They never looked or listened or turned my way. In an instant, the three lumbering, cloddish animals disappeared cat-like into the thicket.

That morning also serves to illustrate a few other rules to follow when bears are onto berries. Clear, crisp, still mornings and evenings provide the best conditions for several reasons. First, bears are most likely to be in the patches then. I don't know if it is light intensity, the breezes that normally blow when the sun is high, or Indian summer heat, but I seldom see bears eating berries in the middle of the day.

Sound also carries farther on frosty mornings, and like that day, you'll often hear bears tearing up the countryside before you sight them. Lastly, still air won't blow your scent or the leaves around, which sets the scene for what has proven to be the end for most of my berry bears.

When bears feed on high-bush plants like chokecherry and service berry, they lust for the prime, ripe fruits that festoon the uppermost branches. The bushes are too supple to climb, so the bears pull them down, paw over paw, and then strip the berries by mouth or claw. When they're done, they release their grip and the bush catapults back into an erect position. On a calm day it's a real attention-getter and proof positive of your quarry, even if you can't see it.

One afternoon last fall I joined Russ Kipp, a good friend and professional guide, on a fishing trip down the Beartrap of the Madison River. The Beartrap is renowned for wild whitewater and top trout fishing, but as local history goes, it was originally named for the unusual amount of bears that were killed in the rugged canyon.

Still, I was taken back a bit when Russ packed a .357-magnum pistol in the pannier of his raft. When I asked him what the heavy artillery was for, he announced, "I just might kill a bear."

I had been down the river many times in the summer and had never seen a bear, so I considered his boast to be wishful thinking.

Two-thirds of the way through the float Russ jumped like he was snake-bit. "Quick … pull to shore," he hissed. "Did you see that?"

I leaned hard on the oars, and followed his eyes. A chokecherry bush 50 yards above us was quivering like jelly. "That's gotta be a bear," he whispered, bailing out over the tubes, pistol in hand. It was, and still is, I'm sorry to report. The bear caught wind of Russ, and by the time my friend had scrambled up the slope and into open country, the big black was 100 yards away and hightailing it for the ridge, too far for a clean shot with the sidearm.

Russ's misfortune, however, points to better ways to take advantage of telltale trembling in berry patches. When tracks, scat, and broken limbs suggest an area is being visited regularly by a bear, take a stand high. Berries tend to grow thickest in low, damp areas, so natural geography often provides a place with a good overview. In flat terrain, a portable climbing tree stand is ideal. Getting above your quarry does more than give you a better look at bears and bushes, too. It helps disperse your scent, and when alarmed, bears tend to run uphill rather than down.

There are a few other tricks to this special trade. Berries ripen in warmer regions first. This rightly suggests that there will be zones of maximum bear activity, beginning in early fall in the southern parts of the country, then progressing northerly as fruits and autumn mature. The same thing is true on a smaller scale in mountainous terrain. Bears visit low-lying valleys first, then gradually move upcountry to harvest foods from higher elevations. If you follow this seasonal peak, you will enjoy about a month of prime bear hunting.

Best news of all, you will also enjoy the eating. I have killed spring bear, and it makes for debatable dining. Spring animals are usually poor in flesh, and they often feed on winterkills, which results in some funny flavors. But berry bears are always fat, tender, and make delicious table fare, so when you down one of these animals, you can have your rug and eat it too.

By Bob Robb

A Sacred Moment in GRIZZLY COUNTRY

THERE IS LUCK, AND THEN THERE IS THE KIND OF LUCK THAT MAKES YOU SIT DOWN, LOOK SKYWARD, AND GIVE THANKS.

THE FAINT RUSH OF the distant river muted the tinkle of horse bells and the grunts and belches and moans of waking men. Saddle-sore from a two-day ride over a mountain pass that had not been crossed in decades, we were still a half-day's journey from abundant game. Reluctantly, we arose and prepared to leave the comfort of the wall tent and its cheerful wood stove for a small, cold spike camp.

With breakfast downed as a farewell toast, we packed and saddled the horses and mounted up. We lined out eight riders—three hunters, three guides, and two packers—and eight head of pack stock, a familiar caravan on lower-48 elk hunts but a rarity in Alaska. Unlike much of the Rocky Mountain West, where hunters can ride on well-marked and maintained trails, riding in Alaska is mostly brush busting: you follow the remnants of an old trapper's trail, a moose path, a cobbled riverbottom or creek-bottom, or you make your own way, fighting brush and bogs, blowdowns and mud. It's a moral victory if you don't lose your hat more than three times a day.

Outfitter Terry Overly and I had talked about hunting this country for years. Tucked in the shadows of the glacier-glazed Wrangell Mountains, the area was one Terry had flown many times in late Septembers past. Over those years he had spotted numerous big bull moose that moved into the protected bowls and basins of the foothills from the swamps and flats below. There they would rut, and there they would be easier to spot and stalk. There was fine grazing for the horses and plenty of water—an ideal place to camp—yet the country was so remote that no one had hunted it seriously in decades. How remote? Terry's base camp is 75 miles from the nearest road; our hunting grounds were three days on horseback from there.

While moose hunting such magnificent country is an exciting challenge, another animal occupied our thoughts on the ride in. On each flight over this rugged land Terry had seen numerous interior (or mountain) grizzlies gorging on berries and the odd ground squirrel in anticipation of winter. Like the moose, the bears could be spotted in the evening from afar as they fed above the brush line. Unlike the moose, grizzlies are just as capable of stalking as of being stalked.

The grizzly bear is awesome in its power and speed. It sits at the top of the food chain, with no enemies save for man, nature, and other grizzlies. A mature mountain grizzly may weigh 850 pounds, though most are smaller and a very few are larger, depending on where they live and what they eat.

The grizzly gets its name from the whitish tips of its body hair, which give it a frosted or "grizzled" look. This remarkable coat, which can range from yellow to chocolate-brown to nearly black, is coarse and long and sheds water well, protecting the animal from cold and wind. A thick layer of fat further insulates the bear from North Country cold.

Grizzlies are omnivores, eating anything and everything from roots, grasses, berries, and woody browse to carrion, fish, and fresh meat—whatever can be readily found or caught. Grizzlies prey heavily on gangly-legged moose and caribou calves during the spring, and on weak, sick, and careless adults at any time. Boars will kill and eat all the cubs they can catch. A boar may fight to the death with a sow protecting her brood. If he wins, he'll eat the cubs and the vanquished mother. A boar grizzly is not an animal to trifle with.

Like all bears, grizzlies have poor eyesight, though they can detect outlines and motion quite well. Grizzlies have very good hearing, but it is their nose they trust implicitly. Never hunt bears without the wind in your favor. You might trick a grizzly's eyes, and you may confuse its ears, but you'll never fool that remarkable nose.

It was the nose that guide Striker Overly had in mind when he spotted a beautiful blond grizzly rolling in blueberry bushes at the head of a drainage a mile from our spike camp. Our half day ride in had been uneventful, though painful to our saddle-bruised butts. We were leisurely setting up camp when Striker spotted the bear. His hunter, Dick Farnan of New York, was anxious to stalk a grizzly, so hunter, guide, and packer Brian Anderson quickly saddled up and closed the gap on the gluttonous bruin.

A half-hour later we finished our camp chores and from a nearby hill watched the stalk through our binoculars. The trio had worked into the wind, had tied up the horses, and were approaching the bear on foot. A small rise separated predators and prey. The hunters got within 50 yards of the bear before it detected something and shambled off, disappearing from our view. We were convinced Dick had blown a slam-dunk, when we heard shooting, followed by Striker's whoops and hollers. Dick had his bear, a 7-footer with a flawless blond and chocolate coat, highlighted with silver.

With the chores completed and 2 hours of daylight left, my guide, Dick Peterson, and I weren't about to stick around camp after watching all that. We saddled up and rode a mile uphill to the edge of a small bowl. The evening air was clear and crisp. We tied our horses below the crest, then duck-walked to the edge to glass the open ground below.

Grizzly and moose hunting is an eyeballing game. One rides or hikes into good country, climbs to a vantage, and lets eyes and optics do the walking. Evenings usually produce at least a moose or two, and when your dues are paid, a good bear. What makes grizzly hunting so special is the magical way in which such a large animal can appear out of nowhere. On those rare occasions you may not need binoculars. As a friend once said of grizzly hunting, "It's 95 percent boredom and 5 percent pure terror."

After an hour of glassing, I'd seen only a cow and calf moose. Then Dick whispered, "There's a bear." I put the spotting scope on him. He was a good bear, not overly large but no adolescent. He gorged on blueberries in a small saddle near the top of a steep hill. A grizzly hunter should never turn down a mature boar (as one might pass on a six-point buck or a raghorn elk). Spotting one such bear in a week's hunt is good luck. We decided to try for him.

An hour of daylight was left, and the bear was across the bowl and on the other side of a shallow river, perhaps 3/4 mile away. We trotted the horses through the bowl, concealed inside a stand of spruce. When we came to the creek, we gave the horses a quick blow and short drink, then rode across the water and through the spruce on the far side.

The bear was out of sight now, hidden by the hill. A light breeze blew softly downhill, square in our faces, so we decided to ride up the 45-degree slope at a walk and see what happened.

When we got within 200 yards of the saddle, we still had not seen the grizzly, so we pulled up. He might have fed over the saddle and down the other side. We chose to keep riding, ever alert, and let things play out.

The bear must have heard us as we approached his berry patch. He was still where I had spotted him from across the river, but he no longer lolled about, contentedly munching fruit. Now he was up on all fours and looking our way. I saw him first and whistled softly to Dick, who grabbed my reins as I dismounted and dragged the .300 Winchester Magnum from its scabbard. Perhaps the bear thought our horses were a pair of funny-looking moose, because he trotted off only 25 yards before stopping to look back. By then I had found a small hole in the head-high brush where I could sit down in a reasonably steady shooting position. When the crosshairs settled on his front shoulder, I squeezed the trigger. He went down in a heap, then got up and groggily headed up the hill. A solid second shot put him down.

He wasn't just another bear; he was huge by anyone's standard. The berry bushes, usually knee-high, were actually waist-high in this lush, wild place. Consequently, we had misjudged his massiveness from our vantage across the valley. His dark chocolate hide later squared an honest 9 feet 1 inch, larger than the average coastal brown bear. His front claws measured 5 1/4 inches long, his front pads over 7 inches wide. After the sixty-day drying period required by Boone and Crockett, the skull measured 25 5/16 inches, placing him 107th in the book.

As Dick tethered the horses, I approached the bear. The light breeze caught the silver-tipped hairs on his back; they shimmered like a surrealistic halo. I sat next to him and stroked his massive head between his ears. In every direction I looked across untamed wilderness stretching to the horizon. The sunset had turned the western sky a brilliant orange, and soon all the memories of those weary miles on horseback, of nights camped on rock and tundra, of cold and wet vanished.

I was filled with that contradictory mixture of emotions—part elation, part sadness—only hunters understand. What uncommon luck, even in Alaska: two outstanding grizzlies in the same afternoon. That, and the thought that such vast tracts of wilderness so necessary for grizzlies still exist, made the moment sacred. I hope generations to come will be able to see such sights and experience such feelings, too.

By Dan Sisson

Bear Hunt at TERROR BAY

FOR MOST HUNTERS, AN ALASKA BROWN BEAR HUNT IS A LIFELONG DREAM. FOR THESE MEN ON KODIAK ISLAND, IT BECAME REALITY.

FOR A BIG-GAME hunter, an Alaska brown bear hunt has to be a kind of ultimate dream—a fantasy of high adventure set in a wild and rugged landscape untouched except by time. Mixed with the dream, of course, is an element of nightmare, for nobody but a fool would imagine hunting these bears without feeling a shiver of fear.

When choosing an actual place to make a real hunt for the big bears, it would be hard to conjure up a more perfect setting than Terror Bay on Kodiak Island, where the biggest of these enormous animals live. Not only is the place name suggestive of the nightmare edge of the dream, but the setting is as wild and beautiful as could be hoped for. Situated on the northeast corner of Kodiak Island, Terror Bay directly faces the Shelikof Strait. This is a cold and lonely place; its shores are pounded by high tides blown by fierce storms off the Gulf of Alaska, and its slate-gray land mass is pelted by wind-driven rains seven months a year. Above the bay are mountains covered with dense alder, and in the open spaces grasses grow over 6 feet high—hiding from view the monsters weighing up to 1,400 pounds that roam this landscape and hold no fear of man.

But Terror Bay is also a beneficent place, rich with shellfish and migrating salmon. Besides the brown bears, the surrounding hills are filled with deer, fox, otter, beaver, hare, waterfowl, and dozens of songbirds. It is, in short, an ideal place to realize a dream.

Although for a novice bear hunter like me—or even for an experienced one—the name "Terror Bay" conjures up images of agile and cunning creatures moving like ghosts through the alders and brush, never making a sound—huge beasts of legendary power, capable of taking five rounds from a high-powered rifle and never slowing their charge–the "terror" may have nothing to do with bears at all. No one is really certain how or why the bay got its name. One source says it was named by a U.S. Coast & Geodetic Survey employee in 1909. Another version has it that the name came from an incident involving an attack by humans, not bears—the story of two coldblooded murders in a gold-mining camp at the turn of the century, when a family's entire adult membership was wiped out and a baby daughter lived to tell of the terror she experienced.

But whatever the source of the name, my anticipation of this bear hunt—my first—was high. My hunting partners, Dave Harkness and Bob Cassell, both biologists with the Alaska Department of Fish and Game in Anchorage, were more casual in their approach. Dave has been a game biologist in southcentral Alaska for seventeen years. He has had a turn at collaring grizzlies, and early in his career he did a short stint on Admiralty Island, a place nearly as well known for its huge bears as Kodiak. Bob, although one of the younger members of fish and game, flies his plane to the Alaska interior on bear hunts with his 110-pound Labrador retriever, Bear, sitting behind him.

Another member of our party was Alan Carey, a wildlife photographer from Montana. Alan has photographed black and grizzly bears in several states, including Alaska, over the past ten years. The only species he had not spent time with was the brown/grizzly on Kodiak Island.

Their combined experience dealing with bears dwarfed mine by thirty-three years to zero. I was not only lucky to be able to hunt with experienced partners, but I was feeling lucky all around, since I was drawn in the Kodiak lottery on my first application.

Harkness and I were the only ones who had drawn permits to shoot a bear, so the four of us had come together for reasons other than to take a trophy. Bob Cassell came as a friend. An experienced hunter and the most agile person I have ever seen going through an alder thicket, Bob was there to help spot game, back up a hunter in case of emergency, or help carry out a trophy. His motive was simply to enjoy the experience and assist in every way he could.

Alan Carey brought to the hunt the perspective of a wildlife artist. Although a successful deer hunter in Montana, Alan had not even brought along a rifle. His purpose was to photograph the hunt, and on several occasions he stated, "It would be impossible for me to shoot a grizzly with anything except a camera."

Dave Harkness, by contrast, reflected the motives of the pure hunter. A lifelong outdoorsman and an expert on Dall sheep and moose, Dave had started dreaming of an Alaskan brown bear hunt years before, as a fifteen-year-old teenager in Michigan. But in the seventeen years he had been a professional big-game biologist in Alaska, he had managed only one hunt, in the early 1970s, when he bagged a small grizzly near Fairbanks. He had never had the opportunity to hunt the large coastal bears, either because he missed being picked for a bear tag in the annual lottery or his job interfered with the short spring bear season.

But now, after thirty years of dreaming about a classic Kodiak hunt, Dave had a chance at the dream. A nagging back problem only doubled his determination to make this the hunt of a lifetime, culminating in a true trophy-sized brownie.

Three decades of hunting experience lay behind Dave's preparation for this hunt, and he knew, deep down, that this might be the only time he would have the opportunity. In Alaska, the hunter who draws a Kodiak brown/grizzly tag is allowed to apply for another only after a wait of four years. There are no guarantees, even then, and Dave knew it might be another seventeen years before he could hunt Kodiak again.

My own motives were mixed. Like Dave, I too had dreamed of going on a Kodiak bear hunt since I was a teenager more than thirty years before. In the intervening years I had shot enough big and small game to establish a certain code for myself. In addition to the provisos that the hunt had to be legal, the chase fair, and the rifle adequate was one specially important condition: The meat must never be wasted. But grizzly hunters are, for the most part, trophy hunters. They do not eat the meat. Once shot, the bear is stripped of hide and skull, and the meat is left for the scavengers. I realized that this was a different type of hunt, and exceptions had to be made, but I had difficulty reconciling my code with leaving 600 or more pounds of bear meat in the field.

Several of my friends, all of them hunters who had taken bears in the past, turned out to have similar feelings. In every discussion we asked one basic question: If every requirement for legality and fair chase is met, is trophy hunting for grizzly compatible with an ethical approach to hunting? No experienced hunter whom I respected was willing to condemn anyone who hunted the big creatures, even if they had given up hunting them themselves. But all expressed ambivalence about the matter.

One friend in particular, Dennis Bromley, a local Anchorage teacher who hunts in Africa as well as Alaska, was to the point: "Don't worry," he said. "You'll resolve the problem the second you start to squeeze the trigger. Last year I had a brownie in my sights and couldn't do it. But that doesn't mean I wouldn't do it this year, or next." It was a relief to know my dilemma was shared by other hunters and that it might be resolved through experience.

As April break-up came we marked time, waiting until the hunt would begin. Harkness met with me twice. He urged me to find a proper rifle, preferably a .375 H&H magnum, and begin practicing offhand. We went over equipment and talked about bears and bear hunting.

Meanwhile our research revealed that several exceptionally large bears had been taken in the vicinity of Terror Bay over the past twenty years. Skulls measuring 8 to 9 inches wide and up to 14½ inches long were on record. One thing seemed certain: We would be sharing our living space with, as Dave put it, "some awfully big critters."

AT THE END of April we made the flight to Kodiak Island and met local biologists Ben Ballinger and Leon Metz. Leon, who runs the bear radio-collaring program, described a 10-foot bear he had collared near Terror Bay. His terms were somewhat odd: "He's like all the others," Metz said. "A big pussycat." But this "pussycat" weighed 1,200 pounds and, after Leon described several 10- to 11-footers he had seen from his spotting plane the past week, I began to see "pussycats" in a new dimension. After picking up our permits and some last-minute supplies we headed for the dock to take a floatplane to Terror Bay. Leon bade us goodbye with a warning: "Don't shoot any of my collared brown bears!"

A decision to make camp at the head of the bay meant we had to take advantage of a short tide change. We were already running late, and after the 15-minute flight to the bay everyone worked together to offload the plane. In the frantic effort to allow the pilot to beat the ebb tide, we put everything ashore in 5 minutes. As the plane receded into the distance the gloomy silence of Terror Bay was broken by

two sounds: the patter of raindrops and a voice that said, "Our fuel never got off the plane."

Our first order of business, once camp was established, was to scout the area. Our camp was situated at the head of the bay, less than 400 yards from the Terror River. Steep slopes of up to 2,100 feet came down almost to the water's edge on one side of the bay, while gently rising slopes led to a 3,440-foot peak on the other.

We chose to walk up the river and glass the mountains directly across from camp. Within an hour we had spotted two sows, one with two cubs, but no single boars. The next day Dave and Bob spotted a large boar, and after working up close to him realized he was wearing a collar. Alan and I spent 6 hours glassing the mountains and watching the rain turn into snow.

The second night we compared notes. It seemed obvious the bears were still up high. The snowline was only about 1,200 feet up from the bay and we started wondering if most of the bears had even come out of hibernation. Bob Cassell had taken a walk and seen "a monster" up high—at roughly 2,000 feet. We decided to go after him the next day.

Leaving camp as soon as daylight permitted, Dave, Bob, Alan, and I walked down Terror Bay and glassed the northeast side. At about 8 A.M. we spotted a good-sized boar. "Maybe a 10-footer," Dave said. We had to cross a half-mile of mud flat and wade the main channel of the river just to begin the climb. Luckily the tide was out and would be out again 12 hours later when we returned.

For seven hours we stalked that grizzly, trying to keep downwind. But at about 1,800 feet, we noticed the wind swirling in every direction above our heads, making it impossible to get close to a wary bear whose nose is his best defense. We'd hoped the bear would take a long nap, but after reaching a small basin we knew he had gone into, it became apparent we had driven him straight over the mountain. A fresh set of huge tracks disappearing into 4 feet of snow at the top confirmed our suspicions.

Our trip back was a gloomy one. The weather, which had alternated between sun and snow flurries all day, had turned into Kodiak's typical rain. When we arrived in camp, however, Dave greeted us with a hot meal and the good news that Leon had flown in to check on us and would see to it that we got our fuel. As far as we were concerned it was the best insurance possible for his radio-collared bears.

The next two days were more of the same. We hunted the opposite side of the bay and the upper Terror River. On several occasions we sighted huge bears up near the mountaintops, well above snowline. But they were moving and a stalk was out of the question. We were encouraged by the amount of bear sign. Tracks were everywhere in the snow, and up on the Terror River we found prints in the riverbed that were bigger than a man's size 11 shoe.

At the end of the fifth day we did receive a treat. An hour before we were ready to start back to camp Alan Carey saw a giant grizzly—the largest one we had yet seen—near the top of a 3,000-foot mountain standing in the middle of an avalanche chute. Through our binoculars we watched the bear walk to the side of the chute, dislodge a big chunk of ice, and throw it down the chute. Then, as the chunk bounced down the mountain, the boar would lean forward and follow its progress until it seemed that he too would go crashing head over heels down the chute. The big grizzly did this over and over, obviously enjoying himself, and we watched him play for well over 30 minutes.

By the sixth day everyone had come to terms with the realities of hunting grizzlies in and around Terror Bay. Thus far we had seen nine bears and stalked three, and no one had taken a shot. We had become bleary-eyed from glassing the hills 8 hours a day. We were so eyesore, in fact, that Alan and I decided to take time off and view some ducks that had flown into the bay below camp. As we approached them we saw a brown-bear-like creature that appeared to be fishing for salmon at the end of the bay. We started to rush back to camp for camera and rifle. As an afterthought I raised my binoculars and put them on the "bear." It turned out to be a very large beaver that was simply curious about life on the mud flats. Alan and I chuckled about how desperately we wanted to see a grizzly below 2,000 feet.

But Dave and Bob had been more fortunate that day. In the afternoon on a high bluff Dave spotted a beautiful golden grizzly in prime condition near the Terror River, about a mile from camp. The bear was probably a three-year-old and not the trophy size Dave wanted. But it was a respectable, even pretty, bear and I was more than willing to try my luck. Over dinner we planned a stalk.

All my ambivalence seemed to vanish as the four of us lay on the bluff glassing the hillside where the bear had been digging. A kind of grim determination gripped us as we sat staring at a vast expanse of alder and grass. Suddenly we were electrified by Bob's voice:

"Look! There's a bear!"

Dave's response was immediate. "Where? Near the creek?"

"Right in the clearing to the left of the creek. About 100 feet up."

Alan was next. "I see him!"

Dave had picked him up by this time. "It looks like the one I saw earlier. That's a nice bear. Get ready, Dan. He's yours."

My stomach tightened. I was watching the bear too and I knew in the next few seconds I would have to make a decision.

I picked up my Winchester .375 H&H magnum and started to check the magazine when Bob suddenly said, "Look! There's another bear just to the left of that first one!"

Again Dave reacted first. "Hey! Now that's a really nice bear. I'll take that one."

But then Alan added to the confusion: "I think I see another bear. It's moving into that meadow."

All of this had taken place in less than 10 seconds, and now Dave's instincts told him the second bear was the trophy he had been waiting for. As he watched he spoke: "It's a boar because its got a large head and long snout. And the color is beautiful!"

Dave realized this was his chance to realize a thirty-year dream. The bear was big. Its hide was in perfect condition. It was also low; low enough for Dave to make a stalk in the next half hour while there was still enough daylight to be able to shoot and maybe get the hide out before dark.

As Dave prepared to stalk his bear, Bob turned to me and said, "C'mon, why don't you see if you can get that golden bear! If think you can do it."

I started, and then shook my head. If I

took a shot, Dave's bear would be over the mountain in 5 seconds. I motioned for Bob to go on with Dave.

In less than a minute the two of them had disappeared into a woods across the Terror River. Alan and I, from our point high on the bluff, tried to keep track of the second bear. The animal kept wandering in and out of the alders, feeding. It wasn't alarmed and had not picked up any scent. Neither Bob nor Dave were visible, and after 15 minutes we lost sight of the bear.

"What a mess," Alan said. "We can't see the bear and we can't see the hunters." At that moment I spied Bob running across the meadow on the other side of the river. He was coming to get directions because he and Dave had no idea where the bear was. We pointed to the general area.

Twenty minutes later Bob and Dave had still not located the bear. It hadn't gone up the creek, and they weren't going to cross because it was too treacherous. If they did cross the creek, they wouldn't be downwind from the bear. Besides, they couldn't see more than 30 feet in any direction. Everything now seemed hopeless.

Suddenly the bear emerged into a clearing about 100 yards above Dave. Alan and I saw him in the same instant. I stood up and yelled at the top of my lungs: "Up above you! Up above you!" Bob heard me and turned. I gave the hand signal to indicate the bear was above them, and both Dave and Bob got the message instantly.

Ten seconds later Dave saw the head of the boar emerge from the alders. He raised his rifle and ripped off the scope covers. Only the head and front two-thirds of the bear's body were visible. But that was enough. The .375 H&H magnum roared once, and the 270-grain slug slammed into the boar's lungs after hitting the tip of the humerus. The big brown bear let out a low growl and then moaned. Seconds later it was dead.

There was jubilation in Dave Harkness' face when he returned to camp. The boar was indeed a beautiful, mature brown bear, perhaps six years old. His face and nose broadened out into a perfect shape and the hide looked flawless with not one rub mark on it. Dave guessed that the bear couldn't have been out of his den for more than ten days. And while it wasn't the 10-footer he had sought, it was a tremendous animal—an 8-footer that looked enormous.

The next day we tried again for my bear. We watched the gut pile and glassed for hours, and finally toward evening we spotted the golden bear. Bob and I followed the same route across the river and into the alders he had taken the night before. We knew the bear was near us, but there in the brush we could have been standing 50 feet away and wouldn't have seen the animal. Visibility was limited to 30 feet, at best. After two hours of walking in circles, rifles ready, watching and listening as intently as we could, we decided to end the stalk and return to camp before darkness descended on us completely. We started back, knowing we had given it our best try.

As we waded across the Terror River an otter slid down the bank with a loud splash and swam under a rocky ledge in front of us. We climbed the bluff to retrieve our packs and spotting scope and sat down, exhausted by the tension. A pair of mergansers flew over our heads, upriver, their white breasts flashing, and we could hear goldeneyes squabbling down toward the bay.

The scene before us was one of absolute beauty. The evening sun bathed the mud flats and snow-capped mountains in pure gold. We sat silent for 20 minutes, watching a small band of blacktailed deer work across a meadow toward the lengthening shadow of the mountain. Finally I broke the silence.

"You know, Bob, I'm not upset about missing that bear. Just making this trip to Terror Bay has been one of the best hunting experiences I've ever had, and I feel good simply knowing all these animals are here."

Bob waited a minute before answering. "Yeah," he said. "I know what you mean. I'm getting to feel more like that all the time."

Author Biographies

Lionel Atwill is a Senior Editor for FIELD & STREAM. He has been the editor of *Adirondack Life* and *Backpacker* magazines. For 20 years he freelanced for *Sports Afield, Sports Illustrated, Geo, National Geographic,* and numerous other publications.

Lloyd Bare was born and raised (and still lives) in Pleasantville, Iowa. A hunter of upland birds and waterfowl since age 8, he started serious big-game hunting in 1973. In 1980, he completed the "grand slam" of North American wild sheep. He is the author of *High Country Hunting* (1989).

John Barsness lives in southwestern Montana, where he writes about hunting, fishing, conservation and Western history. He has traveled the world in search of big game, chronicling his adventures in his latest book, *The Life of the Hunt.*

Craig Boddington took up big-game hunting in the 1960s, beginning a passion that has taken him throughout North America and to all the continents, including 38 hunts in Africa. He is the author of 12 books and more than 1500 articles on hunting and shooting.

Bill Burrows and his wife, Susan, own an advertising agency and television production company in Fairbanks. Bill no longer hunts, spending his time outdoors on the golf course in the summer and the cross-country ski trails in the winter.

Sam Curtis is a Contributing Editor for FIELD & STREAM and a full-time writer of 26 years. His articles and photos have appeared in over 40 national and regional magazines.

Byron W. Dalrymple's articles appeared in FIELD & STREAM from 1945 through 1994. He always retained his enthusiasm for fishing, hunting and travel, as well as for writing about them, until his death in 1994. Byron also wrote under the pen name Christopher Michaels.

Bill McRae is a Montana-based outdoor writer/photographer with more then 35 years of experience. His specialties include wildlife photography, big-game hunting, shooting and sports optics. His work has appeared in hundreds of magazines, books, calendars, technical manuals and commercial advertisements.

Jim Merritt has written more than 140 articles on fishing, natural history, the American West, and other subjects. He is the author of *Bayonets and Buffalo: The British Sportsman in the American West* (1985) and *Goodbye, Liberty Belle: A Son's Search for His Father's War* (1993), and the editor of *The Best of FIELD & STREAM: 100 Years of Great Writing From America's Premier Sporting Magazine* (1995). He lives in Pennington, New Jersey.

Ed Park, a freelance writer and photographer for 38 years, is a past president of the Outdoor Writers Association of America. He's had thousands of articles and photographs published in virtually every major outdoor magazine, and has hunted big game throughout the western U.S.

David E. Petzal joined FIELD & STREAM as Managing Editor in 1972. He became Executive Editor in 1983 and has written the shooting department since 1982. Petzal has hunted in most of the United States, Canada, Europe and Africa.

Jim Rearden has been professionally involved in fisheries and game management in Alaska for 50 years. He is the author of nearly 600 magazine features and 17 books, mostly about Alaska. For 20 years he was Outdoors Editor for *Alaska* magazine and a Field Editor for *Outdoor Life.*

Bob Robb's articles and photographs have been published in virtually all of the major outdoor magazines. Bob has hunted all across North America, as well as on four other continents.

Ross Seyfried, a native Colorado cattle rancher, spent 10 seasons as a professional hunter in Africa and 15 years as a full-time professional writer/photographer. He has guided for both small and big game.

Dan Sisson lives north of Spokane, Washington, in a nearly full-size replica of Thomas Jefferson's Monticello, surrounded by the finest whitetail deer and grouse habitat in the Northwest. He teaches American history at Eastern Washington University.

Norman Strung's stories first appeared in FIELD & STREAM in 1965. He authored over 1,200 articles and 14 books on hunting, fishing, and camping before his death in 1991.

Wayne van Zwoll has written four books and more than 400 articles on big-game hunting, rifle shooting, optics, and the history of firearms. A technical editor for *Rifle* and *Handloader* magazines, he also contributes regularly to FIELD & STREAM, *Bugle* and several other hunting magazines.

Jack Wendling is a retired aeronautical engineer, a part-time gunsmith and cartridge experimenter, a back-country horseman and a 25-year resident of Idaho. In 50 years pursuing big game, he has hunted Montana, Wyoming, Michigan, Ontario and Newfoundland, as well as his home state.

Photo Credits

Photographers

(Note: T=Top, C=Center, B=Bottom, L=Left, R=Right, I=Inset)

Charles J. Alsheimer
Bath, NY
© Charles J. Alsheimer: pp. 8, 146

Chuck & Grace Bartlett
Lynnwood, WA
© Chuck & Grace Bartlett: pp. 38, 41

Alan & Sandy Carey
Bozeman, MT
© Alan & Sandy Carey: pp. 153, 155

Alissa Crandall
Anchorage, AK
© Alissa Crandall: p. 150

Michael H. Francis
Billings, MT
© Michael H. Francis: back cover: TR, CC; pp. 60, 108, 113, 121, 126-127, 139, 140

The Green Agency
Bozeman, MT
© Dusan Smetana / The Green Agency: p. 48

Donald M. Jones
Troy, MT
© Donald M. Jones: back cover: CL, CR; pp. 5, 52, 80-81, 92, 101, 109

Jess R. Lee
Idaho Falls, ID
© Jess R. Lee: p. 156

Tom & Pat Leeson
Vancouver, WA
© Tom & Pat Leeson: p. 107

Keith McCafferty
Bozeman, MT
© Keith McCafferty: pp. 128, 131

Bill McRae
Choteau, MT
© Bill McRae: pp. 21, 97, 98, 99, 100

Wyman Meinzer
Benjamin, TX
© Wyman Meinzer: pp. 35, 35 I, 105, 136

David E. Petzal
Bedford, NY
© David E. Petzal: pp. 76, 79

Mark Raycroft
Trenton, Ontario Canada
© Mark Raycroft: cover; p. 3

Jerome B. Robinson
Lyme, NH
© Jerome B. Robinson: p. 77

Conrad Rowe
Seeley Lake, MT
© Conrad Rowe: p. 30

Rodney Schlecht
Great Falls, MT
© Rodney Schlecht: p. 115

Ron Spomer
Troy, ID
© Ron Spomer: pp. 151, 152

Jeff Vanuga
DuBois, WY
© Jeff Vanuga: back cover: BR; pp. 6-7, 17, 25, 26, 57

Illustrators

Norman Adams
© Norman Adams: pp. 70, 71 both, 74, 142, 143, 145

Luke Frazier
Logan, UT
© Luke Frazier: pp. 42, 65, 67, 68, 82, 83, 85

Craig P. Griffin
Akron, OH
© Craig P. Griffin: p. 45

R. Scott
Galesburg, MI
© R. Scott: p. 13

Shannon Stirnweis
New Ipswich, NH
© Shannon Stirnweis: pp. 87, 117, 118

John Thompson
Dewitt, NY
© John Thompson: p. 133